Advance praise for *Blind to Betrayal*

"Powerful, illuminating, and disturbing, this translation of decades of meticulous scientific research and sophisticated clinical observation is an eye-opener in the best sense for social scientists, clinicians, and any reader interested in understanding the impact of trauma from a unique new perspective. The work Dr. Freyd and her colleagues have done in this controversial and increasingly urgent area of violence and victimization, the description she and Dr. Birrell provide of the paths to recovery that become possible when psychological blindness is recognized and understood, and the compelling case examples in this book, is a groundbreaking and essential contribution."

—Julian D. Ford, Ph.D., professor of psychiatry,
University of Connecticut Health Center

"Drs. Freyd and Birrell have created a masterwork for all of us who struggle to comprehend our own experiences of not seeing, not knowing, and not protecting ourselves and others from betrayal. The pervasiveness of both betrayal and betrayal blindness, and the challenges inherent in becoming able to know and see betrayal, as well as the psychological science making sense of these painful dynamics, come to life in this book. It's one that I'll be buying several copies of, because I know that it'll constantly be on loan to clients and students. A must-read for everyone who has experienced betrayal and betrayal blindness— and that means almost all of us."

—Laura S. Brown, PhD, ABPP, director,
Fremont Community Therapy Project

Blind to Betrayal

*Why We Fool Ourselves
We Aren't Being Fooled*

Jennifer J. Freyd, PhD,
and Pamela J. Birrell, PhD

WILEY

Cover Design: Wendy Mount
Cover Photograph: ©Tooga/Getty Images

Published by John Wiley & Sons, Inc., Hoboken, New Jersey
Published simultaneously in Canada

For general information about our other products and services, please contact our Customer Care Department within the United States at (800) 762-2974, outside the United States at (317) 572-3993 or fax (317) 572-4002.

Wiley also publishes its books in a variety of electronic formats and by print-on-demand. Some content that appears in standard print versions of this book may not be available in other formats. For more information about Wiley products, visit us at www.wiley.com.

ISBN 978-0-470-60440-3 (paperback); ISBN 978-1-118-22069-6 (ebk); ISBN 978-1-118-23448-8 (ebk); ISBN 978-1-118-25890-3 (ebk)

Printed in the United States of America

To JQ Johnson, 1951–2012

Contents

Preface   ix

Acknowledgments   xiii

1   Blind to Betrayal   1

2   Children Betrayed   10

3   The Wide Reach of Betrayal Blindness   20

4   Blind Adherence   35

5   Why Blindness?   49

6   Knowing and Not Knowing   62

7   Mental Gymnastics   71

8   Insights from Research   84

9   Betrayal Blindness Is Toxic   96

10   The Risks of Knowing   114

11   The Healing Power of Knowing   130

12   The Healing Power of Telling   141

13   Speaking Our Truth   153

14   Now I See: Facing Betrayal Blindness   162

Recommended Reading   175

Notes   177

Index   193

Preface

A husband whose wife is having an affair; a child sexually abused by his priest; a soldier ordered into an unsafe battle by his commanding officer; a single mother who is overworked and underpaid in her secretarial job; a group of people sharing the same ethnic heritage who are denied access to leadership roles—in each of these cases, there is mistreatment and injustice. Infidelity, abuse, treachery, workplace exploitation (in a society valuing fairness), discrimination (in a society valuing equality), and injustice (in a society valuing justice) are examples of betrayal. Betrayal can be mundane or a central threat to our well-being.

Betrayal violates us. It can destroy relationships and the very trust we need to be intimate in our relationships. It can and does damage the social fabric that creates the bonds for a healthy society. In the case of children, the effects can last a lifetime. Betrayed children may grow into adults who fail to trust the trustworthy or who too readily trust people who further betray them. Whether being too willing or too unwilling to trust, difficulty with trust not only interferes with relationships, but also eats away at a strong sense of self. Those who were betrayed as children often suffer severe self-esteem problems, as well as depression, anxiety, and even psychosis.[1]

Yet even though betrayal is often in our very midst and of critical importance, we frequently don't acknowledge the mistreatment or notice the betrayal. We shield ourselves from the awareness of it. Whether the betrayal is in our closest relationships, in our workplaces, or in our society, we often have a powerful motivation to remain ignorant.

We remain blind to betrayal in order to protect ourselves. We fear risking the status quo, and thus our security, by actually *knowing too much.* At the same time, there are costs to our ignorance. This is a very real dilemma that we frequently face, yet rarely recognize fully. Too often, we deal with this dilemma by implicitly choosing to remain unaware, in order to avoid the risk of seeing treachery or injustice. The victim who sees the mistreatment is likely either to confront the betrayal or to withdraw from the situation and the relationship.[2] That confrontation or withdrawal may lead to a good outcome, or it may risk inciting a crisis that is very threatening for a disempowered or dependent person. In contrast, by remaining unaware of the mistreatment, the husband, the child, the soldier, the working mother, or the oppressed group may not be able to escape the injustice. The best way to keep a secret is not to know it in the first place; unawareness is a powerful survival technique when information is too dangerous to know.

Knowledge of betrayal is always destabilizing. Whether we are the betrayers, the observers, or the betrayed, to *know* about betrayal is likely to provoke actions that disturb the status quo and threaten our security. Consider the recent crisis in the Catholic Church: denial and cover-up of sexual abuse gave way to acknowledgment and investigation. All sorts of arrangements and power structures were threatened as a consequence of this crisis. Even when we are not the direct victims, a fear of disturbing the status quo and thus jeopardizing our own comfort, perhaps even our survival, motivates us to remain blind to betrayal.

Systematically not seeing important instances of treachery and injustice is an observable, ubiquitous psychological phenomenon that we call *betrayal blindness*. We have discovered in our work as a research psychologist (Jennifer J. Freyd) and a clinical psychologist (Pamela J. Birrell) that this *not seeing* is all around us, ultimately resulting in negative consequences, both in our personal lives and in our society.

Betrayal addresses five primary questions about betrayal blindness: (1) What is it? (2) Why do we do it? (3) How do we do it? (4) What does it do to us? (5) How do we break free of it?

In chapter 1, we examine the story of Julie Stone, a bright professional woman who was completely blind to the infidelity of her husband. Julie is not alone. Her case illustrates aspects of betrayal that we all can recognize and learn from. In chapter 2, we investigate betrayal in childhood through the stories of Rebecca and Kevin, each of whom suffered many betrayals during their childhood. Both Rebecca and Kevin had to remain blind to their betrayal, although the types of betrayal they experienced were different in detail. (In this book, we use real-life stories to explain and illustrate the research and the theory. We have, however, changed the names and identifying details of the people whose stories we used, to preserve their privacy.) Chapter 3 continues to explore the scope of betrayal and betrayal blindness by considering the stories of a sixteen-year-old girl molested on a plane by her coach, and a sixteen-year-old boy captured and imprisoned in a Russian work camp. Their reactions illustrate both the effects of betrayal and being blind to it.

Chapter 4 introduces the concept of institutional betrayal. It is not only people we trust who can hurt us, but trusted institutions as well. For instance, we can remain blind to betrayal by employers, churches, educational institutions, and governments when we depend on them.

What motivates victims of betrayal, perpetrators of betrayal, and those who witness betrayal to remain ignorant of something so significant in their lives? Chapter 5 explores these questions through the story of Hendrik. Concepts such as betrayal trauma, social contracts, cheater detectors, and fight-flight-and-freeze are introduced and explained.

How do we keep information about betrayal from our awareness? How do we know and not know at the same time? Chapter 6 begins to answer this question through the story of Samantha. We first learn about Samantha's blindness regarding infidelity and then, in chapter 7, we examine her blindness to abuse and domestic violence. We learn that blindness to relational betrayal often includes blindness to abuse and other forms of violence. Chapter 8 reviews research on underlying psychological mechanisms that blind us and keep us blind. We explore concepts such as meta-cognition, directed forgetting, and alexithymia in our explanation of underlying psychological processes.

What impact is betrayal blindness having on us? Chapter 9 describes the toxic effects of betrayal and its blindness on individuals, relationships, and institutions. Toxicity includes dissociation, borderline personality, intergenerational abuse, revictimization, and a host of other problems. Cathy's story illustrates many of these effects. In chapter 10, we begin to address the question of how to stop being blind by considering the impact of telling and knowing about betrayal. Telling and knowing can be risky, as we illustrate with a very close and personal story that affected us.

Telling and knowing can also be healing, as Sean Bruyea's story in chapter 11 attests. How would the world be different if we were more aware of what is really happening in our lives? Chapter 12 further examines how healing from betrayal and its blindness can blossom into hope and justice. In this chapter, Cathy shares her healing story and Beth tells her experience of betrayal in therapy and her return to wholeness.

In chapter 13, we continue with our own story and describe coming full circle from betrayal to intimacy to hope. Chapter 14 offers suggestions to prevent betrayal and betrayal blindness and provides approaches to healing. It is meant for those who have been betrayed, their friends and supporters, and the institutions that may have betrayed them. Paradoxically, the very blindness we may rely on for survival in the short run can lead us astray in the long run. Fortunately, if we so choose, we can learn to become less blinded by the treacheries and injustices that are there for the seeing. We need only learn how to transform blindness into insight.

Acknowledgments

We are so grateful for all the support we have received in writing this book.

First of all, we are indebted to the people who gave us their stories. How can we thank you enough? We have protected the identity of those who requested such protection. We have named them Samantha Spencer, Julie Stone, Beth McDonald, Rebecca Brewerman, and Cathy Turner. Their painful and real-life experiences with betrayal are both illuminating and instructional. We cannot express our appreciation enough for their courage, honesty, and compelling witness to the power of betrayal, betrayal blindness, and healing.

There are those whose stories are more public—Jacques Sandulescu, Sean Bruyea, and Lana Lawrence. They show us the power of both surviving betrayal and standing up to the institutional powers who would betray our very survival. Theirs are stories of courage and resolution in the face of almost impossible odds.

Next we owe so very much to our extraordinary literary agent, Edite Kroll, who believed in this book and patiently supported our efforts through years of gestation. Edite's magic touch is everywhere. Edite helped us find our wonderful Wiley editors and staff: Stephen Power, Thomas Miller, Jorge Amaral, and John Simko, as well as free-lance copyeditor Patricia Waldygo.

And where would we be without a wonderful support network of students, colleagues, friends, and family? Students—both undergraduate and graduate—kindle our interest, help us refine our thinking with their questions, challenge our ideas, and generally keep us learning and growing. We would like especially to thank those graduate students who took our Trauma and Attachment seminar in 2012, suffering through an early version of this book. Rosemary Bernstein, Audrey Medina, Melissa Platt, and Carly Smith provided feedback and ideas that added to the quality of this final draft. Specific and crucial help was also provided by Rachel Goldsmith, Sarah Harsey, Kevin Wiles, Ann Yee, Eileen Zurbriggen, and all the other current and former students in the Dynamics Lab. Thank you for your contributions!

Colleagues provide personal support as well as intellectual challenge for our ideas. Holly Arrow, Laura Brown, Deb Casey, Ross Cheit, Sara Hodges, Kat Quina, and Marjorie Taylor have been enormously supportive through difficult and joyful times, adding to our personal and professional web of connections so important for all of us.

Our families have suffered through much as we struggled to write, revise, and polish this book. JQ Johnson, Theo Johnson-Freyd, Brian Gillis, Philip Johnson-Freyd, Sasha Johnson-Freyd, and Bruce Birrell form the basis for our personal lives. Without their support and love, we could not have embarked on nor completed this journey.

1

Blind to Betrayal

B etrayal blindness means not seeing what is there to be seen.
Julie Stone is now a respected lawyer in her forties who told
us about her experience with betrayal blindness. Her story gives
us many insights into the phenomenon of blindness—both how it
happens and why.

Julie told us about a time when she was a young wife, sitting in
a bar and waiting for her husband, who had been traveling all week.
She knew his ritual on returning to town: having a beer or two at
this bar with the guys. Usually, she waited at home with their infant
son, but this time she made an exception. A friend—the wife of her
husband's work partner—had talked her into a rare evening out.
Initially reluctant, Julie was now eager to surprise her husband. She
knew it would be a special evening for them both.

Julie explained to us that she didn't get to town very often, spending almost all of her time minding their young son and caring for
their home and farm: canning fruits, working in the garden, tending
the animals. With her thick curly hair and winsome eyes, she was
lovely. Perhaps because she was so busy as a mother, a homemaker,
and a farmer, she did not appreciate her own beauty, and she was
even less aware of her powerful intelligence. That evening, she was
excited because their son was home with a babysitter, and she would
be free to spend the evening with her husband.

She watched the door closely, and when he finally walked into the bar, she broke into a joyful, loving smile. Yet her husband never saw the smile, because almost immediately another woman—a stranger to Julie—jumped from her seat and ran into his arms. They kissed.

"When they stopped kissing, he looked up, and our eyes met. And I'm kind of watching this, and he walked over to me and said, 'I don't know who that was.' And I believed him."

As Julie said these words to us, we sat in her living room on comfortable contemporary furniture, under a vaulted ceiling, facing a picture window that revealed the forest surrounding the house. A tape recorder sat between us, preserving Julie's story. Outside, the August sun filtered through the tall Douglas firs. Bits of sunlight speckled the ceramic art Julie had created in her "spare time." *How does she manage all this?* we wondered. The room felt warm and light and airy. We felt good, privileged to be there. Julie exuded an air of competence and self-confidence. She seemed to like herself and to enjoy her life, and she could laugh at herself, too. It would be nearly impossible not to like and admire this woman. Yet as we sat there liking and admiring her, Julie told us about a series of betrayals that she managed—in her words—to "whoosh" away from her own awareness.

How did she remain so blind to what was so obvious? we wondered.

The bar incident wasn't the first time Julie had reason to doubt her husband's fidelity.

"My ex-husband was a good-looking guy. Women definitely were attracted to him. In fact, I know that they approached him. I had this friend who kept telling me, sort of kidding, that she was always lusting after my husband. It was sort of a joke between us. One time we were sitting around with a bunch of women. I brought this up somehow, and I laughingly asked her if she still had a thing for my husband. There was a hush in the group. I thought it was funny, but much later I realized that everybody there except me knew that she was sleeping with him. I didn't find out until her boyfriend approached me and said that since my husband and his girlfriend were having an affair, he thought we should get together. That was just shocking to me. I was so surprised. He was really stunned that I didn't know."

Then Julie became aware that her husband was sleeping with yet another woman. Amazingly, the bar incident happened the following year—*after* she had learned of two prior infidelities. So now the mystery was even greater: how could she have "whooshed" away the fact of that kiss between her husband and the other woman? She explained that between finding out about the first two cases of infidelity and the bar incident, the simple passage of time had worked its magic.

"My husband and I had a big fight over it and kind of made up, and time goes by. I was still with him, and it didn't occur to me . . . I thought it was finished."

She went on, telling us in her own words about the bar incident.

"I was kind of a stay-at-home person, and my son was under two years old. One of the standing fights I had with my husband was that he never came straight home after being away at work all week. He always went to a bar first and drank with his buddies. That really bothered me because he had a little boy and a wife, and he didn't want to come home right away to see us? I could never understand that. He said, 'Look, I work hard all the time, and I deserve to have a good time with my buddies.' . . . So anyway, this Friday, the wife of a man he worked with said to me, 'Come on, we're going to surprise them.' She had gotten a babysitter. We were going out—and I never went out, never.

"I decided to go, and we got all dressed up. We got to the bar in this small town before my husband and his coworker arrived. It had a local band, and the place was filled with people. We were kind of excited, waiting to surprise our husbands. They walked through the door and as my husband came inside, a woman jumped up and went over to him, and they kissed. When they stopped kissing, he looked up, and our eyes met. I'm kind of watching this, and he walked over and said, 'I don't know who that was.' I believed him. I seriously believed him. I thought, 'That was weird' and . . . whoosh! That was it. I spent the rest of the evening with him, dancing. . . . I never questioned him again about that woman."

"Whoosh?" *What exactly is this mental process?* we wondered, while replaying the audiotape of our interview with Julie. We are psychologists—we should know. We do in fact investigate the ways people can forget and remain unaware of important events. You could even say we study "whoosh" in the laboratory and observe it in the consulting room. Although we must admit that it remains something of a mystery to us, there is much we do understand.

We have come to call this "whooshing" away of important betrayals "betrayal blindness."

Betrayal blindness means you do not or cannot see what is there in front of you. The information that her husband was unfaithful was there the whole time. When Julie later replayed the bar incident in her own mind, she finally saw what she couldn't see at the time.

"It wasn't until much later, after we were divorced, I was working as a gardener, and when you work as a gardener, you have a lot of time . . . to just mull things over in your mind, and I remembered that night, and I thought, 'Oh, my God, he must have been having an affair with her.'"

How could Julie be blind to her husband's infidelity when she already knew of at least two of his previous affairs? Her husband kisses a strange woman and she accepts his claim: "I don't know who that was"?

What would it take for Julie to acknowledge the betrayal? Julie provided the answer: "Did I have to see it right in front of me? Yes, I did, because the final event that happened, when I could no longer deny it, was when a mutual friend of ours came to spend the night, a woman. I can't remember exactly the series of events leading up to this, but I was downstairs, and they were upstairs, and all of a sudden I thought, 'What is going on?' I tip-toed upstairs, and they were making love in our bed. I saw them. And I couldn't exactly . . . There it was. So I just went back downstairs again."

Some months after finding her husband in flagrante delicto with another woman, Julie did manage to leave him. Yet her reasons for doing so were as much about his marked cruelty toward her as they were about his infidelity. Her husband had become scary: alcoholic, emotionally abusive, and threatening violence. By that point, his infidelity was less significant than his reign of terror, and maybe that is why Julie let herself creep up the stairs and get the hard evidence for what was probably so obvious already. Staying with her husband was becoming a risk to her safety and her son's well-being.

The human mind is marvelously convoluted. Julie almost surely knew about her husband's betrayals in some sense of the word *knew*, even as she didn't let herself know in another sense. Betrayal blindness requires this convolution, so that one can be in the dual state of simultaneously knowing and not knowing something important.

Why would Julie not know something that's there for the knowing? The answer likely resided in her need to survive. During the initial period of her marriage, Julie had a powerful—although unconscious—motivation for remaining blind to her husband's betrayal: she was utterly dependent on her husband. Knowing about the betrayal would have required some action, yet she could not afford to rock the boat. Sometimes ignorance can preserve the relative bliss of the status quo when knowledge would inevitably lead to chaos. Ignorance *is* bliss when it allows you to survive.

"You know, people always look at other people's marriages and their bad relations and say, 'Why does she stay?' There are so many reasons to stay, and it's so hard to leave, because everybody says no relationship is perfect, and you have to go through the bad times, and you have a child with someone, and also you have no resources. I had no resources at all. . . . I spent all of my money, $250, on a car, and I drove it away, and it threw a rod and died completely, and there I was in the middle of nowhere with a two-year-old in the backseat. I thought, 'Okay, this sucks,' and then I went back, and he had moved back into the house. . . . So you wonder . . ."

We asked Julie how her financial situation had affected her ability to leave him.

She explained, "I had no money of my own. I wasn't working. I was isolated. I was completely dependent on him. Once I got out of that relationship, I knew I could never again be financially dependent on a person like that, to not have any kind of options."

With Julie's financial dependence, how did she manage to leave her husband? Partly it was her willingness to call on other relationships.

"I had to get help to leave him. A girlfriend said she would send me the money to get out. I was dependent on him to take me to the airport. I didn't have a vehicle. We lived in the country. The airport was really far away, so I had to lie to him. I had to pretend I was just visiting my mother, so I couldn't take my stuff. I had a lot of really nice things I had to leave because he would have known, and he wouldn't have driven me to the airport."

"It sounds like an escape," we said.

Julie agreed. "It was an escape. I had to escape."

So Julie did escape, and over time she re-created herself into the successful professional she is today. She is very happily remarried. We asked Julie to think back to her friends: "You said other people knew at the time. Do you know how they knew?"

"That one friend wasn't the only one in the group who was sleeping with him, as it turned out, so some of them knew through firsthand experience, and some knew from gossip. They talked. It's amazing that nobody told me."

Why didn't her friends tell her?

Julie saw part of the answer: "I think we tend not to tell others because we don't want to set the ball in motion that might break up a marriage. It feels like none of our business."

We were getting a sense of Julie's first marriage, the betrayals, the blindness, the collusion of those around her. Yet the psychological mystery persisted: Where did the information in front of her eyes go?

Julie tried to help us understand. "If we take the event where I actually saw a woman kiss him, it didn't even seem like a special event. I didn't even think about it again, until I began to think about my marriage when I was gardening. I was remembering that night, the excitement of getting together and going out because I never went anywhere. I had a really good time, actually. And then I remembered that kiss, and I stood up, and my jaw kind of dropped. I thought, 'Oh my God, what an idiot I am! What do I have to do to . . . ?' See? I had to see him actually having sex before I could really accept it. So, yeah, where does the information go? It feels like it just completely didn't register. And he walks over and says to me, 'I don't know who that was.' He'd just kissed her, for God's sake!

"Because I'm not a stupid person, right?"

No, Julie is not a stupid person at all. She's quite brilliant. So imagine our surprise when she told us about being blind again after she left her first husband.

"Later I had another relationship where the guy had an affair, and this was *after* my marriage. It was actually the next really important relationship, which was a few years later. I was vigilant. At that point, I had become obsessed with the possibility that somebody could be having an affair. I looked for all signs of this activity, and I never felt like that was happening with this guy. . . . But when we were leaving to go on a long trip—we had some dogs—all of a sudden, he had rented the house to this woman who was going to look after the dogs. It struck me as weird that I had never met this woman before. He had just made this arrangement, and she had come over one night to see the house and look at the dogs. I was very friendly to her, and she was strangely reserved around me. I thought, 'Who is this woman?' She was a very attractive young woman, and I thought, 'Wow.' Then, years later, I found out that he had been having an affair with her!"

We were struggling to understand. We asked Julie, "Do you remember suspecting and discounting it, even though you were being vigilant?"

"When my other friend said, 'Remember the woman who looked after the dogs?' I was not surprised. I felt like, right, okay, and a long time later, confronted the guy."

How could Julie fail to detect betrayal in a new relationship after living through her husband's betrayal? "The second time is puzzling," we said. "You described yourself being observant, and we still don't understand what went through your mind when you met the dog-sitting woman."

"Well, I remember thinking, 'We have this problem: we have these dogs, and we need someone to look after them in this house.' Also, the dogs were very important to my boyfriend. The person who was looking after the dogs had to be someone he could really trust. He said, 'Well, I know this woman, and she is going to do it,' and I thought, 'Who is this woman?' You know, it crossed my mind. I was puzzled because it seemed that you would have to know someone quite well if you were going to leave your beloved pets under her care. And then I remember her being very attractive and very quiet. She was exactly the way you might be if you were meeting the woman whose boyfriend you were having an affair with. She was uncomfortable and reserved. I was quite friendly to her, and she didn't reciprocate. But it didn't occur to me then that he was having an affair with her."

Julie reflected on her own process of remembering and figuring out the betrayal. "Where does the information go? To me, it is interesting that when I was remembering the event—going out to surprise my husband . . . Then just replaying the event, I remembered the woman, and then in light of later events and my understanding of who he was, I realized what I had missed, and it just stunned me. So the information was all coded in memory but not interpreted as evidence of his having an affair."

Perhaps some people don't suspect infidelity because they don't think it is possible. Yet by the time Julie saw her husband kiss the woman in the bar, she had already learned of two of his prior infidelities. Perhaps before the very first fight she had with her husband, she didn't suspect infidelity because she didn't really believe it was possible. After the fight, though, after she had learned of his first and then his second infidelity, she must have known it was at least possible that he could be unfaithful. And yet she had accepted his explanation of the kiss, and she didn't think about the matter again for years. How could this be?

"I had the idea, but in terms of information, I think it was just unprocessed, somehow—it's there, but it's just totally not processed. Yet it's available if you recall the incident for some other reason."

We wondered how much of it was motivated by a desire not to know. Julie answered, "I wanted to believe that we had a happy marriage, that it was going to work."

The need to trust is a powerful agent, a blinding agent.

Were Julie's experiences unusual? From our research and interviews with many other individuals, we know that Julie's experiences of remaining blind to infidelity are fairly common for both women and men.[1] Furthermore, betrayal occurs in many domains besides infidelity. People can be betrayed at work, in the family, and in society. Betrayal can occur at the individual and at the societal level. Betrayal can be the act of a terrorist or the act of a friend. Parents can betray by abandoning or abusing their children. Treason is betrayal. Social injustice and oppression often entail betrayal and betrayal blindness, as will be illustrated in the next chapter by the case of Kevin, who remained blind to being a victim of racial discrimination for so many years.

Although not all betrayal involves blindness, ongoing or repeated betrayal is intrinsically linked with unawareness.[2] Ongoing betrayal can occur only when there is some deception that is not fully detected. Sometimes this lack of knowledge is the result of insufficient information, but other times the obliviousness is in part the result of *betrayal blindness*—unawareness of information that is present but is somehow "whooshed" away. Moreover, the discovery of betrayal always seems to prompt a profoundly new awareness:

the world is not the same. Someone who was trusted is now considered unsafe. On discovery of betrayal, a key response is to reorganize one's perceptions of what has happened—to rewrite history. Betrayal therefore has a fundamental impact on one's perceptions of reality. As one woman who had been betrayed by an unfaithful husband said to us, "Betrayal is so contrary to what one expects that it throws you off balance. It tips you over. It's like, where have I been? Everything that I know to be true is not true. It's insidious, it's got tentacles that reach in and make you question everything."

And yet, although betrayal is so common and insidious, very little has been written about it in the psychological literature. Psychology as a discipline may suffer from betrayal blindness. Part of the problem stems from a tendency in clinical psychology and psychiatry to focus on individuals and individual symptoms. As a result, the relations between people—betrayal and its blindness— are not seen. Betrayal, depending as it does on interpersonal and institutional relationships, never quite makes it onto center stage. Perhaps beginning to look at betrayal in scientific ways can also make the discipline of psychology question everything it thinks it knows.

2

Children Betrayed

Consider the situation of a child who is betrayed by his or her parents. Most children are not strong enough within themselves to confront betrayal by a parent on whom they depend for their very existence. The relationship with their parents is far too important for them to risk losing it. Yet there are many ways that parents can betray a child in his or her vulnerability. One of the greatest fears for a child is the fear of abandonment; children must trust that their parents will not hurt or leave them. Abandonment can occur in purely physical ways, that is, through actually leaving children when they are helpless. It can also occur in emotional ways, through rejection and withdrawal of love. The free fall and disorientation for these children may result in the lack of a coherent sense of self. What is wrong? They can't know about the betrayal or name it that way. So children will dissociate into parts, develop strange fears, or experience a myriad of other reactions to hide from themselves and others the deep betrayal.

One way that children may manage betrayal at the hands of their parents or caregivers is to turn the blame inward. Similar to being blind to the betrayal or forgetting about it later, such shame could protect the relationship by allowing the child to maintain an attachment to the abusive caregiver by blaming him- or herself instead of the true perpetrator. Although this seems unlikely and perhaps unbelievable to our adult minds, it is a real strategy to maintain family ties in the face of ongoing betrayal.

With repeated betrayal, the shame becomes chronic. Debbie, a psychotherapy client, had been constantly criticized and blamed by her stepmother for her failure to live up to adult standards. In other words, Debbie's "sin" was being a child. As a result, she developed a chronic sense of failure and an almost total lack of self-esteem. As an adult, when things started to go wrong, either at work or in the family, she suffered a sense of internal collapse, blaming herself. Although the shame allowed Debbie to stay in a relationship with her abusive stepmother, it exacted a tremendous cost on Debbie's well-being as an adult. In current research in our laboratory with Melissa Platt, we are investigating the relationship between betrayal trauma and shame. Our preliminary findings indicate that shame is indeed associated with exposure to traumas that have a high level of betrayal, but not to traumas with a low degree of betrayal. This preliminary finding is consistent with our hypothesis that shame, similar to unawareness and other aspects of betrayal blindness, helps preserve necessary relationships.

Children need secure and trusting relationships to grow and thrive. Their very sense of self and emotional stability depends on it. Betrayal damages that web of relationships on which we all depend. Imagine for a moment a free-fall feeling of betrayal with no comprehension of its source. The confusion and disorientation can't be understood by young children, so they go into a kind of internal whirling and feeling of craziness. As adults, we can give a name to the events that caused our free fall. Children only whirl—attempting to hold onto *anything* stable in their world. If there are no other trusting relationships, and the betrayal is widespread, children can find stability only by locating within themselves the badness that happened.

Judy's mother died in an automobile accident when Judy was four years old. Shortly afterward, Judy's father abandoned her to distant cousins who did not particularly want her. It's easy to imagine four-year-old Judy's internal falling and whirling. She had to have something to hold onto, so Judy did what almost all young children do in that situation. Her foundation in this internal maelstrom became the very firm belief that she had caused her mother's death because she somehow hadn't been a good enough little girl. She also settled on a deep conviction that she was a bother and that her emotions were too much for other people. She put them away, even from herself.

As an adult, Judy was haunted by self-doubts about her competence and basic goodness. She was highly anxious in relationships, often panicking when difficulties arose. She was constantly fearful that she would be left, and that it would be her own fault. So when relationships failed (as happens with all of us), Judy was quick to blame herself and become depressed.[1]

As Judy began to understand the roots of her anxiety and depression, her internal world started whirling once more. When the anchor of her belief in her own badness and culpability began to erode, Judy initially grew more anxious and depressed, as is often the case. Yet this time she found herself in a therapeutic relationship that she could begin to trust, and the depression and anxiety that she had always felt now had meaning and could be rooted in her early experiences of betrayal and loss. Her anxiety, instead of being a "symptom" of a mental "disorder," became an impetus to find another foundation for her life—one rooted in her innate goodness and trust in people around her. Her depression became a mourning for her years of isolation and for her mother, for whom she had never been able to grieve.

Kayla, another psychotherapy client, suffered betrayal of a different sort. One night when she was six, her caring and loving father came into her room and molested her. Kayla's world was shattered. She, like all of us, depended on that interweaving of supportive relationships to understand herself and the world. Her father's betrayal of their relationship and the family's subsequent denial of that betrayal left Kayla no choice. The knowledge of the incident and others that followed was too dangerous for her to keep in her awareness. To maintain the only family she had ever had and the only reality she had ever known, Kayla put the knowledge of the molestation away deep inside, where it remained for years.

As Kayla grew older, she had continuing problems with relationships. She could not become intimate with anyone, men especially, without feeling a sense of panic. Even friendships were problematic for her, because closeness to others meant closeness to herself and her secret—something Kayla could not risk. Kayla became isolated and depressed. She attempted suicide on numerous occasions.

After a nightmare when she was thirty, Kayla began to know and understand the depths of the betrayal that had been perpetrated on her. As she gradually began to trust more and reveal more of herself in a therapeutic relationship, she began to know more about what had happened and how it had affected her. Her depression turned to rage, and her rage woke her to a new life and a new reality—one in which unconscious fears of another betrayal gave way to a conscious ability to relate to others and herself in a truly intimate manner.

Rebecca's Story

Judy and Kayla couldn't know their betrayals, although they had both suffered severe and clear betrayals. Their stories illustrate the importance of human connection and the damage that can be caused by the disruption of those bonds. They also illustrate how early betrayals can make us appear as if, and think we are, crazy. Let's examine a true story in more detail, as Rebecca Brewerman told it to us in her own words. Rebecca is an intelligent and sensitive woman in her early sixties. She was molested by her father during her childhood. We interviewed her at her home on the Oregon coast. Rebecca lives alone and is highly artistic. Her home was warm and welcoming, and the rare Oregon sunshine came in through ruffled curtains. Her big dog slept on the floor at her feet. Rebecca seemed at peace, but here's what she said about her earlier life: "For the first forty years of my adult life, I was in the depths of confusion, anxiety, guilt, and depression. In the last few years, I have finally achieved mental/emotional peace and respect for myself, and I really work very hard not to descend again into my previous horrifying state of mind.

"I just couldn't cope with the world around me. I was always in financial trouble, I was losing jobs. I had originally—when I was in teenager—expected to have a PhD and teach at the college level, and I certainly have the smarts for that, but I never could do it because of what I call 'scrambled brains.' I was just barely surviving, and it was getting worse."

Rebecca remembered vividly the terrors of her childhood— the early deaths of her brother and sister and her father's nightly visitations: "Yeah, I would wake up, he was on the evening shift, and I would wake up with his penis in my mouth in the middle of the night, choking. And then when we were picking strawberries, he would stick a great big strawberry in my mouth and just laugh 'cause he thought that was just so funny. So . . . I don't know how long, I think by the time I was in high school, he wasn't doing it anymore. 'Cause I was probably getting too big and strong for him. And as a bereft child, actually society let me down after my sister died because there was no help for children in the '50s. My mother was physically but never emotionally there for me. I had a wonderful second-grade teacher, and I was in second grade then, and she gave me a book of common prayer because she knew I was Episcopalian. She kinda took good care of me, but after that, by the time I was in fourth grade, my fourth-grade teacher asked me why I was acting out, and I told him my sister died. He asked, 'When was that?' and I said, 'Two years ago,' and he said, 'You should be over that by now.' Betrayal."

Scrambled brains, as Rebecca called them, made life more and more difficult to cope with. She lost a teaching job at a small college because she couldn't manage anymore: "I experienced this black chasm, I thought I was going to fall into it. I was just so overwhelmed, and there was no support for me, being the head resident. I lived in a dorm. So I simply quit that job, which I really wish I hadn't because it was an outstanding college, and I wish I was still there. But that was more than forty years ago."

In her forties, Rebecca began to figure out what was happening to her after she went into therapy for the first time: "I went to her for a year until I felt like she had abandoned me. During that time, she didn't make any suggestions at all. She just listened. But I started having flashbacks, major flashbacks, and that was about twenty years ago. It was horrible. . . .

"Mostly at night. But while I was awake, it wasn't dreams 'cause I didn't dream for decades. I didn't think I dreamed. I didn't remember them. It would be kinda like I might be half awake, but I actually had to get out of this house I was living in because it was just so terrifying to wake up and have these visions. And it was a horrible, horrible house, too, it had holes in the wall because I was so poor by then."

Rebecca's story is ultimately hopeful, though, and you'll read her inspiring words in the last part of the book. In the meantime, we'll leave her cozy warm house and look at a bigger picture of betrayal.

Kevin's Story

Child abuse is an intimate and personal betrayal. Other betrayals can occur at societal levels. Racial discrimination involves numerous people and organizations. Although it has a shared existence, it nonetheless affects individuals intimately and profoundly. Similar to the child abuse described earlier, discrimination can result in betrayal blindness, as illustrated by the case of Kevin.

The year was 1973. Kevin Nakamura was a boy in school in the Midwest. His parents were born in Japan and immigrated to the United States before he was born. Kevin considered himself American. He spoke excellent English without any accent. He did what most American boys do—he played basketball, traded baseball cards, ate hot dogs with ketchup and mustard. Despite his ethnic heritage, Kevin did not know about Japanese culture, nor did he consider himself Japanese, not even Japanese American. Kevin was a smart boy, a good son, and a loyal friend.

What Kevin did not see—at first—was the way he was the victim of racial discrimination. On the phone, Kevin could pass for a "regular" American, his flawless English conjuring an image in the listener's mind of "a white kid." Yet in person, Kevin looked different. This difference in appearance was behind all sorts of subtle and not-so-subtle slights he experienced. Kevin was not selected for a role in his school musical performance of *Oklahoma!* despite the fact that he was a talented singer and actor, and few boys had auditioned for the school play. Kevin's homework assignments that he turned in for English and American history were superb, yet he got B+ marks. Kevin got invited to fewer birthday parties than average, although he was friendly and cooperative with the other kids in class. In high school, when it was time to select a date for the school dance, Kevin was rejected by all of the girls he asked, despite his being an attractive, considerate young man.

It was only when Kevin went to college (his standardized test results helped him get into a very good school) that Kevin's eyes were opened wide. In college, Kevin learned about the history of Asians in America. He learned about the depth and the pervasiveness of discrimination, and he realized that some of his childhood suffering may have been due to prejudice and discrimination. He also realized that he might have known all along on some level, while being unwilling to see the discrimination and thus remaining ignorant of it on another level. Kevin's hunch about his own state of mind was insightful. As we explore in later chapters, the human mind is adept at knowing and not knowing at the same time—compartmentalizing knowledge so that it is not available for conscious reflection but is there for other purposes. In college classes, Kevin was no longer primarily surrounded by a culture that accepted only one main culture and skin color. Although discrimination still existed, there was more tolerance and certainly more diversity in his immediate world. Why would Kevin the child have remained unaware of discrimination perpetrated against him that Kevin the young adult was able to acknowledge?

As a young child, Kevin had a strong motivation to remain blind to his betrayal. During childhood and adolescence, we are learning who we are, how we fit into the world, and how to be accepted. We all remember how challenging this time can be. If Kevin had acknowledged to himself that he was being excluded and marginalized for reasons (such as skin color and facial features) he was powerless to change, it could have been a realization of devastating proportions. Living in a community without other Asian American families and without resources for minorities, he had little to gain and much to lose from knowing the true reasons for his rejection. Knowing about the prejudice would have meant Kevin might have felt alienated and thus behaved in ways that made him even less accepted by others. His alienation might have caused him to withdraw from the very community in which he needed to get along.

Knowing about the discrimination would have undermined Kevin's ability to meet at least some of his social and educational needs. Furthermore, it is likely that Kevin's blindness supported his parents' approach, and if Kevin had seen things more clearly, he might have alienated not only his peers and teachers, but his parents as well. Seeing the truth would have rocked the boat so much, it might have failed to float.

Kevin's experiences involved betrayal because he had a deeply held belief that he would be treated fairly. This belief grew naturally out of a value system that stresses equality, equity, and fairness; these values are taught repeatedly throughout grade school in this country. From reading Horatio Alger to learning about a grading system based on merit, Americans are socialized to value justice and equality.[2] The catch is that often injustice and inequality exist all around us, but we don't recognize them. Injustice and inequality are a kind of betrayal because they are reneging on a trust; they are breaking an initial promise that we all are free. Equally free.

Another version of Kevin's experience was described by author and lawyer Frank Wu, whose parents came to America from China:[3]

I am about as American as you can be. You know, I don't speak Chinese. I'm really bad with chopsticks.

I held up my end of the deal. When I went to school as a five-year-old, thirty years ago, teacher said to me and the kids said to me—and if they didn't say it, they made it clear—that if I assimilated—the deal was, if I assimilated, they'd accept me. But if I didn't assimilate, they wouldn't. If I continued to eat funny-looking foods, if my English wasn't good, well, then, their view was it was right for them to pick on me because then I would be different. But if I became like them, they'd accept me.

So I did. I learned how to shoot marbles. I collected baseball cards. I built model airplanes. I knew nothing about Chinese culture. I went to college; I was told "You have to study the Western canon." So I did. I know Shakespeare. I'm a huge Shakespeare fan. I can recite for you the opening 45 lines of *Richard III* from memory. And I have no accent. I can pick up the telephone; I could pass as a Smith. I could tell you my name's Frank Smith, and until I showed up and you look at me and say, "Smith? How did you get to be a Smith?" I could, for all practical purposes, if I were invisible, be a Frank Smith.

So the irony here is the more I fit in, the more I realize there's a dichotomy. I'm not bitter about it, but I realize others—they reneged on the deal. The deal was I'd fit in, you'd accept me. And yet sometimes I'm still treated as if I'm fresh off the boat.

Both Frank Wu and Kevin Nakamura did the best they could to fit in as children. They lived as if they were white Americans, rather than Asian Americans. This was a survival strategy. Kevin's blindness to this betrayal helped him survive his childhood by allowing him to remain connected with a community that provided some positive benefit, despite the injustice. Had Kevin seen the unfairness and reacted with anger or withdrawal, he would have risked disrupting the tenuous positive connections with his community that did exist. As a child, Kevin was probably powerless to change the prejudice and discrimination in his community through any direct confrontation. In contrast, once Kevin was in a different environment, a college community that had more diversity and that was less discriminatory toward Asian Americans, Kevin had less to risk and more to gain by becoming aware of the reality of discrimination. Indeed, Kevin's growing awareness had many benefits for Kevin and the world. As he recognized the parallels between his own past and the history of discrimination he was learning about in college, Kevin experienced intellectual and emotional liberation, despite the pain of accepting betrayal. As college progressed, he found he was able to seek out and find more open-minded friends who did not discriminate against him. Kevin's deeper understanding of these issues inspired him to pursue a career in social justice, so that future generations would suffer less discrimination. His contributions to society would not have been possible if he had not survived his childhood with so much of his sense of self intact; betrayal blindness might have been his best option. Kevin would like to help create a world that does not put children into such a bind.

Betrayal as a Violation of Trust

Trusting relationships are the basis for personal well-being and growth, for intimate and loving partner and friend relationships, and for justice and peace at the societal and international level. However, at all of these levels betrayal is ubiquitous. It harms us on a personal level, it destroys relationships and the ability to trust, and it finds its way into national and international relationships and is often the cause for wars. Logically, it seems that when we are betrayed, we confront the situation, deal with the betrayer, and go on with our lives. As we've described previously, though, it's often not that simple. Either the relationship is too important or we are not strong enough within ourselves to deal with the betrayal.

Yet there are other complications. Sometimes we know we've been betrayed—we read a love letter our spouse has written to someone else, or we find evidence that our government has lied to us. Most often, however, the evidence of betrayal is not that clear, as in the case of Kevin, but we know something is wrong. We don't know what it is, but there is discomfort, perhaps guilt, or anxiety. As we've described, children who are abused can't recognize betrayal, so must blame themselves when trusted parents turn on them; sometimes spouses who are cheated on take a very long time to understand what is happening. It is an emotional and cognitive conundrum. We can't live with the feelings and knowledge about the betrayal, yet in some ways we *do* know.

It is important that we come to respect the impact of betrayal and its consequences if we encounter it in our lives or the lives of others. It very likely will affect the degree to which we can give ourselves in trust in other situations in our lives. It can even have an effect on what we call the capacity of individuals to trust that life is good, and to trust that they can make their way and find what they need from their lives. Those who cannot trust cannot grow and thrive.

3

The Wide Reach of Betrayal Blindness

The idea that you or I—that *we*—could be betrayed is off-putting, to say the least. "Not me," we say. "No one would want to betray me; I am a good person." Furthermore, most of us like to think that if we were betrayed, we would spot it immediately. After all, we're intelligent people, right? Yet intelligence has absolutely nothing to do with it. Did Hillary Clinton—an inarguably intelligent woman, no matter what your political leanings—know about Bill and Monica? According to her biographer Gail Sheehy, Hillary did not let herself know about the affair: "And so, just as countless times in the past, *Hillary's choice* was not to know what she knew."[1] This unawareness lasted until the betrayal was made so very public that Bill had to confess to her, and Hillary could no longer not know about it. According to Sheehy, Hillary and Bill both relied on a vast amount of studied avoidance of the facts of their marriage and the inevitable consequences of Bill's unfaithful behavior. It wasn't only Monica, but a whole string of women and messy relationships that Hillary failed to see, despite the evidence all around her. Hillary, a brilliant, strong, and exceptionally accomplished woman, was apparently an expert in remaining blind to her own betrayal.

The 2003 documentary *Capturing the Friedmans* examines some of the complexities of knowing and not knowing about betrayals.[2] In the late 1980s, Arnold Friedman was accused of sexually abusing

20

more than a dozen boys in his computer classes. Arnold first came to the attention of the authorities after child pornography on its way to him via the U.S. mail was intercepted. This led to law enforcement officials obtaining a warrant to search his house, where large amounts of child pornography were discovered. Much later, during filming, Arnold's wife at the time of the search, Elaine, described her initial inability to see the child pornography lying in plain sight around her house:

> Somewhere along the way, I think it was the Nassau County cops, they showed me this magazine. And they said, "You see? Look at this magazine." And they showed me the magazine. They were embarrassed to show it to me because of what the pictures were. And you know, I didn't see it? My eyes [motions downwards from eyes] were in the right direction. But my brain saw nothing. Because, when it was all over, the lawyers showed me the magazine and then I saw it. For the first time, I really saw it. And, I just, couldn't believe what I saw. [Sighs] I mean, I had no concept that this thing even exists in the world. That this magazine would even exist in the world. I mean, we had a middle-class home, educated, I had a good family, right? Where did this come from?

When Elaine said, "And you know, I didn't see it? My eyes were in the right direction. But my brain saw nothing," she was giving an exact description of betrayal blindness. It is because of this inability to see what is right there in plain sight that we use the word *blindness*. Although this word captures our intended meaning, in some ways it is troubling. The fact that this same word— *blindness*—denotes a physical condition and also has a more abstract meaning may both reflect and contribute to "ableism"—an assumption that there is a normal correct body versus a disordered incorrect body. We have struggled with the use of this word for this reason.

We all currently swim in a cultural and linguistic system that conflates having limited eyesight with ignorance. You may have already noticed that it is very difficult to talk about knowing without using vision terms. For example, "I see what you mean." "My perspective is different from yours." "Your argument is crystal clear." This interlocking of vision and knowledge may be an inevitable result of the tendency known as embodied cognition, because a primary way we know things is through our bodies.

In the case of the word *blind*, the connection between knowledge and vision is explicit. The earliest known meaning of the word root was not "sightlessness" but "confusion and darkness." The word *blind* has evolved over time to have two interrelated primary meanings: (1) unable to see, and (2) unwilling or unable to perceive or understand. We use the phrase *betrayal blindness* to include both of these meanings, although we do not mean to include physical blindness or contribute to a kind of institutional betrayal that sees the idealized body as standard and all other bodies as less able. In addition to betrayal blindness occurring when we don't see with our eyes, it can also happen when we do not hear, feel, or know something that should be obvious to us. Furthermore, a physically blind person could be more fully aware of betrayals than a sighted friend is. We use the phrase *betrayal blindness* because it so closely captures what we intend to convey, and we know of no other phrase that communicates this full meaning. We hope that someday there will be language that more clearly distinguishes between sightlessness and not seeing at a more abstract level.

Betrayal blindness is not a game. There are times when we know about a betrayal and consciously pretend not to know, in order to ease social relationships. Steven Pinker describes games people play when they know or think something that is too risky to say out loud.[3] For example, one would not offer a bribe to a policeman in explicit terms but might manage to imply willingness to bribe using more cautious language, such as, "Can I pay the ticket right now?" The quintessential example is the story "The Emperor's New Clothes." Everyone knows that the king is naked, but no one risks saying it. Once the words are spoken out loud, however, everything changes, not because people learn that the king is naked (they already know that) but because they learn that it is now common knowledge. Pinker points out that when information rises to the level of common knowledge (which means I know that you know that I know that you know, and so on), one can no longer plausibly deny the reality. In the case of betrayal—such as infidelity in a marriage—one conceivably might know about it and decide it is too risky to discuss. Yet in cases where one is greatly dependent on, and attached to, one's partner, it is very difficult to *pretend* that one has not been betrayed. The natural reactions to betrayal are either to withdraw or to confront the person, and these are difficult reactions to consciously suppress, over and over. At a minimum, that degree of pretending would require a substantial amount of attention and effort. Worse, the charade would break down, and the true feelings would leak out, risking the very relationship that needs to be protected. Imagine the plight of a young child who doesn't have the cognitive and social maturity to play these social games. In these cases, we argue, nature has a better solution: remaining blind to the betrayal in the first place removes the need to pretend. Elaine Friedman described this kind of blindness when she was presented with her husband's pornography: "And you know, I didn't see it? My eyes were in the right direction. But my brain saw nothing." This was not pretending not to see; it was not seeing.

Betrayal, especially by a close and trusted person, can have far-reaching and damaging effects. Psychotherapy clients regularly report sexual, emotional, and physical abuse at the hands of parents—a severe betrayal from those who are supposed to love and protect us, although clients may not use the word *betrayal* or even recognize these events as betrayals.[4] Therapy clients also report infidelity, workplace harassment with no institutional support, friends who have turned on them, and a wide variety of major and minor betrayals. Yet with the current psychological emphasis only on symptom reduction and mental disorders, therapists and well-meaning friends can often miss this all-too-common thread in the lives of those who suffer. We instead try to lessen depression or anxiety without addressing the underlying reasons for it—one of the most common of them being betrayal in all of its disturbing forms.

Another example is that of Howard Friedman, Arnold's brother. According to *Capturing the Friedmans*, Arnold wrote a letter describing what he did to his brother:[5]

> This story goes back 50 years to when I was a child. When I reached adolescence I sought out partners for my emerging sexuality. My first partner when I was 13 was my 8-year old brother. I had overt sexual relations with him over a period of a few years.

Howard has no memory of his abuse. In *Capturing*, he explains,

> I know my brother has said he messed around with me when I was a kid. And, I don't remember any of it. I don't remember anything. I have nothing up here [covers forehead with hand] that has me yelling or screaming or crying or trying to get away or unhappy or . . . I, I, there's nothing there that . . . Maybe someday a door will open but it better hurry up because I'm 65 and at this point in time I could care less!

We have heard stories of betrayal and betrayal blindness from many women and men. Some of them have told us of horrendous acts of violence that were forgotten or very greatly minimized. Others have spoken about lives relatively free of violence but nonetheless peppered with intimate betrayals. We relay some of these stories of intimate betrayal in this book.

Betrayal occurs in many areas besides infidelity and in many contexts that are not entirely intimate. People can be betrayed at work, in the family, and in society. As we learned in chapter 2 from the stories of Kevin Nakamura and Frank Wu, even social injustice and oppression often involve betrayal and betrayal blindness. The factors that make these society-wide acts ones of betrayal are twofold. First, society-wide acts involve individual human interactions, and many acts of injustice or oppression at the individual level look just like other personal betrayals. Second, we have implicit and explicit assumptions in our society of equality and justice. These implicit and explicit assumptions form a "social contract" between members of society. When discrimination occurs, this is a betrayal of the equality contract. When there is an injustice, this is a betrayal of the justice (or fairness) contract. In this chapter and in chapter 4, we consider these issues further, as we explore some of the many ways humans betray and are betrayed.

Girl on a Plane

In August 2008, we attended a trial in federal criminal court in Portland, Oregon. Jennifer Freyd served as a consultant and an expert witness for the prosecution. She was asked to educate the jury about what we know from research about victims' responses to sexual assault. It became clear to us that this expert testimony was needed only because of the widespread ignorance about the reality of sexual assault in the general public and thus in the population of potential jurors. The experience was a stark reminder of the importance of disseminating research and educating people about societal and criminal justice. Our research can have an impact only when it reaches the right people. In the case of a jury trial, the right people are the jurors. Without this education, victims may be betrayed all over again by the court experience.

Jurors are asked to rely on their common sense and reason. This works well when common sense and reason coincide with empirical reality. However, the criminal justice system is at risk when jurors show pervasive ignorance or, worse, adhere to dangerous myths. Rather than holding accurate knowledge of victim psychology, many individuals endorse some degree of belief in what research-ers have called "rape myths" and "child sexual abuse myths." Rape myths are false beliefs that tend to blame the victim for the rape and absolve the rapist. They are false in the sense that they conflict with scientific evidence. An example is the belief that victims of rape cause the event by the way they dress. Another example is the belief that men cannot control their sexual urges. Similarly for child sex-ual abuse, an example of false belief is that children cause the abuse by the way they act or dress. These myths can work against justice in profound ways, causing victims—who were already betrayed by a crime—to be betrayed all over again in the courtroom.

The criminal case for which Freyd served as an expert witness involved abusive sexual contact aboard an aircraft. The victim was at the time a sixteen-year-old girl, and the defendant was her thirty-two-year-old coach. The case was federal because the offense oc-curred on an airplane that crossed state lines.

The defendant admitted to FBI investigators that the sexual acts did occur. There was no prior romance, flirtation, or invita-tion between the coach and the athlete. They were returning from an athletic event. The victim had fallen asleep under a blanket in the window seat, and the defendant was seated next to her. It was nighttime and dark on the plane. She woke up to him touching her under her clothing. The victim displayed a fairly passive or "frozen" response to finding herself in this predicament.

The age of consent in federal sexual assault cases is sixteen. The defense attempted to portray the events as consensual sex, relying heavily on the implicit question: If she didn't want the sexual intrusion, why didn't she actively object? In closing arguments, the defense attorney suggested that the victim and her coach had together created a "bubble of intimacy" on that plane that was later burst, causing the victim to feel "sexual regret" and to claim the sexual acts were without her permission.

Consent in sexual assault cases remains a vexed issue in American courts. In the excellent book *Unwanted Sex: The Culture of Intimidation and the Failure of Law*, Stephen Schulhofer, traces the history of consent laws.[6] He notes that in the sixteenth century, "the common law of theft protected an owner's property only when a wrongdoer physically removed it from the owner's possession, against the will and by force" (p. 3). However, "the law evolved, slowly at first, to fill the intolerable gaps" (p. 3). Today the law "punishes virtually all interference with property rights without the owner's genuine consent. Yet there has been no comparable evolution and modernization of the law of sexual assault" (p. 4). In other words, if your front door is unlocked and someone you know walks into your house and takes your laptop computer while you cower in the corner, this is a crime unless you have explicitly given affirmative permission. There is no argument to be made that you have implicitly consented to engage in giving away your possessions by your open door, by the prior display of your product, or by your silence during the theft. Compare this state of affairs to current beliefs about sexual assault, where victims can be blamed for their clothing and are often held responsible for not actively resisting. Furthermore, sexual assault law currently draws inconsistent lines regarding the age of consent and is largely insensitive to other aspects of the power differential (such as formal roles of authority and power) that can vastly reduce a person's ability to freely consent.

In Freyd's testimony, she drew on research about victims to educate the jury that a passive response to sexual assault is not uncommon, and she discussed some of the research regarding factors that are associated with such a response, such as fear and perceived powerlessness. Most important was the concept of betrayal. The girl on the plane was dependent on her coach for her position on her team, and she trusted him. He was twice her age, and she was under his care. Her passivity was entirely consistent with betrayal blindness. During closing arguments, the prosecutor was able to remind the jury that crime victims often do respond passively, and she brought up all of the substantial evidence contrary to the defense's argument of consent. The jury found the defendant guilty.

Mark Walker: Another Case of Betrayal

In April 2011, a federal parole officer named Mark Walker pleaded guilty for engaging in sexual contact and sexual abuse with female parolees who were directly under his supervision between 2006 and 2009.[7] Walker had used his enormous power to manipulate and co-erce the women into performing sexual acts they did not want to engage in. Walker was a bold and masterful perpetrator, able to use his substantial institutional power for his own gratification. At least fifteen of the women Walker had supervised accused him of inap-propriate contact, although not all of these instances were included in the criminal case, due to matters such as the statute of limitations. This sort of abuse involves a great deal of betrayal, and much of that betrayal is due to the social and institutional context in which the abuse occurs.

The women Walker targeted were vulnerable to him for a number of reasons. First, many of them had already been abused by others close to them, and as we see in chapter 9, one way betrayal is so toxic is the way it sets up victims to be revictimized. Second, their fates were all under Walker's control. He could grant them favors (such as not requiring drug testing), or he could punish them (such as reporting them as violating parole) to the point of sending them back to prison.

Jennifer Freyd was again a consultant for the federal prosecution on this case. One of the issues the prosecution faced, prior to the guilty plea, was that the victims initially did not report the abuse. It took quite some time and probing on the part of the FBI to uncover the extent of Walker's abuse. Furthermore, in some ways it might seem as if the women consented to the sexual acts because they did not initially file reports to complain. This silence could potentially be confusing to a jury, just as in the case of the girl on the plane who was passive during her assault. However, we can understand this response in terms of betrayal blindness. These women were entirely under the control of Walker. Many of them initially trusted him and wanted him to like them. In some cases, the women did not at first realize the extent to which they were being mistreated. Furthermore, when they did realize, they had reason to fear they would not be believed if they spoke out. The women's initial silence makes very good sense for their own survival.

Fortunately, Walker was ultimately held accountable for his crimes, and the federal government acknowledged the terrible betrayal. A federal judge, Chief Judge Beistline, apologized to the victims on behalf of the U.S. government.[8] He commended them for their courage and integrity in coming forward.

In July 2011, Walker was sentenced to ten years in prison. After the sentence hearing, U.S. Attorney Dwight C. Holton said this:

> Walker's betrayal of trust is staggering. He victimized people he was entrusted to supervise, and on top of that, he undermined the credibility of people in law enforcement and the courthouse community. I hope his lengthy prison sentence makes clear that we will hold accountable those who breach the public trust.

A Special Case of Betrayal Blindness: Stockholm Syndrome

For six days in August 1973, a group of bank employees were held hostage in Stockholm, Sweden. To the surprise of the world, many of these hostages became attached to the terrorists who were their captors. Some of the hostages even defended their captors after they were released. You might wonder how and why this happened. The term *Stockholm syndrome* was created to name what at first seems a paradoxical reaction to being held hostage. This reaction is characterized by a victim having positive feelings toward the captors. Stockholm syndrome applies to the special case of those feelings developing after a hostage takeover, as when an individual or a group is kidnapped and held for a ransom. From a theoretical perspective, the Stockholm syndrome reaction may be understood as a special kind of betrayal blindness.

The unusual aspect of Stockholm syndrome, compared with most betrayal blindness situations, is that the strong emotional attachment occurs *after* the abduction and without the preexisting context of an enduring caretaker or trusting relationship. Law enforcement officials believe that for Stockholm syndrome to occur, the captors must show a certain amount of kindness (or, at least, lack of cruelty) toward the hostages. From the perspective of betrayal blindness, the most important elements that predict Stockholm syndrome would not be kindness, per se, but rather caretaking behavior on the part of the captors and an implicit or explicit belief on the part of the victims that survival depends on the captors. Thus, we believe the victims would have to experience the captors as a source of caretaking and as necessary for survival in order to develop the emotional attachment necessary to create a betrayal trauma. Once the captors are experienced as necessary caretakers, a process much like that in childhood could occur, such that the victims have a good reason for attaching to the captors and thus eliciting caretaking behaviors. So, just as children do, the victims would need to become blind to the betrayal by the captors. To see the captors in a positive light, victims might distort reality in order to survive their predicament.

Anecdotal support for the premise that the victims' dependence and survival are at the heart of the development of Stockholm syndrome can be found in an online FBI article about Stockholm syndrome.[9] A related article states:

> In cases where Stockholm syndrome has occurred, the captive is in a situation where the captor has stripped nearly all forms of independence and gained control of the victim's life, as well as basic needs for survival. Some experts say that the hostage regresses to, perhaps, a state of infancy; the captive must cry for food, remain silent, and exist in an extreme state of dependence. In contrast, the perpetrator serves as a mother figure protecting her child from a threatening outside world, including law enforcement's deadly weapons. The victim then begins a struggle for survival, both relying on and identifying with the captor.[10]

The Story of Jacques Sandulescu's Betrayal Blindness

A powerful experience of betrayal blindness in a captive situation occurred to the late Jacques Sandulescu, the author of the autobiography *Donbas: A True Story of an Escape across Russia*.[11] In 1945,

Sandulescu, a Russian boy of sixteen, was captured by the Soviet Red Army. He was shipped in a cattle car to the coalfields of the Donets River Basin (from which comes the name "Donbas"). There Sandulescu became a slave laborer, mining coal. His life was tremendously harsh, and he almost died more than once. Ultimately, Sandulescu escaped the mines and made his way to the United States, a rare survivor of the slave labor camps.

Jennifer Freyd (JF) had the opportunity to interview Sandulescu (JS) while he was still alive. She asked him about his ability to survive the camps. He spoke about his success in befriending the Russian guards, who then ended up helping him survive. Sandulescu's wife, Annie Gottlieb (AG), was also part of the conversation.

JF: It seems to me, reading the book, that the guards are kinder to Jacques than to many other prisoners, like giving him extra things. Is that true?

JS: They were kinder because in a way I had reached out to them, too. I talked with them, and the other prisoners were very sullen.... They hated them. It's like ... this guy's got a job. The government tells them ... Why should you hate him? I did not view the guards with hatred.

AG: So you reached out to them, then, in a way that other prisoners didn't.

Jacques explained that during the day he would talk to the guards, even laugh with them.

AG: Other prisoners did not do that much? Most of them?

JS: No, no, no, no. Not at all. I think that was one of the keys. That's why the guards liked me.

AG: Yeah, because it wasn't just that you were a strong worker, because Omar was also a very strong worker, but he wouldn't talk to them.

JF: So, I think I understand your point that the guards were doing a job they were told to do, and so there's no point to hate them for just doing their job. But at the same time, it sounds like sometimes the guards were cruel in a way they didn't really have to be.

JS: Sometimes they used to go out of their way to be cruel!

JF: And when you saw that, what did you do? Did you—

JS: What could I do? I couldn't do anything. I just thought this guy's a stupid asshole, you know.

JF: Right, well, you couldn't really do anything, but I mean what were you thinking? What were you feeling when you saw them being cruel, more than they needed to be for their job?

JS: I sometimes used to see them be cruel to girls—

AG: Cruel in what way?

JS: Well, you saw the other guys . . . hit that lady . . .

AG: With a stick?

JS: Yeah. That type of thing.

AG: Driving them to work harder?

JS: Yeah. I don't know, sometimes I used to get in the way. . . . Those were girls from families where there was no physical labor involved, like a daughter of a professor. What did they know about a shovel, grab a hard shovel and lift the shovel and empty a coal car? They didn't know, they had soft hands, they . . .

AG: You said sometimes you used to step in and do it for them, you said?

JS: Yeah, quick, the guards shouted, "Quick, quick." They needed an empty car. I got it done.

AG: The guards didn't object to that?

JS: No.

Jacques went on to explain that not only did the guards let him help the girls, but they brought him treats.

JS: Some of them, they used to bring me roasted sunflower seeds. They gave me a couple of handfuls.

AG: But I'm still trying to figure out, Jacques, when you say that the guards were cruel to prisoners sometimes. . . . Were those the same guards that you laughed and joked with at other times?

Jacques explained that he felt compassion for the guards.

JS: Some, they, they used to get lonely too, sometimes needed to talk to somebody. Stand there with rifles, cold all day, get lonely, nobody to talk to.

AG: It sounds like that was really unusual behavior for a prisoner.

JS: Yeah.

JF: Do you think that it helped you survive? Keep alive? That you were friendly with them?

JS: Well, you know, there is, in friendly communication, the passage of time. Of course, it's helpful.

JF: When you were friendly with them, were you just pretending to be friendly, or did you actually feel friendly?

JS: In a situation like that you cannot really pretend, because if you pretended, he says get the fuck away and kicks you in the ass and walks away.

JF: They can tell if you're pretending?

JS: Yes. If you *feel* friendly, then you act it out.

Although Sandulescu survived his imprisonment and slavery by befriending his captors, ultimately he did escape with their help. His book stands as testimony, not only to the power of the human spirit, but also to the overwhelming importance of human relationships in survival. Jacques knew with one part of his brain that these guards were cruel and sadistic. Yet his attachment to them, the attachment that eventually led to his survival, did not "know" of their sadism. Eventually, Sandulescu told his story in *Donbas*. The telling became a crucial step in his healing, as we discuss in chapter 11.

Jaycee Lee Dugard

When Jaycee Lee Dugard was eleven years old, she was kidnapped at a school bus stop in South Lake Tahoe.[12] Jaycee was within sight of her home when the kidnapping occurred, and there were witnesses to the crime. Despite this, Jaycee was not rescued for eighteen years. In those eighteen years, Jaycee was held captive by Phillip Craig Garrido and forced to bear two of his children. Finally, in 2009, Jaycee was freed from her ordeal. Her children were eleven and fifteen years old when she was finally reunited with her own parents. This case has drawn a great deal of media attention from the very beginning.

When Jaycee was first rescued, she surprised the world by describing her relationship with her captor as "almost like a marriage."

She seemed to be defending her abuser, and it appeared she had developed a bond with him. While at first this might seem odd, it is completely consistent with what we know about betrayal blindness. In order for Jaycee to survive her ordeal, she had to attach to Garrido and his wife.

Reporter Clara Moskowitz wrote about the Dugard case in 2009, shortly after Jaycee's rescue. The question on the public's mind at that time was why Dugard would defend her tormenter. In an article about the Dugard case, Moskowitz explained the application of betrayal trauma theory to Dugard's behavior:

> Bonding with a kidnapper is not just a mental coping skill, but a physical survival strategy. Since Dugard's life was at the mercy of the Garridos, and she depended on them for food and shelter, it was in her best interest to bond to protect herself from further abuse.[13]

As Moskowitz understood, someone who is kidnapped as a child might make an unconscious decision not to fully see the abuse and to bond with the person providing food and shelter. The victim might respond by putting it out of her mind and acting as if it's not happening. It's more important to protect the relationship. Responding or fighting back may only cause the abuser to become even more abusive or to stop taking care of the victim in a way that's needed for survival. In other words, if you're in a situation where you're completely empowered to say no, you generally will. But if your captor is your only source of support, you're going to be really stuck if you alienate that person.

Stockholm syndrome is rare, whereas betrayal blindness events and reactions are, unfortunately, fairly common. What is also fairly common is institutional collusion in the betrayal. In the case of Dugard, a whole other side of the story has come to light, one involving institutional betrayal. It turns out that there were numerous missed opportunities to rescue Dugard during her eighteen-year ordeal. These missed opportunities included failures of law enforcement to act on tips. Yet most disturbingly, it has become apparent that the state of California also failed to properly supervise the perpetrator Garrido, who was already known before the kidnapping to be a sex offender.

In an extraordinary statement issued to the press on November 4, 2009, by David R. Shaw, the inspector general of California, titled "Corrections Failed to Properly Supervise Parolee Philip Garrido," the errors were made public. It is as though he is admitting to betrayal blindness:

> Corrections failed to properly supervise parolee Phillip Garrido and missed opportunities to discover his victims according to a report released today by California Inspector General David R. Shaw. Garrido was arrested along with his wife in August for the 1991 kidnapping and sexual assault of then 11-year-old Jaycee Dugard. During the course of the following 18 years, Garrido reportedly sexually assaulted Jaycee—fathering two children—while holding her captive on the grounds of his residence in Antioch, California. For the last 10 years, Corrections' parole division supervised Garrido. . . .
>
> The department missed potential opportunities to discover the existence of Garrido's three victims, by failing to investigate clearly visible utility wires running from Garrido's house toward the concealed compound at the rear of his property; talk to neighbors and local public safety agencies; and act on GPS and other information clearly showing Garrido had violated his parole terms.[14]

Once again, we can see that betrayal blindness can lead to not seeing what is there.

4

Blind Adherence

As we saw with examples such as California's failure to moni-tor Phillip Craig Garrido in chapter 3, betrayal and betrayal blindness operate in a larger context beyond interpersonal relation-ships. Anita Hill has described her sexual harassment by Clarence Thomas at a time when she had little power and needed to stay in his good graces.[1] A similar dynamic occurs when a secretary puts up with a boss who asks him to do personal and degrading chores not in his job description. These are examples of blindness to institu-tional betrayal.

Blindness is also a standard response to oppression in society. As you remember from the examples of Kevin Nakamura and Frank Wu in chapter 2, victims of oppression can be motivated to remain blind. This blindness to oppression may play a role in the continued audience for Holocaust deniers and denial by the victims of sexism and racism, even when that same sexism and racism can be demon-strated to be objectively present. Also, those who hold more power or are perceived to hold more power often play a role in motivating other people's betrayal blindness.

In 2003, when Colin Powell told the American public that Iraq held weapons of mass destruction, was betrayal blindness a factor in the collective willingness to believe what was not true?[2] Eileen Zurbriggen, a professor of psychology at the University of California, Santa Cruz, has used betrayal trauma theory to

35

analyze the belief in lies such as this told by government officials, including U.S. presidents. Zurbriggen suggests that betrayal trauma theory predicts that citizens who are emotionally or financially dependent on the person lying will be most blind to signs of deception.[3]

In situations of explicit mistreatment, perpetrators may manipulate their victims to remain silent and unaware. For instance, leaders who want blind adherence can engage in fearmongering. When citizens are afraid, they are more dependent on their leaders and thus more at risk of remaining blind to the leaders' lies and betrayals. Indeed, oppressors may encourage the ignorance of the oppressed in many ways. What follows are a number of examples of institutional betrayal and blindness to it.

Institutional Betrayal by Employers

One particularly common, but often subtle, type of institutional betrayal occurs in the context of employment in a large organization. If the employee is being betrayed by his or her employers and if the employee feels the employment is particularly necessary, the ingredients for betrayal blindness are present. For example, a large company may have structures in place that systematically oppress some employees, perhaps on the basis of gender or race. When the employees confront such injustices, they are at risk of losing their jobs; thus, they have an implicit reason not to see the injustice. This is all too common. Another way that employers can betray employees is by failing to protect them when they are vulnerable, such as when they fall ill or become pregnant. This is such a serious problem that the government has enacted the Family Medical Leave Act (FMLA) to protect employees from just such betrayal.[4] However, FMLA lasts only for a short while, and it is insufficient in cases of prolonged illness. In those situations, employees are at great risk of losing their jobs. For instance, Tom worked as a manager at a large company. He fell ill with cancer and used his FMLA benefits. After the FMLA leave had run its course, Tom still had earned sick leave to use. While he was at home recovering from chemotherapy, his employer attempted to reorganize the company so that Tom's job would no longer exist. Although Tom or any individual who faces such a betrayal by his employer may no longer have a motivation to be blind to the betrayal, all of the surrounding coworkers may remain highly motivated not to see the injustice, for fear of losing their own employment. Thus, institutional betrayal and betrayal blindness flourish.

Cover-Up of Church Sexual Abuse

Perhaps the best-known example of institutional betrayal is the cover-up of child sexual abuse in the Catholic Church. This has been in the news for more than a decade and continues to surface. This child sexual abuse was clearly a betrayal of the individuals victimized by their priests. The cover-up is a betrayal of those individuals and of many others. The cover-up allowed the abuse to continue, creating a kind of shared betrayal blindness. The denials and the continued cover-up eventually caused a great deal of harm and distress.

In 2011, a new set of allegations and related cover-ups came to light in Ireland. The *New York Times* reported in July 2011 that "The Roman Catholic Church in Ireland was covering up the sexual abuse of children by priests as recently as 2009, long after it issued guidelines meant to protect children, and the Vatican tacitly encouraged the cover-up by ignoring the guidelines, according to a scathing report issued Wednesday by the Irish government."[5]

In one case, described in July 2011 by the *Independent*, an Irish newspaper, a north Cork woman was sexually abused in the Diocese of Cloyne.[6] According to the article, she "found her trust in her local cleric replaced by an unending nightmare of shame and betrayal." The *Independent* went on to explain the betrayal:

> The woman, who does not want her identity to be revealed, has since rebuilt her life despite the trauma of having been abused before she was even 14 years old. In an almost unbelievable breach of trust, she was abused by two Cloyne clerics for a period lasting several years.
>
> "I was abused by two priests over a period of time starting from the late 1970s and running into the early 1980s," she said.

The woman finally decided that she had done nothing wrong and that she would join other victims in pursuing the abusers through the justice process. Yet when she did join the effort to hold the perpetrators accountable, she found more betrayal:

> It took years to find the courage to bring the abuse to light, only to find that the diocese was dragging its feet over numerous abuse complaints.
>
> What has appalled the victims most is that those who should have been trying to protect them were apparently more focused on protecting the church from any whiff of controversy.
>
> The worst hurt is over the fact that, had the diocese acted properly and immediately on the receipt of the first abuse allegations, at least one of the clerics involved would not have continued to be around children.

Research on Institutional Betrayal: Violations of Members' Trust Surrounding Incidents of Sexual Assault

In a recent survey study, Carly Smith and Jennifer Freyd have proposed that the harm of sexual assault may be made much worse by institutional failure to prevent sexual assault or to respond supportively when it occurs.[7] They examined the involvement of institutions (for example, universities, churches, fraternities, or sororities) in events surrounding experiences of sexual assault. In order to conduct this research, Smith and Freyd first had to find a way to measure institutional betrayal. They created the Institutional Betrayal Questionnaire (IBQ), which measures institutional betrayal both leading up to a sexual assault and following the assault. Using the IBQ and other measures, the researchers collected self-reports of unwanted sexual experiences, trauma symptoms, and experiences of institutional betrayal in a sample of 345 female college students.

Nearly half of the women (47 percent) reported at least one experience of sexual assault. More than a third of participants reported experiencing some form of institutional betrayal. Of the participants who reported institutional betrayal, nearly half reported still being members of the institution. Perhaps most strikingly,

institutional betrayal predicted that trauma symptoms would occur, even after controlling for sexual assault. In other words, women
who had reported experiencing institutional betrayal in the context
of their unwanted sexual experience reported increased levels of
anxiety, sexual trauma–specific symptoms, and problematic sexual
functioning. It is clear that institutional betrayal is particularly toxic.

A startling example of institutional betrayal came to light in
late 2011, in the case of assistant football coach Jerry Sandusky at
Penn State University. Sandusky was convicted of forty-five counts
of child sexual abuse that had taken place over a number of years. It
became clear that university authorities had known about the abuse
and had not reported it. In fact, the special investigative counsel report (known as the Freeh Report), released on July 12, 2012, states
the following:

> Our most saddening and sobering finding is the total disre-
> gard for the safety and welfare of Sandusky's child victims
> by the most senior leaders at Penn State. The most power-
> ful men at Penn State failed to take any steps for 14 years
> to protect the children who Sandusky victimized. Messrs.
> Spanier [former president of Penn State], Schultz [former
> Penn State vice president], Paterno [head football coach]
> and Curley [former athletic director)] never demonstrated,
> through actions or words, any concern for the safety and
> well-being of Sandusky's victims until after Sandusky's
> arrest.[8]

When Joe Paterno was eventually fired for his role in the cover-
up, many people reacted with anger—not at the child abuse but at
the firing of Paterno. Even after Paterno's death and the conviction
of Sandusky, there are those who support Paterno. One might wonder why people would flock to the side of someone who had colluded
with a child molester. Paterno, by his blind eye, had created the context for Sandusky to repeat his acts of abuse on child after child. The
initial cover-up of the abuse and the later protests from some people
are examples of institutional and societal betrayal blindness.

The denial displayed by the protesters also makes sense from
the perspective of avoiding a personal awareness of abuse that might
be very close to home. Many at Penn State who were not directly

involved in the Sandusky or Paterno case were themselves or have close family or friends who are victims or even perpetrators of abuse. By denying the abuse at Penn State, they help themselves remain blind. At the same time, the subsequent attention and outrage this case has inspired are a positive sign. Sexual abuse of this magnitude and its related cover-up are a common story, but rarely are charges filed, officials held accountable, or outrage expressed. The uproar at Penn State is much better than the alternative: silence.

Military Sexual Trauma and Betrayal Blindness

One context in which institutional betrayal has recently come to light is that of military sexual trauma.

Military sexual trauma has been occurring for a long time, probably for as long as there has been war. Yet the very high prevalence of military sexual trauma and the extensive damage it causes are relatively new topics in academic trauma research. Military sexual trauma is related to institutional betrayal because, historically, the military has been so unwilling to prevent, acknowledge, or respond appropriately to reports of military sexual trauma. This has led to a great deal of silence. As Dahr Jamail reported for *Al Jeezera English* in December 2010:

> Billy Capshaw was 17 when he joined the Army in 1977. After being trained as a medic he was transferred to Baumholder, Germany. His roommate, Jeffrey Dahmer, by virtue of his seniority ensured that Capshaw had no formal assignment, no mail, and no pay. Having completely isolated the young medic, Dahmer regularly sexually assaulted, raped, and tortured him.
>
> Dahmer went on to become the infamous serial killer and sex offender who murdered 17 boys and men before being beaten to death by an inmate at Columbia Correction Institution in 1994.
>
> Capshaw reflects back, "At that young age I didn't know how to deal with it. My commander did not believe me. Nobody helped me, even though I begged and begged and begged."
>
> The debilitating lifelong struggle Capshaw has had to face is common among survivors of military sexual assault.

Dahr Jamail also noted,

Military sexual trauma (MST) survivor Susan Avila-Smith is
director of the veteran's advocacy group Women Organizing Women. She has been serving female and scores of male
clients in various stages of recovery from MST for 15 years
and knows of its devastating effects up close.

"People cannot conceive how badly wounded these people are," she told *Al Jazeera*. "Of the 3,000 I've worked with,
only one is employed. Combat trauma is bad enough, but
with MST it's not the enemy, it's our guys who are doing
it. You're fighting your friends, your peers, people you've
been told have your back. That betrayal, then the betrayal
from the command is, they say, worse than the sexual assault
itself."[9]

In late 2010 the Service Women's Action Network and
the American Civil Liberties Union filed a lawsuit against the
Department of Defense and Department of Veterans Affairs for
their "failure to respond to Freedom of Information Act requests
seeking government records documenting incidents of rape,
sexual assault and sexual harassment in the military." The goal
of the lawsuit is to "obtain the release of records on a matter of
public concern, namely, the prevalence of MST within the armed
services, the policies of the DOD and VA regarding MST and
other related disabilities, and the nature of each agency's response
to MST."

A press release issued by the Service Women's Action Network
(SWAN) and the American Civil Liberties Union (ACLU) noted:

"The government's refusal to even take the first step of providing comprehensive and accurate information about the
sexual trauma inflicted upon our women and men in uniform, and the treatment and benefits MST survivors receive
after service, is all too telling," said Anuradha Bhagwati, a
former Marine captain and Executive Director of SWAN.
"The DOD and VA should put the interests of service members first and expose information on the extent of sexual
trauma in the military to the sanitizing light of day."[10]

The press release included this information:

"The known statistics on military sexual trauma suggest that sexual abuse is all too prevalent in our military," said Sandra Park, staff attorney with the ACLU Women's Rights Project. "But we know that many service members who suffer from abuse are not receiving the treatment they need. The truth about the extent of this abuse and what has been done to address it must be made known."

The realization that this is institutional betrayal is clearly part of the motivation for the lawsuit:

"The government is failing to care for the overwhelming number of women who so desperately need help coping with something as devastating as rape, sexual assault and harassment," said Andrew Schneider, Executive Director of the ACLU of Connecticut. "These women have already put their lives on the line by serving their country. The least that the government can do is disclose the scope of the problem."

Isn't one kind of betrayal bad enough? Isn't the betrayal of being raped by a fellow service member sufficiently terrible? To then have to endure lies and denial by the organization entrusted with protecting victims adds a whole new dimension of devastating betrayal.

Institutional Betrayal in the Courtroom

In chapter 3, we discuss the case of the girl who was abused on an airplane. The outcome in that case was ultimately good—justice was done—but it could easily have turned the other way, due to the public's misunderstanding about victim psychology. Indeed, the combination of insufficient legal clarity about the standards for consent and widespread ignorance about victim response opens the door for a defense that blames the victim and potentially holds her responsible for sexual assault, while leaving the perpetrator not accountable. This is a betrayal in a larger social context. It is thus crucial for justice that we do even more to educate the public.

Here are some of the things we learned from research in trauma psychology that are likely not sufficiently known by potential jurors or perhaps even by interested readers like you. You can educate yourself on these issues and, in so doing, help bring understanding and justice to victims of sexual assault, betrayal, and betrayal blindness.

Passivity during sexual assault is a common response of both child and adult victims. Studies suggest that anywhere from one-third of adult rape survivors to one-half of child sexual abuse survivors display a passive, even frozen, response during the assault.[11] Naturally, people wonder why and how this passive response occurs, but it is important to recognize that separate from questions of motivation and mechanism, we know from empirical scientific research on sexual victimization that such a passive response is quite common. In the scientific literature on sexual assault, this constellation of passive or freeze responses from victims is sometimes called "rape-induced paralysis." There are research studies that attempt to answer the "why" and "how" questions regarding victim passivity. A number of factors (such as power disparity and betrayal blindness) are associated with victims having a passive response. These factors can range from victims making a conscious decision to be passive, based on their judgment that it is a wise course of action, given the dangers of resisting, to involuntary mental processes, such as dissociation and the involuntary physiological responses of paralysis or freezing. We discuss these in chapter 9.

Sometimes victims forget all or part of their assault experience. Numerous studies have shown that some percentage of trauma victims either display or later report a period of forgetting the event.[12] Forgetting can occur even after a period of remembering.[13] In 1997, Diana Elliott published her investigation of memory for a wide range of traumatic experiences in a carefully executed research study using a representative sample of Americans.[14] Elliott reported that overall, for various types of trauma, 17 percent reported partial forgetting and 15 percent reported a period of complete memory loss (for a total of 32 percent who reported delayed recall) for various traumatic experiences. Rates of forgetting were higher for certain interpersonal victimization experiences (such as childhood abuse and completed rape) and lower for other noninterpersonal traumas (such as motor vehicle accidents). Forgetting is apparently more likely in cases involving a betrayal trauma, such as when the victim trusted, was very close to, and/or was dependent on the perpetrator.

Often, victims do not disclose the assault at all or disclose it only after a delay. Sometimes victims retract a legitimate accusation. Numerous studies have discovered that nondisclosure, recanting, and delayed disclosure are common reactions to sexual assault.[15] Most people who experience child sexual assault do not disclose it until adulthood, and many never tell at all.[16] Studies have also revealed a pattern of recanting and redisclosure.[17] Nondisclosure, delayed disclosure, and retraction are particularly likely in cases in which the perpetrator is close to the victim.[18] The same logic of betrayal blindness that can keep people unaware of intimate victimization can also motivate victims to keep silent. Later in this book, we discuss both the riskiness and the healing potential of disclosure.

Assault by a familiar person is both more common and potentially more toxic that assault by a stranger. Most sexual assault is committed by individuals who are known to the victims, which increases the likelihood of delayed disclosure, unsupportive reactions, and worse outcomes.[19] Widely held stereotypes about "stranger danger" reflect perilous confusion about both the relative risk of assault and the likely harm caused by someone known versus not known to the victim. For instance, if a girl was on a plane next to a man she didn't know, and she fell asleep and woke up to him touching her and later explained that she felt too scared to do anything, would the defense attorneys attempt a consent defense? Would this have a chance with a jury? Our intuition is no, that this defense has a chance only if the victim and the assailant were acquainted. What is it about the fact that a victim knew a perpetrator that potentially opens the consent door, despite no prior invitation? Perhaps people believe that females enjoy being sexually touched by men they know simply because they know them and/or that because they know someone they have more freedom to object to an unwanted touch and/or that men have implicit rights to touch females they know. None of these ideas are at all correct. Women or girls assaulted by someone known to them are even more likely not to disclose the assault and to experience negative aftereffects than if the assailant was not known to them.

Victims often display a constellation of reactions after the assault. Responses to adult sexual assault and child sexual abuse are diverse. Some individuals display great distress, whereas others do not. Immediate reactions are likely to include fear, anxiety, confusion, and social withdrawal.[20] Because of intense feelings of shame, victims often report not wanting to be seen by others, as well as a desire to shower or cleanse themselves repeatedly for days to months after the assault.[21] Long term, these crimes increase the risk of a host of negative outcomes, including post-traumatic stress disorder, depression, suicide, and other mental health problems.[22] As we discuss later, the probability of experiencing particularly damaging reactions is greatest in the case of betrayal trauma.

When people react negatively to a victim's disclosure, notably by disbelieving and blaming the victim, this can compound the damage done by the assault. Disbelieving and blaming constitute additional betrayal and can be especially harmful to the well-being of victims of sexual assault.[23] As Brian Marx explained, "In our society, the validity of reports of sexual violence is often questioned, and survivors are blamed for their sexual assaults. Furthermore, the consequences of these experiences are often trivialized or ignored by family, friends, police, legal officials, and sometimes even mental health professionals. Unfortunately, such social conditions further create stigma and shame for survivors, thereby compounding the destructiveness of their experiences."[24]

This list of relevant research findings not generally known by the public is far from exhaustive. There is much more we know about trauma psychology in general and the response of victims to sexual assault in particular. If the public and thus potential jurors were better educated prior to serving on a case, expert testimony about victim psychology would not be needed. An educated public would help create a more equitable situation in both the criminal justice system and society more widely. An educated public would make it more likely that eventually the laws themselves would be improved to better reflect the reality of power dynamics and victim response. An educated public could more effectively defend our freedom from assault. The results of our research are often highly relevant to making fair and good decisions about the treatment and the responsibility for—as well as the prevention of—interpersonal violations. Knowledge of that research is also often highly relevant to how helpfully and successfully we interact with one another in society. We hope that your knowledge of these ideas will make a difference in the treatment of sexual assault victims.

Betrayal Blindness in Bystanders

One of the most perplexing aspects of our shared social world relates to our ability to ignore the injustice, oppression, treachery, and betrayal that are all around us. Although the betrayal blindness of bystanders is terrible in its way, it is also understandable. Just as victims may have a need not to see the betrayal they experience, so, too, may bystanders have such a need. We are each designed by eons of evolutionary history and a lifetime of cultural learning to be moral individuals. Morality is part of our human evolution and a central part of every culture and religion. A fundamental tenet of all moral codes is that of fairness. Another is that of caring for or not harming others. Although different traditions also have other moral concerns (for instance, obedience, loyalty, and purity), fairness and caring are central to all known moral systems. Both fairness and caring can be violated by others, and when that happens, it can create a sense of betrayal not only in the victim but also in the minds of bystanders, who experience a betrayal of justice, of *what is right*. Yet we may remain blind to this betrayal for all of the reasons we have already discussed—to see the betrayal might risk too much.

As Judy Herman has famously noted,

> It is very tempting to take the side of the perpetrator. All the perpetrator asks is that the bystander do nothing. He appeals to the universal desire to see, hear and speak no evil.

The victim, on the contrary, asks the bystander to share the burden of pain. The victim demands action, engagement and remembering.[25]

Implicit in this eloquent statement is the idea that bystander blindness protects the bystander by maintaining the status quo and helping him or her avoid risk, whereas to see the betrayal puts the bystander in the position of having to do something that can risk the bystander's status and comfort.

Bystanders' betrayal blindness may be a fundamental factor in what has been called "psychic numbing" to horrific events such as genocide. In these cases, the bystanders risk their own well-being in society if they dare to be fully aware of the mistreatment. An example of this sort of bystander betrayal blindness may be found in the *Vel' d'Hiv* Roundup, also known as the French Roundup.

Not far from the Eiffel Tower in Paris, the *Vélodrome d'Hiver* was a large indoor cycle track. In July 1942, the velodrome was used in a most terrible way. French police, under Nazi occupation and order, arrested thousands of Jewish citizens, particularly women and children, and brought them to the velodrome as prisoners, simply for being Jewish. These individuals were eventually transported to Auschwitz, where most of them were killed. This horrific event is notable for being both orchestrated and implemented by French police, rather than by Nazi officials, and for the massive forgetting that seemed to happen around the event. Even today, many people would be astonished to learn that many of those killed in Auschwitz were French citizens who were arrested by their own countrymen.[26] Eventually, and more recently, certain citizen groups have demanded that this event be acknowledged. In Paris, one can now find plaques commemorating the victims, but there was a time when the official French position was largely to deny accountability. Finally, in July 1995, then president Jacques Chirac ruled that it was necessary for France to be accountable for the role it had played in victimizing Jews and others during the German occupation:

These black hours will stain our history forever and are an injury to our past and our traditions. Yes, the criminal madness of the occupant was assisted by the French, by the

French state. Fifty-three years ago, on 16 July 1942, 450 policemen and gendarmes, French, under the authority of their leaders, obeyed the demands of the Nazis. That day, in the capital and the Paris region, nearly 10,000 Jewish men, women and children were arrested at home, in the early hours of the morning, and assembled at police stations. . . . France, home of the Enlightenment and the Declaration of the Rights of Man and of the Citizen, land of welcome and asylum, France committed that day the irreparable. Breaking its word, it delivered those it protected to their executioners.[27]

The levels of betrayal here are extraordinary, of course, but so are the levels of betrayal blindness. It is good to know that in recent years, more light has been shed on these terrible betrayals. In chapters 10 and 11, we discuss the risk and the healing power of removing blinders, of being aware of past betrayals.

5

Why Blindness?

B etrayal can be deeply traumatic, but we don't usually think of betrayals when we think of *trauma*. We all know about war, earthquakes, tsunamis, and car accidents, and often we assume that this is what trauma is. We so often miss the trauma of betrayal and its effects. Some betrayals are fairly mundane, but many betrayals are traumatic events in their own right. For instance, child abuse committed by a parent, rape perpetrated by a partner, or societal events such as the Holocaust are both betrayals *and* traumatic events. We call these events *betrayal traumas*.

Jennifer Freyd first developed betrayal trauma theory in the early 1990s to make sense of one particular puzzle: *Why* would some people forget traumas that happened to them? Let's consider the case of Hendrik Janssen, an accomplished physician, who told us about forgetting a major trauma—his experience of being sexually abused as a child by his minister.

Hendrik wrote to us:

> I was sexually abused by a minister when I was in the age range of six to eight. It was not something I ever recall having a conscious memory of until I was an adult. Over the years, I did frequently remember getting sick when I went to church, but I never knew why. I first sought help for a worsening depression in 1990 during my residency.

I was undergoing therapy at the time the memories started coming—seeing a therapist about once a week. At
the time, I also took a seminar with a group of about 20
other people over about four separate weekends. During that group, there was a lot of discussion about people's pasts, and so on. It was in this group setting when
everyone was individually sharing their past experiences
(some painful) that I first started having the memories.
The group was the first people that I told. The general
memory that I was sexually abused by a male figure came
back immediately—I knew right away I was remembering being sexually abused by a male. I think at that
point, though, there was still a lot of denial on my part.
The details around the abuse—when it happened, what
all he did, where it happened, number of times, who
knew—all came back in bits and pieces. As I continued to talk about it more and started discussing it with
my family, I would remember more things. Some of the
memories were confusing at first—came back more like
pieces of puzzle, bits of memory that I wasn't always sure
at the start of where it fit with the rest of the memories.
Once I started talking about it, some of the memories
came back, much like any memory—talking about, going
back to where it happened—triggered more memories.
Most all of these pieces would just come back to my
mind as was thinking about what happened/journaling—
then would go back and share/discuss it more with my
therapist.

Hendrik also explained,

When these memories started to surface, I did go back and
do a lot of things. This minister was then deceased but was
apparently discharged from the church (secretly discharged)
for abusing his grandchildren, which he apparently admitted at that time. Since then, I have found there are several
victims—mostly all from his own family. For several reasons, including learning that one of their leaders had knowledge of my abuse, I did pursue a civil suit against this church

and won the suit. We really found quite a lot of supporting information.

There was indeed strong corroboration of Hendrik's memories of his childhood sexual abuse. During the legal proceedings, Hendrik introduced various types of compelling evidence, including testimony that the minister had sexually abused his grandson and eyewitness testimony to one of the incidents of sexual abuse of Hendrik himself.

What happened to Hendrik was a terrible trauma. It was also a huge betrayal. We wondered about his family context. Perhaps that would help us better understand his story. We asked Hendrik, "Do you remember your relationship with your parents and family members when you were six to eight years old? What sort of parents and family did you have?"

Hendrik responded,

There were seven children in my family, twenty-year age difference from oldest to youngest. I am the third to the youngest. We grew up on a farm—Father was very busy trying to make ends meet. My mother had recurring problems with depression for much of her life as I was growing up as a child. She spent a couple spans of several months hospitalized for this depression and some smaller periods as well. The longer spans occurred prior to my abuse (the minister had knowledge of when she was hospitalized). As children, we were always concerned about her health/well-being. During my six- to eight-year-old period, I was concerned about my mother's well-being. We had a fairly good relationship, but at times I felt more like a caretaker for her, instead of vice versa.

My father was generally very quiet, and overall, we didn't communicate about our problems or what was going on with us. He would often get very quiet and not talk for few days—I thought then that he was angry during these times. He never hurt me directly, and generally he was always good to me. He did, though, sexually abuse/hurt some of my sisters to varying degrees (in the same general time period)—part of which I had some knowledge of as a child.

We asked Hendrik to tell us more about his father's sexual abuse of his sisters.

[With] my sister Patty, it involved only attempted inappropriate touching and did not go any further—he attempted to remove undergarments. He stopped when she resisted. I did not know about this until this issue was brought up in the family ten years ago. My father has admitted such, and it seems like it was no more than this incident, and my sister Patty has been open about it.

My sister Jane was abused to a much greater degree, involving intercourse. What I knew predated what happened to me by a short time (age ages five to six or so). I think the only thing that I knew at the time was that he hurt her in bed together. My father has admitted to abuse, although not entirely to that degree. I know that it was not an isolated incident and probably occurred mostly when my mother was hospitalized. I do not know for certain when it started or over how long a period of time. I was quite young at the time and really don't remember any specific clues, other than what I mentioned above. I know that she saw a physician, and when she was bit older, I always remember my father being very concerned (overly) she was going to be pregnant—but at the time I thought he was relating to her dating. My oldest sister remembers Jane coming to her saying something about him trying to touch her and that she had gone and talked to him after that incident.

My sister Jane had an eating disorder that started after the abuse ceased (bulimia), which is something I also suffered with for a period.

Hendrik described being sexually abused by someone he had reason to trust: the minister in his church. He also described a family in which sexual abuse was rampant. Hendrik was betrayed by both his church *and* his family, and for a long time he forgot all of these betrayals.

Betrayal trauma theory was first created to account for massive forgetting and unawareness of this sort. The core idea is that forgetting and unawareness help the abuse victim survive. The theory draws on two facts about our nature as social beings and our dependence and reliance on others. First, we are extremely vulnerable in infancy, which gives rise to a powerful attachment system. Second, we have a constant need to make "social contracts" with other people in order to get our needs met. This has led to the development of a powerful cheater-detector system. These two aspects of our humanity serve us well, but when the person we are dependent on is also the person betraying us, our two standard responses to trouble conflict with each other. To understand this better, let's consider these concepts one by one.

Dependence on the Caregiver and Attachment

Human infants emerge from the womb with almost no ability to fend for themselves. If you think about almost any other animal at birth, you'll appreciate how relatively helpless the human baby is. Although the human baby gradually acquires various skills that can aid survival, this maturation process takes a very long time. In fact, human infants are almost entirely dependent on adult caregivers for months, and after that they remain very dependent for years. This long period of dependence is possible in part because of our highly inbred attachment system. The *attachment system* is the name researchers have given to all of the various processes that together ensure that babies love their caregivers and that caregivers love their babies. This includes the smiling and cooing sounds a baby makes, the desire to hold and be held, the pleasure in the scents of a baby, and so on.

It is important to realize that both the caregiver and the baby have attachment systems—that the relationship is reciprocal, in the sense that attachment depends on both parties behaving in ways to inspire the attachment of the other. If a baby consistently fails to smile or coo or if a young child will not hug or make eye contact, that child is risking not only his or her own attachment to the caregiver, but also the caregiver's attachment to the child. Without caregiver attachment, the baby or the child is at risk of not being cared for, and this means at risk of dying. This is a crucial point, because it means that the baby and the child have an essential "job"—to attach to a caregiver and thus promote the caregiver's attachment and care. Attachment is essential when there is dependence. Humans are often dependent on others, even after infancy and childhood. As we will see, this attachment system and the need to maintain relationships, even in adulthood, drive our blindness to the betrayal of people who are important to us.

Social Contracts, Trust, and Cheater Detectors

In addition to being dependent on one another for caregiving, we are interdependent in another sense: we make deals with one another constantly. These deals have been called "social contracts," and they include everything from explicit major contracts, such as marriage, to much more mundane everyday agreements that occur when I give you half of a sandwich in return for half of your piece of pie. We exchange goods, we exchange work, we trade, we barter, and we are constantly making cost-benefit negotiations. This extremely high number of social contracts is at the heart of what makes us such social creatures. Our most intimate relationships are no exception to this. In fact, in close relationships we have some of our most important social contracts: you keep my secrets and I keep yours; you remain faithful to me and I to you; and so on.

Social contracts depend on trust. This is particularly the case whenever there is a time discrepancy between the agreement and the resolution of it. I agree to keep your secret—that is an agreement about time. I agree to send you a check after you provide some service—that is an agreement that takes place over time. When an agreement is made at one point in time but can be completed only at another point, trust is required.

Whenever there is a social contract, and especially one depending on trust, there is also the opportunity for a violation of that contract. In other words, for every deal we make, there is the chance we can get cheated. With every social contract, we risk betrayal. When there is betrayal, the pain of that betrayal is highest in close relationships that depend on mutual trust for their maintenance.

Because we can be cheated in social contracts, we have developed—through evolutionary history and our individual life experiences—the ability to expertly detect cheating in others. In fact, we are so good at detecting cheating that evolutionary psychologists have come up with the term *cheater detectors* to describe our specialized skills. A series of research studies conducted in the

1990s by evolutionary psychologists Leda Cosmides and John Tooby demonstrated that humans can reason about violations of social contracts—that is, cheating—at a much more rapid rate and at a more accurate level than they can reason about other sorts of problems that involve the same reasoning logic.[1]

The exquisite ability we have to detect cheaters is a very important survival skill because it means that we can reduce the probability of getting cheated. Most of the time, when we realize we have been betrayed or cheated, we also have a strong emotional reaction—a very negative reaction that washes over us, like the free fall or disorientation described in previous chapters. This sort of predictable strong emotional reaction in response to a thought or a perception is the hallmark of a highly important process—the strong reaction motivates our behavior. If we experience cheating or betrayal, we typically take one of two actions. One action is to confront. The other action is to withdraw. Either action may protect us from the harm of cheating. For instance, if you are cheated by a friend, you can confront the friend and demand that the situation be corrected, or you can withdraw from that relationship and protect yourself from future harm.

Betrayal Blindness When Attachment and Cheater Detectors Collide

What should you do when the person perpetrating a betrayal is also a person you are dependent on? This is the core bind of a betrayal trauma victim. The standard response to betrayal—confrontation or withdrawal—might only make the situation worse for the person who depends on the perpetrator, because confrontation and withdrawal are generally not good for inspiring attachment and care giving. In this case, the victim might be better off remaining unaware of the betrayal in order to protect the relationship. Indeed, this is what leads to betrayal blindness.

Analogy to Fight, Flight, and Freeze

You have probably heard about *fight* or *flight* reactions to threats. When an animal—or a person—is under threat, the first response is to fight back or to flee the situation, if that is possible. If neither fight nor flight is possible, the animal then has only one option left: to freeze. This freeze reaction is sometimes called "tonic immobility" when observed in prey animals under attack from a predator. Fight, flight, and freeze responses in predator-prey situations are highly evolved defenses that involve distinct physiology. Some researchers have observed humans display exactly this same set of responses and physiological changes.[2]

An interesting analogy between fight, flight, and freeze can be seen in our response to betrayal. If we are strong enough and in a good enough situation, we confront (fight) the betrayal to correct the situation. If we cannot do that, we withdraw from the person or the situation (flight) to avoid future harm. If that option is too dangerous—for instance, because we are dependent on the betrayer—our next best defense is to block out awareness of the betrayal; in other words, a kind of mental freeze (betrayal blindness) is our next best option.

Betrayal Trauma Theory and Research

Since its inception in the early 1990s, we have been further developing betrayal trauma theory. We have also been conducting research to test our theory and to better understand the psychology of betrayal traumas. Betrayal trauma theory explains why betrayal traumas—abuses perpetrated by someone the victim trusts and depends on—pose unique challenges to the victim, creating a conflict between the need to maintain a relationship and the need to respond to betrayal with protective action. As we have just explained, the core idea is this: although a protective response to betrayal might usually involve confronting or withdrawing from the perpetrator, the requirements of maintaining a necessary relationship may make such a response dangerous. In other words, often the need to preserve the relationship trumps the need to take protective action against betrayal. Protective action in response to betrayal—such as confrontation or withdrawal—may risk a crucial relationship by alienating the perpetrator, who is also the caregiver. This means that the victim—the person being abused or betrayed by someone close to him or her—may need to remain blind to the betrayal in order to protect the relationship with the caregiver.

Betrayal trauma theory has caused us to reevaluate the very idea of psychological trauma. Traditionally, psychological trauma was understood to be the result of terrorizing, life-threatening events

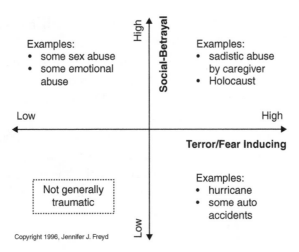

Two-Dimensional Model for Traumatic Events

that cause extreme fear.[3] These events can be very traumatizing, that is true. Yet what we and our colleagues have come to understand is that an equally traumatizing aspect of the events is social betrayal. In the above graph, we illustrate these concepts. The point is to show that events can be high in two very different kinds of traumatizing features—they can be terrifying or they can be highly betraying.

If we look at Judy, whom we describe in chapter 1, in the way that we usually look at trauma (the horizontal dimension in the graph), we see that difficult things happened to her, but nothing that would have caused her to be terrified, as might have happened if she were raped by a stranger. Judy, however, was terribly betrayed (the vertical dimension in the graph). It is important that we begin to see such events as traumatic, for in research we have discovered that the effects of betrayal are often even more psychologically problematic than what we usually mean when we think of trauma—car accidents or natural disasters.[4] Those occurrences can cause lasting psychological trouble, but betrayal traumas are especially likely to cause distress and serious problems in adjustment.[5]

Betrayal Traumas Are Toxic

After twenty years of research on betrayal trauma, we now have compelling evidence that betrayal traumas can be powerfully toxic to the victim.[6] Betrayal trauma theory explains that the double bind a victim faces (on the one hand, a need to protect against betrayal, but on the other hand, a need to remain attached to a caregiver) leads to a host of reactions, including blindness about the betrayal, memory impairment about the betrayal, and eventually even an increased risk for developing mental and physical distress.[7] Our research has confirmed that exposure to traumas that are high in betrayal (such as an assault by someone who is close to the victim) is linked to poorer mental health outcomes, including symptoms of depression, anxiety, dissociation, post-traumatic stress disorder, borderline personality characteristics, and increased physical health problems, as well as an even a greater risk of further victimization.[8] Later in the book, we explore in detail how betrayal trauma is toxic to the victim.

An interesting aspect of our development of betrayal trauma theory has been the particular issue of recovered memories. In the early 1990s, we first became curious about the issue of delayed recall of trauma, and this led to our initial conception of betrayal trauma theory—and to the false memory syndrome foundation that we discuss later in the book. According to betrayal trauma theory, forgetting abuse is a way to preserve the attachment relationship when the abuser is someone the victim is dependent on. Although there are various ways to remain blind to betrayal, perhaps the most effective way is to forget the event entirely.

Betrayal Traumas Are Frequent, Particularly for Girls and Women

We also know from two decades of research on betrayal trauma that people, particularly women, report alarmingly high rates of exposure to traumas that are high in betrayal.[9] A close interpersonal relationship to the perpetrator is a distinguishing characteristic of traumas commonly suffered by girls and women. For example, Lewis Goldberg and Jennifer Freyd discovered a startling relationship between gender and trauma exposure in a large adult community sample in the Eugene and Springfield, Oregon, area.[10] Men reported more traumas with a lower degree of betrayal (such as assault by someone who was not close to them) and women reported more trauma with a higher degree of betrayal (for example, assault by someone close to them).

In order to find out whether people have had experience with betrayal trauma events, Lewis Goldberg and Jennifer Freyd created a measurement tool called the Brief Betrayal Trauma

Survey (BBTS). This tool has been used in many studies now and translated into four languages (German, Swedish, Japanese, and Mandarin Chinese). The BBTS is short and easy for people to complete. There are a number of versions available. One version that has been used many times, including by Goldberg and Freyd, has fourteen items. For each item, participants report on exposure both "before age 18" and "age 18 or older." In some other versions of the BBTS, three different age categories are used: "before age 13" and "13 to before age 18" and "age 18 or older." Response choices are: "never," "1 or 2 times," or "more than that." Participants who complete the BBTS are first asked: "Have each of the following events happened to you, and if so, how often?" You might try asking yourself what your answer would be to some of these items.

1. You were in a major earthquake, fire, flood, hurricane, or tornado that resulted in significant loss of personal property, serious injury to yourself or a significant other, the death of a significant other, or the fear of your own death.

2. You were in a major automobile, boat, motorcycle, plane, train, or industrial accident that resulted in similar consequences.

3. You witnessed someone with whom you were very close (such as a parent, a brother or a sister, a caretaker, or an intimate partner) committing suicide, being killed, or being injured by another person so severely as to result in marks, bruises, burns, blood, or broken bones. This might include a close friend in combat.

4. You witnessed someone with whom you were not so close undergoing a similar kind of traumatic event.

5. You witnessed someone with whom you were very close deliberately attack another family member so severely as to result in marks, bruises, blood, broken bones, or broken teeth.

6. You witnessed someone with whom you were not so close deliberately attack a family member that severely.

7. You were deliberately attacked that severely by someone with whom you were very close.

8. You were deliberately attacked that severely by someone with whom you were not close.

9. You were made to have some form of sexual contact, such as touching or penetration, by someone with whom you were very close (such as a parent or a lover).

10. You were made to have such sexual contact by someone with whom you were not close.

11. You were emotionally or psychologically mistreated during a significant period of time by someone with whom you were very close (such as a parent or a lover).

12. You were emotionally or psychologically mistreated during a significant period of time by someone with whom you were not close.

13. You experienced the death of one of your own children.

14. You experienced a seriously traumatic event not already covered in any of these questions.

How did you do? Clearly, some items involve great betrayal, while others are asking about traumas that can occur without the betrayal component. Was it easy for you to see which questions described betrayal traumas? If these were things that you experienced, did you always recognize the betrayal in the event?

This survey was designed to allow researchers to quickly measure a person's exposure to traumas with lots of betrayal and traumas with less betrayal. If you look at the previous list, you'll see that the traumas on the list that have the highest betrayal are items 7, 9, and 11. These items pertain to physical, sexual, and emotional abuse by someone very close to the participant, such as a parent or a lover. The other events are also traumas but not the sort of very-high-betrayal trauma that occurs when the victim is being abused by someone very close to him or her. In some studies, we have further divided the remaining events into medium and low betrayal. Medium-betrayal events involve interpersonal abuse by someone not so close to the victim. Low-betrayal events involve non-interpersonal traumas, such as natural disasters and accidents. It is important to realize that any trauma can involve betrayal, even a natural disaster (as occurred to some people in the aftermath of Hurricane Katrina), but these events are categorized based on the certainty of high betrayal. Any time a parent or a lover abuses someone, high betrayal is certainly a result.

Using these questions, Goldberg and Freyd looked at the rates of women and men who reported at least one event that was high in betrayal or lower in betrayal. The answers were somewhat surprising. Although there were very high rates of betrayal trauma, there was also a big difference between the experiences of men and women. Men and women did not differ very much in their overall rates of trauma exposure; however, they differed greatly in the types of events to which they were exposed. Women were much more likely to be betrayed than men.

It is instructive to consider our findings regarding physical abuse. Rates of exposure to physical abuse are about the same for men and women overall.[11] However, women report more physical abuse by someone with whom they were close in both childhood and adulthood.[12] These findings reveal that even for an event such as physical assault that appears to affect men and women at a comparable rate, women experience assault by people who are close to them more often than men do.

What about other groups of participants? We have now observed the high rate of exposure to betrayal trauma in numerous samples, including those with more ethnic diversity. With the collaboration of researchers at the Oregon Research Institute, Bridget Klest and Jennifer Freyd surveyed 833 members of an ethnically diverse sample in Hawaii.[13] Ethnic groups with lower socioeconomic status generally reported more exposure to both high- and low-betrayal traumas. Yet once again, we found that although men and women are exposed to similar rates of trauma overall, women report more exposure to traumas that are high in betrayal, while men report exposure to more lower-betrayal traumas.

Betrayal trauma theory gives us a framework for understanding betrayal and its effects. In this book, we draw on this theory to understand human reactions to betrayals that span the spectrum from everyday events to severe traumas. We have seen that betrayal traumas are frighteningly common. Next, we consider the impact they have on people who experience them.

6

Knowing and Not Knowing

We have seen that betrayal is common and that very often, people respond to betrayal by not fully seeing it, by not knowing about it. We have discussed why this is often an adaptive strategy: by remaining blind, victims or bystanders protect their place in the world, in society, and in relationship to others. By not seeing betrayal, victims are not motivated to disrupt the status quo. This is *why* people remain blind, but what about *how*? What are the mental and social mechanisms that allow one not to see something that is right in front of one's nose?

Part of the answer to the "how" question resides in social factors—how people can deceive others; how perpetrators groom victims to be blind; how governments hide their own betrayals; how society conspires to turn a blind eye. Another part of the answer to the "how" question is psychological—how people can deceive themselves; how the individual human mind can put on blinders to filter out incoming information; how the individual mind can channel information out of awareness; how people can forget.

In this chapter, we examine the "how" question by focusing on one particular account: the story of Samantha Spencer. In chapter 7, by following Samantha further, we see that not knowing one sort of betrayal can contribute to not knowing about a broader range of betrayals. Then, in chapter 8, we explore the issues further, considering a range of experiences and research findings.

Samantha's Story

Samantha Spencer—Sam, to her friends—was happy. She was happy to be at this fine restaurant with Mark, her husband of eleven years, and Rosalie, their infant daughter. They didn't get out often; money was tight, and recently their daily life had been dominated by Mark's recovery from alcoholism.

Mark had been in treatment for his drinking problem. Treatment was hard work for all of them; even Sam had to attend sessions for wives of alcoholics. Yet that night Sam was feeling hopeful. Things felt as if they were finally on the right track, and to Sam, this evening out promised a new beginning. Things were going to be okay. Even Rosalie was being an angel, turning her head from Sam to Mark and back again as they discussed the food. Roast duck. Sam's favorite. Mark had insisted that they splurge a little. The dimly lit restaurant and Mark's easy smile suggested romance. Sam smiled, too.

Years after that evening, Sam told us what she was thinking at the time: "He's treating me nicely. He wants to make things good." They were a family together, a happy family, enjoying the evening out. Sam felt good. They ate and ate and talked about new beginnings and bright futures. Mark reached across the table to brush away the freckles from Sam's face, like the old days.

After blackberry pie, Mark excused himself to go to the men's room, and Sam began packing up Rosalie's toys: a cloth picture book, her yellow rattle, a well-chewed stuffed bunny. The waiter brought the check, and Rosalie began to fidget. Sam realized that the whole evening had been charmed, but now it was late and Rosalie was tired. Soon she might start to fuss and cry. So Sam, a good mother and a polite diner, knew it was time to get Rosalie out of her highchair and then out of the restaurant while things were still so nice. She decided she'd pay for the meal and meet Mark when he exited the restroom. As she headed toward the register, Rosalie on her hip, she glanced at the bar.

Sam explained to us, "There he is, having a shot of tequila at the bar. I am just horrified because I have this desire always to believe what he says."

He was standing—half-turned toward Sam, half toward the bar—and when he saw her, he set the empty glass on the bar and rushed toward her.

"So now you are spying on me!" Mark yelled.

"I can't believe you are drinking!" replied Sam, as she pulled Rosalie close to her chest.

Mark and Sam threw accusations at each other, back and forth, back and forth. Rosalie began to cry. Then Mark said with a sudden surge of anger: "By the way, I'm required to tell you . . ." Mark blurted out a new confession, claiming his treatment program insisted that he confess as part of his "coming clean." Mark then told Sam, at the end of their nice evening, that he had had an affair with another woman.

"It was like being hit by a train, because I had no clue."

Sam said these words a decade after the events of that confession-in-the-restaurant evening. She was visiting her old friend who lives in our town. Her old friend is our new friend. Our now-mutual friend had told Sam about our interest in betrayal, and Sam, visiting for a few days from Ohio, offered to tell us her story.

So there we sat on the bedroom floor belonging to one of our young children on a lovely October day. The bedroom offered us privacy. Outside, the maple trees had recently turned brilliant fall colors, and the sunlight entering the bedroom was saturated with red and yellow tree light. We opened the windows wide; the gentle breeze was spiced with autumn leaves.

A tape recorder sat between us, preserving Sam's story. Sam often spoke in the present tense about long-ago events: "He is treating me nicely; I have a desire to believe what he says." Yet she felt very present, too, very grounded in the here and now. It's as if she were in her past and in her present, both at once. Sam is a striking woman with a mane of fiery red hair and a warm smile. Quick to say she has low self-esteem, she seemed to be outgoing, talkative, and full of joie de vivre. Although we offered to set up chairs for the interview, she indicated that she was happy sitting on the floor. With her legs casually tucked under her long flowing skirt, she did seem comfortable. We were grateful for that; we preferred the floor, too.

Sam is now a graduate student at a fine university in Ohio. After she divorced her husband, she managed to complete college and enter graduate school—an accomplishment we came to admire deeply as we replayed the audiotape and considered the story of her sixteen-year marriage. Many years have passed, but Sam brought the past to life as she told her story.

"It was like being hit by a train, because I had no clue," she had told us. No clue? Did Sam really have no clue that Mark had had an affair? As Sam talked, she complicated the picture: "Now, looking back, I think, 'How could I have not had a clue?' He went to bars all the time, and I couldn't even go out to a movie with my girlfriends without him saying, 'I know that is not where you are at.' He didn't like any of my friends, and 'every man was flirting' with me . . . and still he could go to bars. There was really a huge double standard."

We learned more as Sam talked to us. We discovered that Mark hadn't just "gone to bars all the time"—Mark often spent the whole night out "at bars." Mark was also intensely jealous and possessive of Sam, apparently projecting all of his own betrayals onto her. Sam's friends easily put two and two together. They witnessed the obsessive and entirely misplaced jealousy, they were aware of the all-nighters, and they knew what was going on. Sam told us that her friends at the time were warning her: "Your husband is not to be trusted. He is spending nights out." Something was not right, but Sam wouldn't accept the evidence or the warnings.

How could Sam have failed to see what was so obvious? We knew from what Sam already told us that the affair Mark confessed to that evening at the restaurant was not his only infidelity.

Sam had found a way to repeatedly ignore evidence of Mark's betrayal. *How* did she do this?

How Did Sam Remain Unaware of Mark's Infidelity?

Of course, part of the answer to Sam's ignorance resided in Mark's deception. Yet Mark really wasn't that good at deception, and Sam's friends saw what was going on. Sam's unawareness of Mark's betrayals must go beyond Mark's limited ability to deceive. Sam was doing something in her mind with the evidence: what?

Consider Sam's answer to our question: "When he confessed, did he say it was still going on, or did he claim it was over?"

"No, he said it was a one-time thing. One night in the bar he was really drunk, and this woman just talked him into going home with her. He was like, 'I couldn't even get it up.' Almost like it really didn't happen, like it was an aborted attempt. So I ended up after the fact feeling almost sorry for him. And being angry at the woman and angry at [the treatment program]."

So one thing Sam could do in her head was change the story around. Mark became the victim, not the responsible party. Mark didn't have a real affair, just an aborted attempt. Sam felt anger at the woman and the treatment program for making Mark confess to something that hadn't even really happened.

After the restaurant fight and Mark's quasi-confession, Sam found a way to stay with Mark. She found a way around the promise she'd made to herself to immediately leave him if he ever cheated on her. To do this, she needed to believe Mark didn't have a real affair, and she also needed to ignore any evidence of continued infidelity. Sam pulled it off: "So I stayed for another five years after that."

Sam told us about her friend's attempts to warn her during those years. "She told me, 'No, he goes to the bars all the time. My friends see him. You don't know him. He's always flirting with women.' And he was. He went to bars all the time, stayed out all night, and for some reason I just didn't want to believe it because he told me, 'Oh, no, I don't do that, it was a one-time thing.' And I saw him as so incapable of being conniving. He's one of those—you know—doesn't have a poker face, doesn't really even plan things. So he just would go to the bars, and I think I just decided, 'No, I need to believe him, he's just drinking because he's alcoholic.' But my friend said, 'No, you don't know what he's doing.' And I remember defending him to her. Like, 'Well, I know, he told me.'"

Yet of course, Sam's friend was correct about Mark.

"So I find out about two years ago about this girlfriend he had had. And I said, 'Oh, I hear that you were with Liz before we were even divorced, which I think is pretty crappy.' I said, 'Two years before we were divorced.' And he said, 'No, we were actually together before Rosalie was born,' which would have been nine years ago, and at that point I felt completely betrayed because not only had he been going out on me, but I had been defending him to my friends, so it was almost a betrayal of my notion of who he was. I just didn't even know who he was! That really shook me, because I felt that I had at least had a concept of a person."

Betrayal blindness involves not seeing what is there to be seen. Like Dorothy's ruby slippers, the information is there the whole time. As Sam realized later, she had all of the evidence she needed to see the sad truth: "Looking back now, I can think, 'Well, he was going to bars all the time, he was staying out all night, my friend was telling me these things . . .'"

Sam had given us some clues about how she managed to transform the evidence in her mind. She denied the obvious to herself. She ignored her friends' warnings. She looked the other way time and time again. Perhaps, similar to others who have talked to us about their betrayal blindness, Sam even forgot unpleasant facts about Mark when that forgetting helped her remain unaware.

Sam and Betrayal Trauma Theory

Let's revisit betrayal trauma theory for a bit. Now that we know the basics, we can begin to see Sam's reasons for not knowing.

Why did she overlook Mark's infidelity? Sam dropped some clues. First, she told us that before Mark's confession in the restaurant, she had told Mark that the only way she would ever leave him was if he "went out on her"—Sam's words for infidelity. In fact, Sam gave Mark an absolute ultimatum: if he went out on her, she *would* leave him. Sam remembered the crisis this created for her after Mark's confession of the supposedly "aborted affair."

"Here I am with this baby, and what's going to happen? I am going to have to go out and get a job and put my baby in day care and live on my own, which I had never done in my life. I went from living with my parents to getting married and being with him, so I was unable to even envision myself living alone. So I was just devastated for weeks. I felt at the time it was for what he had done, but I think I was most devastated by the notion of having to change my life and figure out how to be on my own. . . . How was I supposed to manage? . . . So I ended up putting my stuff aside and saying, 'Okay, we'll be fine as long as you never do this again.' Of course, he convinced me it was a one-time deal, he couldn't even actually have sex with her because he couldn't get an erection, and she had come on to him at the bar when he had been out having a drink. I look back now, and I think I almost turned it around. He was seduced; he was in this position; it was a one-time thing. So I ended up deciding, 'Okay, it was a one-time thing, and we'll work on things.' I realize now it was more important for me to continue to stay home and be with my daughter—live in the home we bought together, instead of creating this huge upheaval in my life."

Sam's words resonated with our core theoretical premise about betrayal blindness: people remain unaware of betrayal when the un-awareness helps them stay in a relationship they believe they need for their own survival. Sam felt totally dependent on Mark. She simply didn't know how to live without him. Her own survival, and that of her daughter, seemed dependent on staying with Mark. The empowered response to perceiving infidelity is to leave or challenge the unfaithful person, but Sam didn't consider leaving to be an option. She didn't know how to live on her own. Leaving was out, but what about insisting that Mark change? Confronting Mark with ongoing distrust and demands for accountability would likely have rocked the boat and perhaps even have caused Mark to want to leave. Indeed, Sam reported that for the first few weeks after his confession in the restaurant, she did withdraw from Mark, and he began to complain. His complaining likely scared Sam; perhaps he would leave her. We believe that Sam found a way to overlook Mark's infidelity because she felt as if she needed Mark for her survival, and awareness of the infidelity would threaten a relationship that felt absolutely necessary to Sam.

Sam stayed with Mark for five years after the restaurant confession. During those five years, she acknowledged no further infidelity. Sam found out about Mark's long-term affair with Liz only after the divorce. Even now, she had trouble seeing Mark as deceptive, and she struggled with reconciling her image of Mark: "I don't think he's a particularly clever person, so I don't see him as necessarily trying to be deceptive to me, and at the same time I think if he was doing this for years, he must have . . . I don't know . . . been living in fear that I'd find out. . . . I don't think he's really someone who feels cocky about things. He's sort of a humble person. But I don't know. He made it like: 'It was a one-time thing' . . . but, yeah, obviously he had been with Liz, so I don't know if this was a different woman, or this was just a story he concocted, or if that had happened and then he had ended up with Liz."

Sam believes she began to think about leaving Mark only after *he* told her he was thinking of leaving—a few years after the restaurant event. "He told me about two years before I actually left that he had decided he was going to leave. I was devastated because I had never actually had to think about what I would do if I was on my own. We fought all the time, and it had always been an unstable marriage, but that was the first time I had to really think seriously about developing strategies. At that point, when I figured he was leaving, I thought, 'Well, what will I do? Well, I will go to college because I was going to the Ohio State extension program, and my dream would be to go to Columbus and get the degree that I want.' So, boy, from that point on, when I had to develop strategies for being on my own, I just started slowly . . . not even consciously planning, but unconsciously thinking, 'This is what I want, this is my dream.' It took two years just to get to the place emotionally— I was going to counseling; I was talking to friends; every strategy imaginable just to get myself to the point emotionally that I could leave, and even so, it was so difficult."

When Sam understood that Mark might leave her, she was forced to think about a way to survive without the relationship. She had already been doing her part to keep things going by not seeing the infidelities, but now it wasn't working, so further unawareness wasn't likely to help Sam. Thus, Sam began to realize that her survival might depend on her ability to function independently. This dawning awareness represented a fundamental shift in Sam's strategy. The shift allowed Sam to move away from unawareness into awareness, and this shift encouraged her growth as an independent adult.

"I think from about the point where he said he was going to leave, I think from that point, we were living in the same house . . . and I was not even consciously planning to leave at that point. . . . It still took me a little while longer to really start plotting, saving money, figuring out bank accounts, separating my stuff out. I even figured out a budget for him and how things would be okay for him and what bills he would have to pay and how he would be okay with the income he had, so that I could decide what to go ahead and agree to for spousal support. So we actually lived together. . . . I filed for divorce that May, and we still lived in the same house for the next four months. I said, 'I'm going to leave, I'm going to leave,' but I don't think he really believed I was going to leave until I actually left. Even after I filed. I think I even wondered if I would have the courage. It's one of those things that is very stressful, but I wanted it a lot. It was so painful just to have to leave somebody, to hurt somebody like that. I realized I'd rather be the person who gets hurt and has to deal with things than be the one who really dumps this on someone else. It was a long emotional process, not even the physical move, it was more the emotional. How can I extract myself, take my daughter away from her dad, leave this man who is alcoholic and drug-dependent, everything else, with nothing? It took a long time to get myself to the point where I believed that was okay to do."

As Sam told us how desperately she wanted to leave Mark, yet how hard it had been to actually leave, we felt an increasing sense of foreboding. We sensed something dark in Sam's past. Dared we shine a light on that darkness now?

7

Mental Gymnastics

There on the floor of a young girl's cheerful bedroom, amid the stuffed animals and the little-girl toys, surrounded by the gentle breeze and the fall sunlight, we asked Sam about the unthinkable: "Did you have to worry about your physical safety?"

"Yeah, in fact, he . . . I was trying to figure this out because we lived in Alabama shortly after we were married for two years. I was isolated from my family. That period was really the most abusive. I didn't have friends. I didn't live near anybody. There was quite a bit of abuse. . . . I don't think there was that much physical abuse for [our first years after our move to Ohio], but during the last six months to a year, there were a few times he hit me. . . . I have to say that the primary thing that pushed me to the point where I could leave was that I had a daughter, and I realized I didn't want him to repeat . . . because his [Mark's] dad had beat his mom, and I realized even if I don't matter, I do not want my daughter to develop these same qualities. I used my daughter as an excuse to leave. At least two times, he did. He hit me or grabbed me by my hair. He was doing a lot of drugs toward the very end. He was taking crank, doing a lot of crank [a type of methamphetamine, or 'speed,' that is smoked], and becoming almost delusional. He'd wake me up in the middle of the night in my room and say, 'Did you just get here? I heard a car door in the street.' It's like two o'clock in the morning, and he's just whacked out, and I've been in here sleeping, and he thinks I'm out running around.

"So the last six to nine months were really stressful. I don't think he had hit me for years, and suddenly it sort of escalated. So yeah, I was just very worried. In fact, there was one incident where I was trying to leave with our daughter, who was five and a half then. I have her in my arms, and he's trying to pull her out of my arms as I'm trying to get in the car, so we are fighting and yelling for all the neighbors to hear, and she's crying. So it did even get to the point where she was in the midst of these struggles. I think that actually helped me, though, to really have conviction to leave. Because if it had just been me, I don't know if I would have ever got to the point where I would have said, 'Okay' . . ."

"When you were struggling with your daughter, was that when you were actually leaving him?" we asked.

"It was the summer before I left," Sam replied. "And I think that was just an incident when I think he had even hit me, and I was just like, 'This is not going to happen, and we are leaving.'"

"So it's like you were running away."

"Yeah, so I'm like: We are leaving, and you are not taking my daughter!"

Now we understood: Sam was a battered wife. This husband was dangerous: alcoholic, drug-addicted, and emotionally and physically abusive. By the time Sam left, Mark's infidelity was less significant than his reign of terror. Staying with her husband was becoming a risk to her safety and her daughter's well-being.

So the inevitable questions arose about the many years of abuse she endured before she finally left: Why did she stay? Listening to the tape later, remembering our thoughts during the interview, we chastised ourselves: Why did we first question her motivations, rather than his? Why didn't we ask ourselves, "Why did *he* do it?"

Now we are still probing: Why did she stay, and how did she justify things in her mind to make it okay to stay? Just as Sam could whisk away evidence of infidelity, she found a way to transform the abuse into something not so terrible. Why? How?

Even when Mark was not physically abusive to Sam, he was often emotionally abusive. Thus, emotional abuse likely played a part in Sam's inability to envision herself as capable of living independently. At the end of her relationship, she enrolled in an extension program. "I started taking courses through the college and just realizing I did have a brain. For years, he had said, 'You're stupid,' and I really had to build up this knowledge that I was intelligent, that other people did like me, that I did have worth, that I needed self-worth. I probably still have lower self-esteem than most people."

Mark's emotional abuse helped keep Sam trapped. She did not believe in her own competence. Without competence, she was dependent on Mark for her survival.

Once more, we asked Sam to tell us about her marriage, and this time she connected her ability to overlook evidence of infidelity with her disregard of emotional mistreatment.

Again, we asked her to review the signs of Mark's infidelity that she had ignored at the time. Sam began, "He never wore his wedding ring, but I thought—" Sam interrupted herself at this point, as she often did while talking to us. Later we learned that Sam explained the lack of a wedding ring to herself by attributing Mark's behavior to his dislike of the style of the ring itself. Sam told us that she had picked out the wedding ring, and Mark let her know that the style was too ornate. Probably Mark didn't wear the ring because a wedding ring is an inconvenience when philandering. His excuse put the blame on Sam (for choosing the wrong ring), and Sam accepted this version of reality.

Sam continued, "He liked to tell me stories of women hitting on him, and him as this innocent victim being tried and true . . . as far as other things, it was the fact that he would periodically stay out all night. I have memories that come back to me now of before we were even married, memories of how he was supposed to meet me somewhere, and he'd never show up and me waiting for hours, listening to every car that went by, thinking, 'Oh, that must be him!'

"Looking back, it's chilling to realize that there were things that happened before we were even together that I did to protect the relationship. I remember my friend telling me a couple of years ago about a time when we were in high school: 'Yeah, I remember coming over one day and thinking you never get out anymore. You are always with Mark, and you never do things with us.' She came over to my family's home, and I remember feeling resentment toward her because I just instinctively knew he would be angry. I remember thinking, 'How dare you come over and want me to go out running around?' He's going to think, 'Why do they want her to go partying with them?'

"So I remember transferring the resentment to them, instead of toward him, and then forgetting it altogether. Always compensating for his behavior. And throughout . . . I never would tell anyone that he hit me. I could never go anywhere because if I went to the grocery store, and I took an hour when I was supposed to take forty-five minutes, he'd say, 'Where did you go?'"

Sam explained to us that she was living in fear, yet she believed her friends viewed her as upbeat. She told us she had not wanted anyone to view her as someone who was abused or who lived a sad life. "I feel like I have this characteristic where I want things to be all right, so I'll do what I have to in my mind in order to justify or fix things. I think I did that a lot with my husband. I wanted so badly to have a good marriage."

The human mind is marvelously convoluted. Sam almost surely knew about her husband's betrayals, in some sense of the word *knew*, even as she didn't let herself "know" in some other sense of the word. Betrayal blindness requires this convolution, so that one can be in the dual state of simultaneously knowing and not knowing something important.

Although we started this interview with the intention of focusing on Sam's blindness to Mark's infidelity, our conversation took us into the difficult territory of domestic violence. In Sam's case, the infidelity, the emotional mistreatment, and the physical abuse became one big swamp of betrayal. Yet for Sam, each element demanded a separate strategy. Sam found a way to be blind to each part, and the blindness for one betrayal type reinforced her blindness for each of the others. In the case of infidelity, Sam chose not to believe Mark's confession and to overlook the overwhelming evidence the rest of the time. In the case of emotional mistreatment, Sam considered it evidence of her inadequacies, so instead of withdrawing from Mark or confronting him for his meanness, she swallowed his judgments as if she deserved them. In the case of physical abuse, she made excuses for Mark and minimized the severity. Yet we suspected there might be more that she did with the knowledge of physical abuse in order to be able to stay with Mark.

Blindness for Battering

We have long wondered about the role of betrayal blindness in physically abusive relationships. Although much of the action of infidelity happens outside the immediate vicinity of the person being betrayed, battering occurs *to* the person being betrayed. Overlooking the *signs* of infidelity seems an easier task than overlooking the *experience* of being physically abused. Yet it seems that Sam did find a way to remain less than fully aware of the battering. How? Pondering this, we returned to the idea that we can know and not know something at the same time. Part of our knowledge may be consciously available, but part may be hidden from awareness most of the time. Thinking about conscious knowledge, we asked Sam, "How much did you *know* he was hitting you?"

"I still struggle with that. Even now, if I see *Oprah*, and she is talking with abuse victims, I can definitely look at their situation and say that was not mine. They profile the guys: this guy is psychopathic, and this guy is more remorseful after the fact. There are different kinds of batterers. I look at them and go, 'No, he wasn't like that.'"

Sam tried to explain why Mark wasn't like the batterers on *Oprah*. She claimed Mark was always remorseful after he hit her. This seems like no distinction at all, because Sam had just told us that some of the men on *Oprah* were remorseful. Then Sam told us she felt she had some power because she knew Mark would feel so bad afterward. This strikes us as not much power at all. Sometimes the dance of unawareness leads otherwise rational people into remarkably convoluted claims!

Sam went on, explaining the typical battering episode: "I wouldn't fight back. He wasn't trying to kill me. I could see that because he had been a state-champion football player. He could easily have hurt me badly. I could see he held back. He was just really angry with me. I knew because I'd be bruised."

Sam was bruised by Mark's attacks, yet Sam still feels that Mark is different from the men on *Oprah*. Did Sam believe her bruises were minor? As she continued with her story, she provided evidence that the physical injuries were sometimes severe. One scar runs the length of her collarbone. Still, she continued to struggle with accepting that she was a victim of domestic violence. "One time in Alabama he kicked me in the back. I thought he bruised a kidney. I could hardly walk for two weeks, it was so painful. Then another time when we lived there, he broke my arm. In the hospital, the nurse said, 'Oh, my God.' It's really strange to me because a part of me doesn't feel as if I was really battered. . . . I think I classically fit the profile of the type of person who would be with somebody like that . . . but at the same time, I don't like to see myself as a victim, and that's why I didn't ever tell anybody. I didn't want my friends to say to me, 'What the hell are you doing with this guy?' I was protecting him, and I was protecting myself from that type of judgment, but at the same time I feel like I was one of those people who always wanted to be happy. So after an incident, I'd go right back to thinking, 'Poor guy, he saw his mom get beaten.'

"There were only two times I really feared for my life. Two different times, he put his hand over my mouth and my nose. He would say it was because I was screaming, but I was scared for my life."

Sam had experienced severe battering on more than one occasion, yet she still felt her experience wasn't like that of the other battered wives on *Oprah*. The human mind is amazing.

Keeping Secrets Supports Betrayal Blindness

We wondered about Sam's history with disclosing the abuse. From her pattern of telling others, we figured we might gain insight into her own awareness over time. If she had explicitly reported Mark's violence as battering, it would be evidence of her conscious awareness of his wrongdoing, which we doubted Sam really possessed at the time. If she had casually mentioned the violence to people, it might indicate that she really didn't know it was wrong. On the other hand, complete secrecy would show that on some level, she knew there was something too awful to tell. "Did you ever report his hitting?" we asked.

"Finally, at the time I was going to leave. I have one friend (whom I became friends with fairly recently) who talked about her ex-husband and how he used to beat her, so I did start telling her. Then I had another friend who actually asked me, when I described his jealousy, 'Did he ever hit you?' It caught me off guard, so I said, 'Yeah.' Those were the only two from back then."

Sam did not tell others until the very end, when her friend's question caught her off guard. She kept it a secret for sixteen years. This strongly suggests Sam knew on some level that the battering was very wrong. Even at the end, Sam didn't tell her family. Her need to keep the truth from her parents was powerful.

"I think actually that was part of the reason I was in the marriage for so long. . . . I tried to keep up this masquerade that we were in a decent marriage, and that made it all the more difficult for them to understand why when I said I wanted to leave. They just thought he was this great guy. . . . What was your question?"

We repeated our question to Sam: "We had asked whether you had reported the hitting."

"Oh, so I didn't even tell anybody, but now it seems a lot of my friends in Columbus know. . . . I really don't like people who act as victims. Like people who are victims of incest, and that becomes what defines their lives. I really don't want to be defined as a person who was abused because, first of all, I don't want pity, and second of all, in the past I certainly didn't want my friends thinking I was crazy and stupid. Actually, I feel bad because my closest friend back there used to talk about . . . I'd say he'd done this or that, and I even told her his dad used to beat his mom, and I'd say, 'But he doesn't hit me'—I'd actually tell her that. And she'd say, "Well, that's amazing," and I kept up this charade that he didn't hit me, and now I feel incredibly guilty because if she were to find out, she'd feel betrayed that I misrepresented him and our relationship. I worry a bit about that."

"What about when you were going through the divorce? Did you tell your lawyer?"

"No."

Sam didn't even tell her divorce lawyer! We were glad to hear that Sam had told some of her current friends about the abuse and that she even experienced this as liberating, although clearly she still struggled with identifying with the experience. We respected her desire not to be defined by something horrible imposed on her by Mark. We also shared Sam's dislike of spending time with people who are overly invested in the victim role. Yet there is a middle ground: one can acknowledge being victimized without being indefinitely consumed by the victim role. One can acknowledge being a victim and be available to others, too. Acknowledging being victimized need not be an obstacle to being a satisfied, even joyful, person.

We worried that Sam was still avoiding the full truth of her experience. As is detailed in the final chapters of this book, social sharing and disclosure are fundamentally part of breaking free of betrayal blindness. Sam seemed on her way to this liberation but still had some distance to travel. For instance, as she was talking to us, we began to suspect that Sam still didn't *really* think of Mark's physical attacks as a crime, as indicated by her reluctance to see

Mark as being like the batterers on *Oprah*. Mark had unquestion-
ably committed many criminal acts in his assaults on Sam. If she
could label these actions crimes, this would be a good sign. So we
asked her, "Do you think about the fact that it was a crime?"

"I don't really. . . . He was a victim, too. He was a victim of parents who had this behavior, so even if his behavior toward me was
reprehensible, I don't really feel like I could pile that on him, too,
that here now everyone is going to know what he did, too. . . . There
were a few times I threatened, when he'd be hitting me, and I'd grab
the phone and pretend that I was going to call . . . which I'd never
do because the notion of the police showing up at my house . . . I
don't think I had the courage for that. Also, I think I had enough
knowledge to know that I would be so horribly embarrassed the
next day trying to deal with it, people would know, he'd be in jail. . . .
I don't think I ever really did think of it as a crime. I don't know that
even now I think of it as a crime, which is funny because obviously it
is . . . and when I hear of other women, I'm very sympathetic. I think
I feel enough sympathy for him. . . . I'm protective of him. . . . So,
yeah, it's hard to think of it as a criminal thing . . . because it seems
there are degrees of it, too, and it's not necessarily even an absolute
thing . . . there is a lot of gray area there. But yeah, it is a crime, I
can't even imagine ever having reported it."

As Sam acknowledged her difficulty thinking of Mark's treatment as a crime, distinct from her ability to see other women as
victims of a crime, we reflected on the many versions of this double
standard. We suspected that this dissociation between the meaning
of personal experiences and the meaning of other people's experiences is an important part of betrayal blindness. Mark imposed
double standards on Sam (he could go to bars; she couldn't even go
to the movies); Sam imposed double standards on herself.

Double Standards and Other Mental Gymnastics That Support Betrayal Blindness

When complete forgetting is not possible, the mind resorts to other
measures. Sometimes it transforms personal experiences into something different from the identical experiences of other people. Sam's
story reminds us of a research study in which children who were
emotionally abused were questioned about their experiences, and

so were their siblings. Here is the interesting finding: the children were more likely to label their siblings as abused than themselves, even when they had had a very similar experience.[1]

Thinking of this study, we mentioned to Sam that people are often resistant to taking on the victim label, not wanting to see themselves that way. We explained, "We hear what you are saying about matters of degree, but in this case it definitely seems he was engaged in criminal activity as defined by the law. It's interesting that when you were talking, you weren't seeing it as a crime . . . maybe more like the drinking . . . a behavior he doesn't have control over. A lot of people who witnessed domestic violence as children don't go on to abuse others . . . so it is related, but not everybody goes on to do that; some people go on to find a way past the abuse.[2] We think about what you have accomplished. Some people in your situation might have become abusive to their kids or something, but you haven't; you have done this whole other thing with your life."

Sam didn't tell anyone, but we were still trying to understand: Did she *tell herself*? She still didn't think of Mark's abuse as a crime, so she could not tell herself, not really, that she was a crime victim. How far did her own unawareness extend? We knew she transformed the meaning and significance of the events from cruel crimes to something forgivable, but did she ever forget the abusive events themselves? This might be hard to find out, because if she did forget any of the events, would she remember them now? And if she forgot for a while and remembered now, would she remember forgetting? This is the sort of challenge that researchers focusing on memory and trauma inevitably face. First, we want to determine what is remembered, but in order to do that, we need to know what really happened. For intimate traumas such as battering, we almost always must rely on the victim's memory, because there are seldom other witnesses, and the abusers rarely will admit to the abuse. Despite these challenges, victims sometimes have good access to their memory for events, and occasionally they can even give detailed descriptions of the way their memories have become more or less accessible over time. Perhaps that would be the case with Sam.

So we returned to our earlier question: "Do you think there were times when you put out of your mind the fact that he hit you?"

"Now I'm really having a hard time remembering," she said. "Definitely in Alabama, there was a lot of abuse. But once we moved back to Ohio, it almost seems to me that there were years and years where I don't remember much happening, so I'm just thinking, 'Did it not happen, or am I just sort of forgetting?' I mean, I don't think . . . I think it changed the way he abused me because he knew my family lived close by, and he liked my parents and my dad especially, so I think maybe that changed . . . but I don't know if I don't remember, or . . . because it seems to me there were years when he didn't . . . and people don't just change like that. . . . I'm thinking about Alabama. . . . I remember there were a number of times I was really bruised, so I couldn't even look in the mirror without remembering, so I know it was very fresh in my mind, but at the same time wanting to forget. Like: make this go away, I don't want people to see me, I don't want to believe this happened."

Did Sam forget years of physical abuse between the early years of her marriage and the later years? She remembered it from the early years—there were the bruises. She remembered it from the last years—she was already preparing to leave. Were the middle years free of physical violence, or had Sam forgotten the violence? Sam did not know. Maybe someday she would ask Mark. At that point, we didn't know. Meta-memory, or having a memory for memory, is a tricky business. There is much about unawareness and forgetting that is hard to uncover and understand, in part because the very nature of betrayal blindness is a distortion of reality. We will struggle with this problem over and over. It's a challenge, but it's not an insurmountable challenge. What we did know in this particular case is that Sam doubted her memory and struggled with feeling that perhaps she had forgotten the abuse. We also knew that she remembered wanting to forget. Of course, we knew she found a way to rationalize Mark's violence and overlook his flagrant infidelity, too. Overall, Sam was a master at being blind to betrayal.

Dependence on the Perpetrator and the Need to Maintain the Relationship

Why would Sam not know something that was there for the knowing? This is the motivation question. As for her blindness to the infidelity, we believe the answer to the *why* question likely resided in Sam's need to survive. During the initial period of her marriage, Sam had a powerful—although barely conscious—motivation for

remaining blind to her husband's betrayal: she felt utterly dependent on her husband. Knowing about the betrayal would have required some action, yet she could not afford to rock the boat. Better
not to know. Sometimes ignorance *is* bliss. Ignorance can preserve
the relative bliss of the status quo when knowledge would inevitably
lead to chaos. Ignorance is bliss when it allows you to survive.

We asked Sam about her financial situation while she was still
married, and how that affected her ability to leave Mark. Our theory of betrayal blindness leads us to predict that unawareness of
mistreatment in marriage is most likely to occur in the context of financial dependence.[3] Sam explained that holding down a job while
she was with Mark had been very difficult, that Mark expected to
drive her home from work every day but would get very angry if she
was late in coming out to the car. One job in particular required her
to close the business each day. "It took a little while, and one time
I came out and got in the car. He was angry and started hitting me,
and one of the managers saw it, so then he told the head manager,
who confronted me about it. And I was, I remember, mortified and
angry with them for knowing about it or whatever, so shortly after
that I quit."

Sam was financially dependent on Mark; Mark made sure of
that. Sam was isolated. Sam had never lived alone. These factors all
made her feel dependent on Mark for her very survival. Eventually,
Sam did get a part-time job she held onto, but by then she had
Rosalie, and Sam didn't know how to live alone, never mind with a
baby.

We wondered whether there was more to the story of why and
how Sam overlooked Mark's betrayal than her adult situation alone.
We suspected that aspects of Sam's childhood in some ways prepared
her to respond to Mark and his mistreatment with denial and sub-
missiveness, instead of with awareness and confrontation. It's hard
to know whether this is a factor in Sam's case, but research studies
indicate that childhood victimization is statistically related to adult
victimization.[4] Abused women are more likely to have been abused
as children than are nonabused women.[5] Such correlations refer
to statistical probabilities, not deterministic patterns. Smoking may
increase the risk of lung cancer, but not every smoker gets cancer,
and not every lung cancer patient was a smoker. Furthermore, there
isn't only one factor that predisposes someone to betrayal blindness.

Many factors interact with one another in complicated ways, including genetic factors, childhood abuse, and gender socialization.[6]

We did not feel comfortable asking Sam about childhood abuse just then. Asking about abuse can open up wounds, and if she wasn't ready to talk about it, and if we were not prepared to help her through the aftermath of opening up issues, then it was too big a risk to proceed that direction. Sam didn't raise the topic, and we didn't either. (Yet later we wondered: Was our own reluctance part of the dynamics of betrayal blindness, too? Hear no evil; see no evil; speak no evil.) Instead, we asked about gender socialization: "Do you think your parents were pretty traditional in their gender beliefs? If you had been a boy, would it have been different?"

"Absolutely," she said. "I look back, my brother was in Little League, and I wasn't. I used to like to watch baseball on TV. I was the one who actually liked to watch sports but was too timid to try them. My brother mowed the lawn, and I dusted and ironed. . . . I was so well educated in how to be a girl in our society. I have all the body image things, all the role-playing things. I really absorbed all of the things I was supposed to absorb, that it made it almost impossible to leave; it was a commitment for life, almost like 'you made your bed.' I took that role very seriously. I made my bed. How can I make this work? I tried and tried and tried. It took me a long time to realize it really was not working, and that was really a hard pill to swallow: that I had failed in marriage. I felt ashamed that I was disappointing my parents, and it would go out through the family network, what people think of me, too. I think I just grew up trying so hard to be the good girl, the person I was supposed to be, trying not to displease my parents. . . . So I was trying to be the good wife. I tried for years. I was so delusional about how bad my marriage was."

Sam had learned to be a "good girl" in her childhood. She was taught to be submissive and to serve others. Sam was taught to put others' needs, particularly men's needs, before her own. This kind of extensive gender socialization can put girls at risk for turning into exploited women should a dangerous man come into the picture; Sam had been taught no skills in conceptualizing or asserting her own rights. "It took me until the very end of our marriage to realize—I had this epiphany and I realized—wait a minute, here I am worried that he had this horrible life. And I stopped to compare the two, and I thought, 'Wait a minute, my life is worse than his is.

He drinks. He beats me, and I'm fearful of him, and I cannot go to the jobs I want.' Even going to college, he said he was proud of me, but then he'd undermine it, like: 'Are you going to be in class all day? What am I going to do? I have to work all week, and if I have to baby-sit . . .' He saw watching his own child as, 'I have to do your job.' So he would do certain things to undermine my going to school, even if verbally he was saying, 'I'm proud of you.'"

Liberation

Sam eventually escaped Mark, taking Rosalie with her. "It's really amazing when I look back. . . . I'm a grad student now, and I'm actually teaching. If somebody would have told me, even five years ago, that I would be teaching college as a grad student, traveling around the world by myself—I mean, I didn't even get my driver's license until I was twenty-five because that scared me, so traveling alone to different countries—India!—I would have just called them a liar. There was just no way on earth. Things that maybe seem like nothing to the average person . . . just to have made the psychological progress to even imagine myself in those places is astounding to me. If people knew that I was even fearful to leave the house, because even if nothing was happening, I just knew that he was thinking that something was happening, and that was all that mattered. So I let every decision I made be based on how he would think about it— even now, to some degree. I know if he is going to call at a certain time, I don't want to not be there because I'm going to have to deal with the consequences. He might be angry. . . . He still has a degree of control."

Sam is on a promising new path, and her future is bright, but she knows she still has work to do. As she discloses her past to other trustworthy people and as she continues to achieve on her own, we believe she will become liberated from Mark. Basking in her energy, we believe the day will come when Mark no longer has any control over Sam.

8

Insights from Research

Samantha Spencer's experiences of pushing information about mistreatment out of her awareness are far from unusual. True, in Sam's case there was a lot of mistreatment to hide away and transform in her mind into something she could accept. Fortunately, not all people are exposed to so much personal mistreatment. Conversely, although Sam's experiences were severe, many others have had equally severe—or even worse—mistreatment. Some of those people have also managed not to know fully about the wrongs they experienced. Other people have committed wrongs or have observed wrongs that they have pushed out of consciousness. Indeed, all of us are confronted with reminders of mistreatment toward ourselves or toward others, reminders that we have a tendency to whisk out of consciousness. Sam was herself the victim of at least two kinds of betrayal by Mark: infidelity and abuse. One largely happened when she wasn't there to observe it directly; the other happened to her directly. She managed to push both types of betrayal out of her full awareness. The infidelity seemed well hidden in her own mind, the abuse well transformed into something forgivable. How can this occur?

In the previous chapter we explore *why* people become blind to betrayal. In this chapter, we focus on *how* blindness occurs. We examine several internal and external psychological processes that make betrayal blindness possible. There is nothing stupid or irrational in how we become blind to betrayal. This process arises from normal mechanisms that serve us well most of the time.

Meta-Cognitions

When people are blind to a betrayal, hiding away the information from their own awareness, do they have any mental experience at the time that might later indicate that something peculiar was going on? A conscious awareness of one's own mental process is called *meta-cognition*—a cognition (or a thought) about another cognition (or thought). Learning more about such a mental experience at the time that it occurs may eventually help us unravel the mysteries of the *how* question. Numerous individuals have told us stories of betrayal blindness, and we have asked them about their experiences at the time of being confronted with evidence of betrayal. Some can remember briefly feeling that something was "odd" or "weird" but then not allowing themselves to dwell on the oddness.

Another woman we interviewed told us about not knowing her husband was having an affair. In her case, the truth came out when her husband left her for the other woman. The woman told us that she was sure she hadn't known about the affair. She felt she hadn't even had an intuition about the affair, but then she said, "My soul knew." She explained, "One night, a week before he left, I went upstairs to this apartment that I have, and I slept up there. . . . I remember thinking, 'That's weird,' yet it was also sort of like my soul wanted to get away from him." Maybe her soul wanted to get away from him, but the rest of her apparently did not. She didn't see the affair until her husband left her and told her about it.

A man we interviewed told us a similar story of discovering his wife had been having an affair for at least a year. He said he was shocked and devastated by the discovery. When we asked him whether he might have overlooked evidence of the affair, he told us about accepting his wife's almost total "avoidance" of him "in the night." He also accepted his wife's claim that it took her three or four hours every day to clean her office after the five o'clock closing. Although this man did not consciously admit to himself that these behaviors were suspicious, he does remember feeling an occasional "worry" that something was "in the air." The need to trust is a powerful agent, a blinding force.

Attention and Memory

Basic cognitive processes involved in attention and memory most likely play an important role in people being able to dissociate their explicit awareness of betrayal traumas. In several studies, we have found evidence for the relationship between dissociation and what we call *knowledge isolation*.[1] Knowledge isolation includes acts such as forgetting and not being aware—the very abilities one needs for betrayal blindness.

In order to study knowledge isolation in the laboratory, Jennifer Freyd and her students have often used a psychological test called the Dissociative Experiences Scale (DES).[2] This test assesses how often people have gaps in awareness, which can range from being lost in the moment (such as missing important landmarks on a familiar drive) to a complete forgetting of events to not feeling real or connected to one's surroundings. In a clinical setting, people with high DES scores are considered candidates for additional testing for dissociative disorders, such as multiple personalities. In a research setting, people with high DES are often classified as "high dissociators." We and other researchers have found a relationship between DES scores and trauma exposure: the more exposure to trauma, particularly betrayal trauma, the higher the DES score is likely to be.[3] We understand this in terms of betrayal trauma theory—that dissociation serves to support betrayal blindness, so people who have had considerable exposure to betrayal trauma develop stronger abilities to dissociate.

In a line of research in our laboratory, we have asked individuals with high DES scores ("high dissociators") to complete various tasks using basic cognitive mechanisms that are involved in memory and attention. We compared their performance to people with low DES scores ("low dissociators") to see what we could learn about the cognitive mechanisms underlying betrayal blindness.

Using this approach and a laboratory task called the "Stroop task," Jennifer Freyd and her colleagues discovered a fascinating result.[4] The Stroop task is very simple and very powerful. Participants see a word printed in a particular color, such as the word *potato* in blue ink. The participant's task is to say out loud the name of the ink the word is written in. In the case of *potato* written in blue ink, the correct answer is "blue." This condition, sometimes called the neutral condition, can be a bit difficult because it requires suppressing the desire to read the word and say, "Potato." The most difficult version of the Stroop task involves incongruous color terms. In this case, the word *red* is printed in a different color, such as blue. The participant's task is to say, "Blue," because that is the ink color, but it is very difficult to suppress the desire to say, "Red," when that is the word. You might want to try this with someone you know. First, write some neutral words, such as *bridge*, in different-colored inks. Then write some color terms in conflicting colored inks, such as the word *green* using blue ink and so on. Ask your friend to name the ink colors out loud, and compare the time it takes him or her to name the color of the neutral words to the time to name conflicting color words. You'll find that it takes people much longer to read the conflicting color list.

There is a black-and-white version of the Stroop task that you can also try. In this case, your task is to say out loud how many characters are on each line. For instance, if you see "C C C C," The answer is "4" because there are 4 C's. Try it for yourself:

D D D D

X X X

F F

H H H H H

Your answers should have been: 4, 3, 2, 5.
Now again try to say the number of digits on each row:

3 3

6 6 6 6

4 4 4

2 2 2 2 2

Your answers should have been: 2, 4, 3, 5.

Most people find this last task with the incongruent digits difficult, and they find the incongruent color version of the Stroop task *very* difficult. That incongruent color task is called the "conflicting color" type of trial. It is difficult because it is hard to overcome the automatic reading of the words and the activation of the meaning of those words, just as it is difficult not to read a sign on the back of a cereal box or on a highway billboard.

Using this basic Stroop task, Freyd and her colleagues found that participants who scored high on the Dissociative Experiences Scale showed greater Stroop interference than did individuals with low DES scores.[5] This suggests that the high dissociators had more difficulty with this *selective attention* task than low dissociators did. Selective attention is the ability to focus on just one thing and ignore everything else. In this case, the one thing to focus on is the ink color. The fact that high dissociators show more interference from the word's meaning suggests they may have difficulty with selective attention, perhaps because their skills in attention were damaged by years of having to keep betrayal information out of awareness. Although perhaps they are in this way damaged, high dissociators might also have developed special skills in order to keep information out of awareness.

In a follow-up study, Anne DePrince and Jennifer Freyd explored whether high dissociators might perform better than low dissociators under the right conditions. They used both a selective attention condition, as in the first study, and a divided attention condition. The selective attention condition was just as before—participants were instructed to say only the ink color and were given no other task. Yet the divided attention condition was different—in this case, participants were instructed to say the ink color *and* remember the word itself for a later memory task.[6]

The results were fascinating. As before, high dissociators had more difficulty with the selective attention task, indicating their inability to focus their attention at will. However, high dissociators had less difficulty in the divided attention task when compared to low dissociators. This suggests that dissociation interferes with selective attention but not with divided attention. In fact, it seems that perhaps dissociation improves the ability to divide attention. We believe that dissociation and therefore betrayal blindness involve some ability to divide attention across multiple aspects of the environment as a way to control the flow of information that is coming into conscious awareness and memory.

To see how this could work, first imagine a young boy who gets molested by his father at night in secret. During the daytime, his father, the primary breadwinner in his family, meets the boy's needs fairly well. For instance, his father provides food, clothing, and even positive attention. This is a classic betrayal trauma situation, because if the child withdraws from his father, he risks losing the good things he gets. So the boy has a very good reason to develop betrayal blindness. This means that during the day, he must interact with his family as if everything is okay, which means he must basically believe it is okay, too. In other words, this young boy has every reason to maintain betrayal blindness. Thinking now about the research on divided attention we just discussed, we can see how this might help the boy. When his father walks into the room while the boy is eating his breakfast, if a little thought starts to form in the boy's mind about the molestation, if he can instead focus his attention on something else in the room, such as his mother's activity at the stove, he can better keep the threatening information out of his awareness. That is divided attention.

In our laboratory research, we also tested people's memory for the words they saw. We included some words that were highly emotionally charged for survivors of betrayal trauma—words such as *rape* and *incest*. We found that the dissociative participants recalled more neutral and fewer trauma-related words than did less dissociative participants.[7] Consistent with betrayal trauma theory, this supports the argument that dissociation may help keep threatening information from awareness. Continuing the example of the boy in the previous paragraph, this memory ability would mean he could remember the color of his mother's clothes (neutral) and forget the look on his father's face (charged).

In two follow-up studies, Anne DePrince and Jennifer Freyd used a *directed forgetting paradigm* (a laboratory task in which participants are presented with items and told after each item or list of items whether to remember or forget the material).[8] Both high and low dissociators remembered words they were told to remember better than words they were told to forget, but what about their memory for different types of words? In both studies, highly dissociative participants recalled fewer charged and more neutral words, compared with less dissociative participants, who showed the opposite pattern for words they were instructed to remember when divided attention was required. As before, this evidence suggests that divided attention helps with betrayal blindness—a way for people exposed to a lot of betrayal trauma to keep that information out of awareness. Also, consistent with this interpretation, we found that the high dissociators in our studies reported significantly more exposure to trauma in general and betrayal trauma in particular.

Kathy Becker-Blease and Jennifer Freyd found a similar interaction with preschool children, using pictures instead of words.[9] In this study, children were asked to look at pictures that were either neutral or charged. After they looked at the pictures, their memory was tested by showing the children a new set of pictures that included some they had already seen and some they had not. The children were told to tell the research assistant in each case if they had seen the picture before. All of the pictures came from story books for children, but some were of mundane scenes, such as a picnic, while others were more threatening, such as a father lurking in a doorway next to a sleeping child.

A divided-attention context was created by telling the children to look at the pictures while also listening to animal names being played in the background. Every time they heard the word *sheep*, they were supposed to squeeze a sheep toy that made a "baaa" sound. In selective-attention conditions, children simply looked at the pictures without hearing animal names. The results with children were similar to those with adults. Under divided-attention conditions, children who had trauma histories and who were highly dissociative remembered fewer emotionally charged pictures and more neutral pictures when compared to nontraumatized children. However, there were no differences between children's memory under selective-attention conditions. As with traumatized adults, the traumatized children seemed able to divide their attention in ways that let them *not* remember information that might cause them to be aware of betrayal.

In summary, these studies suggest that keeping information about betrayal traumas out of awareness and memory may lead to high levels of dissociation. Related to this, people who are high dissociators (and therefore may have experienced abuse and had practice in "not knowing") are more likely to keep emotional information out of their awareness and memory. This dissociation seems to require dividing one's attention. A very interesting possibility is that dissociative individuals may even seek or create environments that require divided attention, such as a hectic workplace. Children who are dissociative may seem to create chaos around them, not because they are disorganized but because they cannot let themselves know. Both children and adults who have been exposed to betrayal trauma may find it easier to manage in environments with a lot of distraction. To low dissociators, this might look like a preference for chaos. It might even appear as if high dissociators are trying to create chaos. Yet in fact they may do this simply because it helps them keep out of their awareness any betrayal information that is too dangerous to know.

Dissociation

As we have discussed, we can know and not know at the same time. This ability to know and not know may depend on the compartmentalization of knowledge that is possible due to the design of the human brain. Consider the case of "Marnie," a thirty-three-year-old woman who has been diagnosed with dissociative identity disorder (previously called "multiple personality disorder"). Marnie is most often depressed. She has been treated in the mental health system for many years. Marnie has participated in research involving brain imaging—scientists have watched Marnie's brain in action using a technique called functional magnetic resonance imaging (fMRI). One of Marnie's alter personalities is "Mimi"—a bright and energetic woman, quite unlike the usually sullen Marnie. Mimi tells about Marnie's past, when she experienced beatings and sexual and psychological torment at the hands of her alcoholic and criminally violent mother.

Marnie, Mimi, and several other personalities agreed to team up with their psychiatrist, Don Condie, and neurobiologist Gouchual Tsai.[10] Using fMRI, Tsai and Condi were able to peer into Marnie's brain as she was switching from different personality states. They found out that a crucially important part of Marnie's brain, the hippocampus, was dramatically smaller than would be expected for her brain size. Shrunken hippocampi have been found in other trauma survivors as well, and we know that the hippocampus plays an essential role in forming memories. When Marnie was switching between different personalities, a child personality named "Guardian" took over, and activity throughout the hippocampus and the surrounding (temporal) cortex ebbed. When Marnie later reemerged, the right side of the hippocampus lit up with renewed activity. The researchers compared all of this to a task in which Marnie was just pretending to switch personalities; in this instance, the brain activity was very different. These sorts of results are preliminary—but very suggestive—of the underlying brain activity involved in the most extreme cases of betrayal blindness. We explore more about dissociative identity disorder in chapter 9, when Cathy has a chance to tell her story.

Knowing and Not Knowing about Feelings

Researchers in personality and clinical psychology have investigated the ways that individuals differ in terms of their disconnection from themselves and others. For instance, some people show high levels of alexithymia. *Alexithymia* refers to the inability to know or state one's own emotional feelings and experiences—probably a very useful condition for maintaining betrayal blindness. You may notice that alexithymia and dissociation are related ideas. Dissociation is the more cognitive disconnection that can occur between one's perceptions, memories, and awareness. People who have a lot of dissociative experiences are considered to be high in dissociative tendencies. Exposure to betrayal trauma is associated with having higher dissociative tendencies.[11] We also know from research, including research conducted in our laboratory with Rachel Goldsmith, that the amount of alexithymia is related to the person's exposure to childhood abuse.[12] It appears as if both the dissociation of perceptions and memories and the dissociation of feelings are ways to remain blind to betrayal.

Perpetrator Grooming and Demands for Silence

In addition to internal processes involved in not knowing about betrayal, the victim may experience social pressures not to know and to be silent. For example, the perpetrator and others (such as family and church) may demand silence. Demands for silence may lead to a complete failure to even discuss an experience. Social pressure interacts with psychological mechanisms so that experiences that have never been shared with anyone else may have a different structure in the mind than shared experiences do. We talk more about this in a later chapter.

Betrayers often help those they betray to remain unaware of the betrayal. For instance, rather than making explicit demands for silence, perpetrators often groom their victims for unawareness and denial. Some perpetrators may do this without even realizing it. Such perpetrators may even remain partly blind themselves, and this blindness may help account for the lack of awareness of others around them. Many betrayers seem to be engaging in a repetition of acts of betrayal that occurred to them. As one therapist who treats young sex offenders said to us, "They are so afraid of betrayal, they betray again." A perpetrator who is himself blind may induce a kind of blindness in the victim and the bystanders.

Other child molesters seem to be more aware of betrayal blindness in their victims and to take advantage of it. It is as if they know how it works, and they then make it work to their advantage. Consider the case of Michael Mattingly. Mattingly was charged with sexually assaulting a nine-year-old boy.[13] He told police that he had befriended the boy's mother years before the abuse began, in order to gain unrestricted access to her son. Mattingly also told police that in other cases, he gained the trust of his victims and their families by offering to baby-sit, take the children to movies, or have them stay at his home for sleepovers. By the time Mattingly actually abused the children, the families had come to depend on his friendship and help with child care. The trust and the dependence were there, making it easy for Mattingly to abuse the children, while he remained protected by the betrayal blindness he helped create.

Groupthink and Government Cover-Up

Betrayal blindness is also helped along by various group processes, including what has been called "groupthink." There are many times when self-censorship can preserve the harmony of the group in the short run, although it may lead to disasters later on. Irving Janis offered the Bay of Pigs invasion as a classic example of groupthink.[14] Although the invasion was planned during the Eisenhower presidency, it was the Kennedy administration that accepted and authorized the plan. Initially, some members of Kennedy's advising team raised important objections to the plan, but group pressure ultimately resulted in self-silencing. The advisers began to believe the impossible, and the result was a fiasco.

Governments can also effectively cover up betrayals. The cover-up of the Tiananmen Square protests of 1989 is an example of blindness to institutional betrayal, in which the government directly contributed to the forgetting. The Tiananmen Square massacre occurred in Beijing on June 4, 1989, when nonviolent protestors were killed by police forces. The protesters, mostly students and intellectuals, began congregating in April to mourn the death of an official who had supported political liberalization. Students at the mourning then demonstrated in support of continued economic reform and liberalization. By May, this was a powerful nonviolent movement in China. The government responded by declaring martial law. On June 4, the government moved into the streets and used gunfire to clear the area. Although it is not known exactly how many civilians died, most estimates are from hundreds to thousands. After the killing, the government arrested many surviving protestors and banned the press from covering the events.

The Communist Party of China (CPC) forbids discussion of the Tiananmen Square protests. Among the actions the CPC has taken to block or censor information are limiting media and Internet resources and requiring textbooks to omit the topic.[15] One cannot even search for "4 June" on search engines such as Google within China without meeting a news blackout. Those who do dare to speak about Tiananmen Square have been arrested. As a consequence of all of this explicit censorship, public memory has been effectively blinded.

Need to Trust

Closely related to betrayal is the concept of trust. Remember that we cannot be betrayed by someone we do not trust.

The headline reads, "Trusted Doctor Found to Be Killer," and below that, "Citizens feel betrayed to discover that the respected Dr. Harold Shipman had a dark side."[16] Shipman was a doctor in Hyde, England, a working-class mill town of thirty-five thousand, who was found guilty of killing fifteen female patients with injections of heroin. Like the notorious American physician Dr. Michael Swango, dubbed "Doctor Death," who was charged with poisoning three of his own patients, Shipman is suspected of poisoning far more of his patients than can be proved in court.[17] Both Shipman and Swango apparently got away with murder—over and over and over. In retrospect, former patients and coworkers point to overwhelming evidence in both cases that the string of patient deaths surrounding these doctors was completely outside of the normal range. How could this evidence have been ignored so consistently and for so long?

The concept of trust—and the need to trust—comes up again and again in both of these cases. Patients, the community, and coworkers all felt a powerful need to trust Drs. Shipman and Swango, and they repeatedly turned a blind eye to the evidence of unnatural deaths. We trust physicians with our lives. Without that trust, we would have a challenge accepting their care and advice. As we said earlier, this need to trust is a powerful blinding agent.

Whenever a person or a group is dependent on others who have more power, it may be advantageous to remain unaware of mistreatment from the power holder(s) to preserve the status quo. Knowing about mistreatment naturally leads to withdrawal or rebellion, which may alienate the more powerful person(s). Such betrayal blindness is almost always a survival strategy. As one mother said in response to her daughter's claim that she had been raped and impregnated by her mother's boyfriend, "I would have a hard time believing that somebody in my home, whom I loved and trusted, would hurt any of my children." By refusing to believe her daughter, this mother was able to preserve her trust in, and thus her relationship with, her live-in boyfriend. People often have a powerful motivation to remain ignorant of mistreatment and betrayal.

Betrayal blindness at its inception is based on an extreme need to keep some aspect of a situation intact, whether maintaining a marriage, keeping a family together, or holding onto one's position in a community. If the marriage, the family, or the community appears necessary for survival, remaining blind to the betrayal is a survival strategy. As we have seen, both internal and social processes operate to keep us unaware. This unawareness is a survival strategy, but it can also prove toxic to the mind, the body, relationships, and society.

9

Betrayal Blindness Is Toxic

We have spoken about the damaging effects of betrayal on many different levels. In this chapter, we examine the effects of betrayal in a more systematic fashion, looking at clinical and research data on the way betrayal affects all of us on three different levels, how those levels interact, and how this results in a toxicity that can permeate a society.

First of all, betrayal affects us individually. Those who have been betrayed develop a number of different psychological and physical conditions. Our research has confirmed that exposure to traumas that are high in betrayal (for example, assault by a person who is close to us) is linked to symptoms of depression, anxiety, dissociation, post-traumatic stress disorder, borderline personality characteristics (which is a syndrome that includes difficulties in relationships), and physical health problems.[1]

The next level where we are affected is the level of relationships. Betrayal, especially in early life, can make it difficult for us to trust and form new, enduring, and enriching relationships. Relational health is as important as physical health in determining the health of a society, and relational health is a predictor of individual mental health, illustrating the continuing and ongoing interaction of these levels.[2]

The third level on which betrayal affects us is the societal level. Betrayal undermines our basic ability to trust one another and our institutions, and lacking trust can feed back on our ability to hold together as a society.

Now let's follow the thread of betrayal from individual to relational to institutional effects.

The Toxic Effects of Betrayal on Individuals

Cathy Turner is a vivacious woman in her mid-forties. She is eager to tell us her story, which began with severe childhood abuse. Cathy and her siblings were brought up in extreme poverty in a small town in Idaho. Cathy has lost track of all of her siblings and the rest of her family. Now Cathy is a student at a community college, where she is studying nursing. Short and blond, she bursts with energy, although that has not always been true. For many years after leaving home, she struggled not only with dissociation, but also with depression and panic attacks.

Cathy's interview took place in a cozy and comfortable office. Outside, lilacs bloomed on a sunny spring day. Cathy showed no indication that she even noticed her surroundings, so eager was she to help others by having her story told. We asked her to talk about what had happened in her life.

"When I think of the word *betrayal*," she said, "I think of a lie, a pretense, whether it comes from family or society or whatever, of an expected norm, and when that gets skewered and manipulated and twisted. And, you know, for me . . . I was abused in many ways by many people in my family. The biggest betrayal for me was the normalization, that there's this incredible lie going on, that parents are supposed to love you and keep you safe, and in my experience those were the most dangerous people I've ever experienced in my life. Throughout my entire life, I have ridden with motorcycle gangs, I have lived with ex-cons, I have done incredibly stupid things because of that, but the dangerous people were the ones who were supposed to love me and were supposed to keep me safe. And, you know, that manifested in horrific physical abuse, psychological abuse, sexual abuse, spiritual abuse."

The lie for Cathy was that her father told her he loved her and then sexually abused her; he told her that she was smart and then punished her for using her brains. "And so, okay, I'm allowed to use my brain, I'm allowed to use my intuition, and then you're going to put me in a box for seven days, and try to break me. That's an extreme situation. . . . But at the same time you're nurturing me and teaching me that I can be this and then taking away any chance to do that. And not having the safe place to learn to develop those things. And learn to be myself and what that meant."

Cathy will come back to the theme of safety and her lifelong search for it—how she never had the chance to grow in many ways because she had no safe and secure base to grow from. Instead, the verbal messages she got were that she was loved and supported, at the same time that she was given other messages that she was disposable. She became very confused and disoriented. "And when you take that away from a child—and children are incredibly, beautifully malleable. I mean, they have these very strong little spirits, you know; they're just these beautiful creatures. And you can nurture them and you can guide them, but . . . they're going to grow in their direction, they're going to grow toward the sun. So this message of 'You're this beautiful, strong spirit and you can do all of these great things, and you're not like your sisters, and you're not like your mother,' and at the same time trying to destroy that . . .

"That was the lie. And . . . the betrayal of the conflict—to me, that was the betrayal. . . . 'Which way is it?' Beautiful or so worthless that you can be betrayed over and over again?

We asked, "So, it left you very confused?"

"Horrifically confused," she said. "And children automatically seek love and approval—everybody does, but especially when we're children—so you're trying to seek some approval and some support and trying to do what's right by the parents, by the role models, or whoever it is in your life, and yet they're eroding it at the same time. And going through life and having studied psychology and trying to go that route, you know, understanding 'Oh, my father was profoundly mentally ill.' He had some profound psychoses, he had profound abuse; so I can analyze and examine it and set it aside, but . . . I can't deal with the betrayal of that four-year-old little girl, you know . . . Because I was also taught to deep throat at two years old and was praised for that, you know. That's messed up. There's no consistency, and it's always conflicting; and I think that's why, you know, I ended up with the 'mental illness' that I ended up with. Because it was always conflicted. Always contradictory."

Betrayal and Dissociation

Like Marnie in chapter 8, Cathy was also diagnosed with dissociative identity "disorder." Yet Cathy looked very much different from Marnie. While Marnie had a few very distinct identities, Cathy's identities were much less distinct and more confused, most probably reflecting the confusion and chaos of her early years. Remember that diagnostic categories are just that—categories—and that people never fit neatly into the boxes the mental health system provides. That is why it is important to listen to the whole of people's stories. As you know, we become blind to betrayal in order to maintain important and necessary relationships. If a little girl (such as Cathy) is sexually abused at night, and during the day her family behaves as though nothing happened, the little girl must put that knowledge aside in order to stay in her family, especially if there is no safe person she can turn to, as was the case with Cathy. Yet the memories and the emotions that go with that knowledge come out in other ways. One part of the personality holds the memories of the betrayal, while other parts can go on. It is basically a life- and psyche-saving strategy.

Understanding the mechanisms of dissociation and the causes of this "mental disorder" in this way makes us begin to question whether it is a mental disorder or whether it is a normal and creative response to what *really is* the disorder: the betrayal of intimate and what should be loving bonds.

Cathy has accepted her dissociation and still lives with it. She reported that she still has problems with losing time (that is, not being aware of her surroundings for periods of time—a way of "checking out"), but it does not happen in the uncontrolled and scattered way that it used to. She now claims the defense that helped her survive her abusive childhood as part of who she is: "But I quit fighting me, and this is who I am. And I'm finally okay with that, you know, and to speak my truth."

This hadn't been true thirty years ago when Cathy was pregnant with her first child (which did not survive full-term). That was a time of extreme confusion for her, when she learned the strategy of dissociation well: "I was taken from my father's home because I was pregnant at ten and a half years old and put into my sister's home, where her husband continued to abuse me. And that taught me, 'Okay, this is going to happen. This is part of life. . . . This is my life; this is the way people are. This is just the way it's going to be. This is the way

the world is. And so [I had] to learn to change it, own it, and rock it.'
. . . And then, thank God, there was truly divine intervention, and
I got pregnant with my first baby who survived full term and who
arrived nine months later. So I had to make a choice to try and be a
good person, but there were still these coping skills, there was still
this tool of . . . shatter or disappear—well, I didn't have that option
anymore because I had this beautiful, beautiful, perfect baby in front
of me. I couldn't join them; I couldn't be one of the abusers anymore,
I couldn't manipulate anymore. I had to be a good person. I had to
teach my son something different. So I tried to leave the manipulation and the gang behind, tried to walk a good path. So if you're not
going to be part of them, then you've got to seek something else out.
And there was this constant seeking, of trying to find some safety. . . .
That's why you go multiple or you dissociate or you check the fuck
out or you do drugs, or whatever it is you do, because you don't have
the surroundings to support that hope. So you scatter, at least in my
opinion or in my experience. You know, adapt to whatever it could be."

With a great deal of emotion, Cathy described the advantages
of becoming dissociative. It was the only option for her in circumstances that could have destroyed her. She learned to check out
from the extreme pain and confusion when her surroundings didn't
support her. It was the only way she could find safety at the time.
Later, we'll see how Cathy found safety in other ways and was able
to bring those dissociative parts of her personality back together.

Dissociation is the disruption of normally connected aspects of
our conscious experience. In the extreme, dissociation can make life
difficult for people. Cathy learned to adapt to her circumstances by
dissociating and creating other "parts." In therapy, those parts were
finally able to express themselves, and they gradually became more
continuous parts of her, although she still uses that coping method
in some ways to the present time.

Our research supports the idea that exposure to betrayal is associated with more dissociation than is abuse that does not involve
betrayal.[3] Betrayal trauma theory explains dissociation as a way that
people can keep away information that poses a threat to the individual's system of attachment. Cathy, as a young child, saw her options
as "shattering or disappearing" in response to the betrayal. She did
this in order to maintain the family and the emotional bonds that,
difficult as they were, were all she had.

Researchers James Chu and Diana Dill compared people who had been abused by family members and those abused by non–family members.[4] They found a pattern of results that can be easily explained by betrayal trauma theory. As discussed, the Dissociative Experiences Scale is a test that measures the degree to which people dissociate. Chu and Dill found that childhood abuse by family members (both physical and sexual) was significantly related to increased DES scores in psychiatric inpatients, and abuse by non-family members was not. What this means is that there is more dissociation—knowledge isolation—when the betrayal is by people we are close to. Other researchers have found that the kind of dissociation that Cathy experienced is more common when the abuse is perpetrated by someone in the family rather than by someone outside the family.[5] This has been found whether the people being studied are juvenile delinquents or students.

Betrayal and Forgetting

Our response to betrayal needn't be as extreme as dissociation. It can be as simple as forgetting. Jack Lavino wrote about his experiences with betrayal and forgetting: "I was sexually abused as a child by a Catholic priest and other adults in a position of trust. My first memories of these experiences began when I was age forty-four. My initial reaction to these memories was denial. I did not want them to be true.

"Three years passed before the memories overwhelmed me. I sought psychotherapy. The rage toward my abusers slowly bubbled to the surface."[6]

Betrayal trauma theory predicts that unawareness and forgetting of abuse will be higher when the relationship between perpetrator and victim involves closeness, trust, and/or caregiving. It is in these cases that the potential for a conflict between the need to stay in the relationship and the awareness of betrayal is greatest and is thus where we should see the greatest amount of forgetting or memory impairment. In her first book, *Betrayal Trauma: The Logic of Forgetting Child Abuse*, Jennifer Freyd reported finding from reanalyses of a number of relevant data sets that incestuous abuse was more likely to be forgotten than nonincestuous abuse was.[7]

Using new data collected from undergraduate students, Jennifer Freyd, Anne DePrince, and Eileen Zurbriggen found that physical and sexual abuse perpetrated by a caregiver was related to higher levels of self-reported memory impairment for the events, compared to noncaregiver abuse.[8]

Other research has found that people who reported memory disturbances and forgetting in general also reported higher numbers of perpetrators and closer relationships with those who abused them than did participants who reported no memory disturbances.[9] In yet another study, participants who reported memory loss in regard to child sexual abuse were more likely to later experience abuse by people who were well-known to them, compared to those who did not have memory loss.[10] One large study even found that general autobiographical memory loss (that is, memory about one's childhood and adolescence) was strongly associated with a history of childhood abuse, and that one of the specific factors associated with this increased memory loss was sexual abuse by a relative.[11]

Betrayal and General Mental Health

Cathy, similar to many of the individuals we have interviewed, suffered betrayals early in life. It is easy to see the effects. These people's stories are important to help us begin to understand how toxic betrayal trauma can be. Our empirical research has also confirmed that exposure to traumas that are high in betrayal (such as assault by someone close to us) is linked to poorer mental health outcomes, such as symptoms of depression, anxiety, dissociation, PTSD, borderline personality characteristics (which is a syndrome that includes difficulties in relationships), and physical health problems.

For example, in a study conducted with Bridget Klest and Carolyn Allard, we found that for adults who had either chronic pain, chronic health problems, or both, exposure to betrayal trauma was strongly associated with anxiety, depression, dissociation, and physical illness symptoms.[12]

In our research, we do our best to measure constructs such as betrayal trauma and depression accurately and with precision. Yet no psychological measurement or study is perfect, so it is important to attempt to replicate the results with different groups of people. Rachel Goldsmith, Anne DePrince, and Jennifer Freyd conducted a similar study with healthy college students and found parallel results.[13] In addition, using a very different set of measurement tools and a large sample of adults, Valerie Edwards and her colleagues at the Centers for Disease Control (CDC) found compatible results.[14]

Other researchers have found similar effects. Anne DePrince discovered that trauma survivors who reported traumatic events that were high in betrayal were particularly distressed.[15] Similarly, Atlas and Ingram investigated the association of histories of physical and sexual abuse with symptoms of post-traumatic stress. Thirty-four hospitalized adolescents (ages 14 to 17.10 years) with histories of abuse were given the Trauma Symptom Checklist for Children.[16] Sexual distress was associated with a history of abuse by family members, as compared to no abuse or abuse by other people, while post-traumatic stress was not. Turell and Armsworth compared sexual abuse survivors who self-mutilate with those who do not.[17] They reported that self-mutilators were more likely to have been abused in their family of origin.

Betrayal adds a dimension to trauma and abuse that is toxic and from which it is difficult to recover. In a recent study of intimate partner violence led by Mayumi Okuda, MD, victims were found to have twice as high a rate of new psychiatric disorders compared to nonvictims.[18] This particular study was part of the National Epidemiologic Survey on Alcohol and Related Conditions. More than 25,000 adults participated, and about 1,600 of them reported being victims of intimate partner violence. Those who were victims had an increased risk of suffering from post-traumatic stress disorder, major depression, substance use, and bipolar, panic, and generalized anxiety disorder.

Many other researchers have found the same thing. Using different measures, different populations, and different research methods, researchers have found over and over again that *exposure to betrayal trauma is bad for the mind and the body*. We say "on average" because these relationships are not deterministic, but rather probabilistic. Betrayal trauma is bad for the mind and the body in the sense that tobacco smoke is bad for the lungs—the toxic elements substantially increase the risk of damage and disease, but there are always some people who beat the odds.

Betrayal Trauma, Gender, and Mental Health

The fact that betrayal trauma is so toxic may help us solve a persistent mystery in mental health. Women are diagnosed with a host of mental health problems, including depression, anxiety, and post-traumatic stress disorder (PTSD), more often than men are.[19] Why? This mystery has inspired countless theories but has remained unsolved. Could these gender differences be related to betrayal trauma? In chapter 5, we explain that girls and women are, on average, exposed to more betrayal trauma than are boys and men. Perhaps some of the increased rates of psychological symptoms seen in women are related to their higher exposure to betrayal trauma. Shin Shin Tang and Jennifer Freyd tested this possibility, using both a large college sample and a community sample.[20] They confirmed prior research that traumas that are high in betrayal are more strongly associated with symptoms of post-traumatic stress than are traumas that are lower in betrayal. Using a statistical technique called "structural equation modeling," they found that betrayal trauma explained part of the association between gender and PTSD symptoms. This preliminary research offers some evidence that gender differences in mental health symptoms may be at least partly due to differences in exposure to betrayal trauma.

Oxytocin Dysregulation: A Possible Mechanism to Explain the Effects of Betrayal

Betrayal traumas are events that involve the serious mistreatment of individuals by trusted others, such as rape by a person close to the victim or child abuse by a caregiver. In addition, betrayal traumas are associated with a number of serious negative outcomes, and that association is above and beyond that linked to other traumas (such as accidents or interpersonal events involving strangers). These negative outcomes include a host of behavioral and health symptoms, such as revictimization, troubled interpersonal relationships, problematic trust decisions, and even increased symptoms of physical illness.[21]

How could betrayal hurt the body? One intriguing possibility is that betrayal can damage the endocrine system—the system that regulates hormones. In particular, we suspect that oxytocin dysregulation is a biological mechanism that links exposure to betrayal trauma (interpersonal violence and abuse at the hands of someone close to the victim) with disease outcome. Although no prior research has looked at these variables together, certain preliminary results and theories from separate studies suggest that possible associations exist between each of the pairs of variables. As already mentioned, there are data indicating that betrayal traumas have negative health consequences above and beyond other forms of trauma exposure. In separate lines of research, substantial evidence indicates that plasma oxytocin is associated with various aspects of human behavior, particularly in the domains of trust, attachment, and interpersonal relationships.[22] This strongly suggests that betrayal trauma exposure has implications for oxytocin regulation.

In yet a third line of research, there is an indication that oxytocin dysregulation is associated with various negative physical health outcomes, such as irritable bowel syndrome, chronic pelvic pain, interstitial cystitis, and hyperemesis gravidarum.[23] Betrayal trauma theory provides a basis for assuming that interpersonal trauma would affect psychological systems associated with oxytocin (attachment and trust) and that the oxytocin system would therefore be vulnerable to dysregulation in cases of chronic betrayal trauma. If so, oxytocin dysregulation may serve as a biological mechanism that connects betrayal trauma exposure to disease outcome. Oxytocin dysregulation, while inside the individual human body, is strongly associated with trust and attachment, both of which are necessary for successful human relationships.

The Toxic Effects of Betrayal on Relationships

Rebecca Brewerman (the woman in her early sixties whom we first met in chapter 2) also remembers the toxic effects of betrayal. It had a different effect on her than it did on Cathy. Rebecca did not have to resort to the extreme dissociation that Cathy did but nonetheless reported confusion and difficulty in functioning. Rebecca was quick to blame herself and was slow to form trusting relationships: "I was a very anxious, needy child, constantly trying to show that I was smart and charming so that maybe someone would love me and perhaps consider that I was a worthwhile person, that it was not a horrible mistake that I even existed.

"By the time I was about eighteen or nineteen, I started to suffer significantly from the effects of the betrayals. Although I was very bright and worked very hard, I had trouble focusing on just what I wanted to do with my life. As a result, I changed my undergraduate major multiple times, all the way from premed to sociology to physical education. I finally ended up with a BS in science and another in health and physical education. I then went on to get a master's degree in PE at a major university. From there, I taught for eleven years at the college level, until I experienced a rapid onset of obesity (from using chocolate and Pepsi as antidepressants). During this time, I was becoming more and more confused and anxious and depressed, to the point that I started wondering just what was wrong with me.

"Whenever anything adverse happened around me, especially at work, I thought that it was my fault. That had been the tenor of my father's emotional abuse, and the message was still deeply embedded in my soul."

Rebecca especially regrets the effects the betrayal had on her ability to trust others and form relationships: "For decades, I had trouble relating to others. I did not understand why, as a highly intelligent adult who had had such promise as a child and a teenager, I was now working part-time or minimum-wage jobs and barely able to survive, financially and emotionally. The pressure would build and build until finally I would explode in a meeting or at work, spewing my agony over everyone present. I scared people. I lost jobs that way. I lost 'friends' that way. I further alienated myself from a world where I felt like a real alien."

Betrayal and Instability in Relationships

Earlier in her life, Rebecca was diagnosed with borderline personality disorder. Borderline personality disorder (BPD) is a severe personality problem.[24] Those diagnosed with BPD are often suicidal, unstable, and unable to tolerate difficult emotions. Rebecca's difficulty with relationships, her seemingly irrational blowing up at coworkers, and her anxiety are all effects of her early betrayal, and yet again, these get diagnosed as a mental disorder, rather than as an adaptation to early betrayal.

Recently, we, together with Laura Kaehler, have investigated the contribution of betrayal trauma exposure to the development of borderline personality characteristics.[25] We have looked at BPD using betrayal trauma theory as our framework. As we have explained, betrayal trauma theory proposes that survivors of interpersonal trauma may remain unaware of betrayal in order to maintain a necessary attachment to the perpetrator. Because of this, their ability to maintain important and stabilizing relationships in the future may be compromised.

In two studies, one with students and the other with community members, we found that betrayal and gender were significant predictors of borderline personality characteristics. For men, all three levels of betrayal trauma were significant predictors of borderline characteristics; for women, only high- and medium-betrayal traumas were significantly associated with borderline characteristics. These findings suggest that betrayal trauma may be a key cause of borderline personality disorder.

A further study that we did with Brent Belford found that having healthy relationships was a mediator variable.[26] One interpretation of this is that people who suffer betrayal trauma but somehow have good relationships—through good luck or good support—show fewer borderline characteristics than those who don't. We examine this more in chapter 11 when we talk about healing. Safe relationships appear to be a requirement for healing from betrayal.

When we asked Rebecca whether she thought that the betrayals affected her ability to have relationships, she said, "I did not have any friends whatsoever for about twenty years. Except, however briefly, maybe three or four months, and then I would just fall apart and storm out. I still don't have any people I call friends, because friends are trustworthy, and they'll do anything for you, and they're not in it just for themselves. I have some really good acquaintances, but I really don't have any friends. So when I have to put down an emergency number, I put down my most recent therapist's. As a friend. Because . . . it's enormously harmed my ability to be in any kind of relationship."

She went on: "I try people out; I semitrust a couple of people. Actually, three, besides my most recent therapist, whom I do trust. But yeah, I've just been let down so deeply, from infancy, that it's really hard to trust myself. And now that I have a peaceful life where I have myself, for the first time in my life, I don't like people messing that up. I feel as if I have to have some control because most of my life I really didn't have any control. Or I didn't feel like I had any control."

Rebecca has faced her betrayal and is doing better now, and we say more about that in chapter 9, but she still suffers from the effects of her early betrayals: "I try to stay out of situations where I'm going to get scrambled brains. That means I'm almost agoraphobic, people might call me agoraphobic. But I just prefer my own company; I'm very introverted, and I like myself—finally! So my neighbor, who I'm friendly with, just loves to talk about other people negatively behind their backs—so God only knows what she's saying about me—but never to their faces. I don't trust that. So, I do things with and for her, but she's not my friend. I give that gift of friendship very sparingly. And . . . I know several wonderful people who I can call on, if need be."

Rebecca agreed that was definitely a change: "I mean, I really never knew anyone because I was just trying so hard to survive and having most of a master's degree and another full master's degree and college teaching experience and having to be a secretary because I couldn't cope with anything else. It was very, very hard."

Rebecca's problems with relationships can be traced directly back to her early betrayals. She did not develop trust in herself or in other important people and was left to try to figure it out on her own. She was aware that she was unstable and reactive to betrayal, and her adaptation to this was to stay out of relationships, for the most part.

Cathy's adaptation was different and perhaps more common. Cathy needed to be in relationships, but she had no idea how to pick partners or friends. Her first husband turned out to be a pedophile. She says of that relationship, "This was the improved life, this was the first upgrade. I had no clue. I had no clue of anything normal or normalcy or stability or safety." She was then married two more times, to men who emotionally abused her. Finally, she is currently with a man who does not abuse her and whom she describes as her best friend.

Betrayal and Revictimization

Cathy's pattern was one of revictimization. Individuals who were abused in childhood are at higher risk for later sexual, emotional, and physical victimization than are people who were not abused in childhood.[27] For instance, Anne DePrince found that the presence of betrayal trauma before the age of eighteen was associated with revictimization after age eighteen.[28] She also found that individuals who report being revictimized in young adulthood following an interpersonal assault in childhood perform worse on reasoning problems that involve interpersonal relationships and safety information, compared to individuals who have not been revictimized.

This cruel aftermath of abuse is a puzzle. Why would early victimization leave one more vulnerable to later victimization? Robyn Gobin and Jennifer Freyd have investigated this perplexing phenomenon. They studied revictimization within a betrayal trauma framework among a sample of college students. They found that individuals who reported experiencing high-betrayal trauma at any time point (childhood, adolescence, or adulthood) were more likely to report experiences of trauma that were high in betrayal during adolescence and adulthood.[29] The effects are strong. Those who experience childhood trauma that was high in betrayal are much more likely to be victimized in adolescence and even more likely to be victimized in adulthood.

Revictimization may be related to the awareness of betrayal. We wanted to investigate this possibility. One of the difficulties with doing research on betrayal and betrayal trauma is finding ways to measure betrayal and the concepts related to it. As we mentioned, the BBTS (Brief Betrayal Trauma Survey) was created to measure exposure to betrayal, but what about measuring awareness of betrayal? It's a sticky problem. That is why, with Robyn Gobin, we created the Betrayal Detection Measure to measure people's ability to detect betrayal accurately and to be aware of it.[30] The Betrayal Detection Measure includes measuring participants' adult history of common betrayals (such as having a friend betray a secret) that are not necessarily categorized as traumatic. Their level of awareness for betrayals, accuracy in detecting them, and reaction to them also are assessed. We wanted to examine instances where individuals are aware that they are being betrayed but simultaneously choose to ignore the betrayal, in effect decreasing their awareness of it. We found that individuals with a childhood history of betrayal trauma showed a lower awareness of some adult betrayals.

One other possible contribution to revictimization is the impact that betrayal trauma has on the choice of a partner. Robyn Gobin investigated the possibility that exposure to betrayal trauma might affect the traits that are desired in potential romantic partners. Betrayal trauma theory suggests that social and cognitive development may be affected by early trauma, such that individuals develop survival strategies, particularly dissociation and lack of betrayal awareness, which may place them at risk for further victimization.[31] Several experiences of victimization in the context of relationships predicated on trust and dependence could contribute to the development of a relational schema whereby abuse is ordinary. Is there evidence for this possibility?

Robyn Gobin asked study participants to rate the desirability of several characteristics in potential romantic partners. She found that participants who reported experiences of revictimization (defined as the experience of more than one trauma perpetrated by someone close to them) differed from participants who reported only one experience of high-betrayal trauma, in their self-reported desire for a romantic partner who possessed the traits of loyalty, honesty, and compassion.[32] Preference for a partner who uses the tactic of verbal aggression was also associated with revictimization status. In other words, people who had been betrayed and then revictimized actually preferred partners who used verbal aggression. These findings suggest that multiple victimizations perpetrated by others who are close to us may affect our partner preferences.

How desirable are these characteristics in a mate? For most people, loyalty, honesty, compassion, reliability, and understanding are highly desirable. Yet for people who have been revictimized, they are not quite as preferred.

How undesirable is verbal aggression in a mate? For most of us, highly undesirable. If you have been revictimized by betrayal, apparently it is not so undesirable.

The seeds of revictimization start in childhood. *Indiscriminate friendliness* is a term used to describe a behavior pattern in young children, in which the children are overly friendly and trusting with strangers.[33] This pattern has been well documented among children who are adopted internationally and also among some maltreated children, including foster children. Researchers assume that inconsistency in caregiving has led to this indiscriminate friendliness. From a betrayal trauma theory perspective, however, we can understand this in terms of damaged trust and attachment mechanisms. In a healthy environment, young children learn to test the waters before being overly friendly or trusting. This learning helps protect them from victimization. If children don't develop this ability, due to early abuse, they are at a much greater risk of being revictimized later because they trust people they should not.

The Toxic Effects of Betrayal on Society

The intergenerational transmission of trauma is a well-known fact in the psychological literature.[34] Studies have found that children of Holocaust survivors are more likely to develop PTSD in stressful situations than are children of people who did not go through the Holocaust.

This intergenerational transmission of maltreatment, also known as the cycle of violence, refers to people who were maltreated as children and later become maltreating parents. Using the National Family Violence Survey, researchers found that men exposed to childhood domestic violence had a 13 percent increased risk of perpetrating child maltreatment.[35] Other researchers documented a 24 percent rate of childhood incest in mothers of maltreated children and 3 percent in the nonabused comparison group, suggesting that mothers of abused children were eight times more likely to be survivors of incest than were mothers of nonabused children.[36] A recent study demonstrated that mothers with a childhood history of multitype maltreatment were at an increased risk of either (a) directly perpetrating multiple types of maltreatment or (b) creating unsafe environments, which put their children in danger of being victimized.[37]

Annmarie Hulette, Laura Kaehler, and Jennifer Freyd looked at the short- and long-term consequences of betrayal trauma in a sample of sixty-seven mother-child dyads.[38] The mothers and the children came to our laboratory at the University of Oregon. We found that experiences of high-betrayal trauma were related to higher levels of dissociation in both children and mothers. Furthermore, mothers who experienced high-betrayal trauma in childhood and were subsequently interpersonally revictimized in adulthood were shown to have higher levels of dissociation than mothers who were not revictimized in adulthood. Moreover, maternal revictimization status was associated with child interpersonal trauma history. These results may indicate that dissociation from a history of childhood betrayal trauma involves a persistent unawareness of future threats to both self and children in the environment. This study provides evidence that betrayal trauma can be passed through generations.

The societal effects of betrayal do not stop at the generational, individual, or relational line. Those effects extend to our institutions as well. Remember chapter 4? In that chapter, we talked about the wide range of institutional betrayal and even the recent research by Carly Smith and Jennifer Freyd showing that institutional betrayal exacerbates the harm of sexual assault. This research shows that institutional betrayal can hurt individuals. We believe it can also hurt societies. When institutions can no longer be trusted, the social fabric begins to fray.

"A time comes when silence is betrayal." . . . Even when
pressed by the demands of inner truth, men do not easily
assume the task of opposing their government's policy, especially in time of war. Nor does the human spirit move
without great difficulty against all the apathy of conform-
ist thought within one's own bosom and in the surrounding
world. . . .

[S]ome of us who have already begun to break the silence
of the night have found that the calling to speak is often a
vocation of agony, but we must speak. We must speak with
all the humility that is appropriate to our limited vision, but
we must speak. . . .

We are called to speak for the weak, for the voiceless,
for the victims of our nation, for those it calls enemy, for no
document from human hands can make these humans any
less our brothers. . . .

I think of them, too, because it is clear to me that there
will be no meaningful solution until some attempt is made
to know them and hear their broken cries.[39]

This quote from a speech by Dr. Martin Luther King Jr., given
in 1967, called and still calls us to action in speaking up for those
who have been betrayed, ourselves included.

Betrayal blindness is dangerous not just to individuals but to
whole societies. By not being aware of our past betrayals, we not
only are at great risk of repeating them, but betrayal blindness can
result in wider betrayals. The best recent example of this is the
happenings in Nazi Germany. There were betrayals on so many
levels that led to the rise of Nazism and the Holocaust. Germans
felt betrayed after World War I and attempted to deal with that
betrayal, not by facing and disclosing the betrayal they felt, but
by turning to what looked safe on the surface—a government and
a regime that established power by increasing suspicion and distrust among its citizenry. Neighbors betrayed neighbors. Children
betrayed parents. Aryans betrayed Jews. The pain of all of these
betrayals and the inability to face them led to a society based on
fear and paranoia. This was the atmosphere that created the soil for
the Holocaust—secrecy and blindness. As we shall see in the next
chapter, later in the twentieth century South Africa took a different

path to deal with betrayal, one that ended blindness to betrayal and resulted in healing and forgiveness.

There can be no doubt that betrayal is toxic. It can cause dissociation and dissociative identity disorder, memory loss, numerous mental health symptoms, instability of personality and relationships, and revictimization. Betrayal and its harm are all too common—from family members to institutions. The picture appears hopeless. Or does it? Our next two chapters examine how we can, as individuals and as a society, overcome the effects of betrayal to become more aware, healthier, and better able to face the future together.

10

The Risks of Knowing

There are advantages to not knowing about betrayal. Relationships can continue, and we don't risk big changes happening in our lives. If we're comfortable enough, it is possible not to know—at least on the surface. We do know that *something* is wrong. We can't trust. We have difficulty growing and thriving in relationships. Perhaps we become depressed and closed in on ourselves, rather than taking the risk of caring and sharing ourselves.

The discovery of betrayal—the breakdown of betrayal blindness—always seems to bring about a profound new awareness: the world is not the same. Discovery inspires new values, beliefs, behaviors, and loyalties. Someone who was trusted is now acknowledged to be unsafe. Perhaps even the world seems less safe. As sobering and frightening as the newfound reality may be, freedom from betrayal blindness also opens up new possibilities for intimacy and growth. Given its insidious underbelly, how does one dare break free of betrayal? Let's examine the risks of knowing and telling.

"Knowing" about Betrayal

First, we must become aware of the betrayal itself. Perhaps the evidence has become undeniable, or we have come to a time in our lives when we are safe enough or have enough social support. Or we meet someone we think we can begin to trust. Whatever the reason, we reach a point where we can risk that free fall of dropping into knowing. Our lives are turned upside-down, and everything begins to look different. The marriage or the relationship ends, perhaps we leave the job, or we can begin to look at our family differently. Our lives become different.

This "knowing" about betrayal is interesting. We usually think we know something or we don't, but it turns out that there are different ways to "know" things. We can know them internally and on the level of sensation or behavior, or we can know them at the level of words. Jennifer Freyd proposed a theory of shareability in 1983 that attempts to describe the difference between our private knowledge versus our public knowledge.[1] Shareability theory proposes that through the sharing of information—that is, through communication—internal knowledge is reorganized into more consciously available, categorical, and discrete forms of knowing. This means that information we have never shared with others is organized differently than information we have shared. So disclosure affects the *way* we know our own experiences internally.

Much childhood abuse and interpersonal violence happen without the opportunity for communication; thus, our knowledge of and memories for these experiences are actually different than those concerning experiences we have communicated.[2] These internal and external kinds of disclosure are mutually influencing each other. By not disclosing to ourselves, we are able to avoid disclosing to others. Once we do disclose to others, it changes how we understand an event ourselves.

Let's put this another way: information inside our heads is often difficult for us to gain access to in words. That "free fall" we've been talking about—how do you put that into words? It's often a long and difficult period of time when we're struggling with finding the right words that seem to fit our experience. When we do find good enough words, we can begin to share our experience with others. It becomes transformed from "free fall" into "my friend betrayed me and it hurt." This is no easy transformation, and as we figure out the words and share our experiences, things become more obvious to us.

You will see this very clearly in Beth's story, because her inner knowledge at first looked (and was labeled as) crazy, until she finally gained the words to speak about it. We can also see that in disclosing her betrayal to another person, Beth was in a way disclosing it to herself. This fact is really at the heart of one of the core aspects of dissociation, when individuals are able to not know of an experience that they have endured. One reason that nondisclosure to oneself (or not knowing) occurs is exactly because internal and external disclosure are so tied together. To the extent that it is not safe to disclose *externally*, it is not safe to know, or disclose internally to, oneself.

Beth's Story

One of the most important things for our psychological well-being is to develop our own unique and true voice. Betrayal not only harms us, it also makes us feel crazy at times and silences us. Whether we are blind to the betrayal or not, we have difficulty telling our story. We don't know whom to trust.

We interviewed Beth McDonald one sunny summer day in July. Beth was a petite woman whose smooth complexion and dark hair gave her the look of someone much younger than her thirty-eight years. Beth was a successful businesswoman and the owner of a camp that had programs to help abused children. Sitting in a private and pleasing office cooled by a summer breeze, we asked her about a betrayal that had almost cost her life.

She told us, "I experienced this firsthand when at seventeen years old, I started having flashbacks of abuse that I experienced when I was four years old at the hands of sadistic teenage boys. I started having weird urges in my late teenage years that had to do with self-harm. It started as giving myself black eyes and goose eggs. It progressed into cutting on my face, particularly around my eye. I don't want to minimize these behaviors, because they were serious cries for help. I could not speak what to me felt unspeakable. I didn't have the words to voice what had happened to me. I couldn't cry. I was numb. Everything—my voice, my memories, and my tears—was trapped inside, with no way out. The act of cutting I now believe was my attempt to free the tears and to 'speak' what I could not voice. Was it the best way? No. Did it appear 'crazy'? You bet. Was there meaning in it? Oh, yeah."

We asked Beth what her therapist had done to help her with her numbness and self-injury.

"I was suddenly diagnosed with a great many labels and medicated to the point of zombie-ism," she said. "Not one of those labels or medications helped cure the flashbacks or reduced the cutting. In fact, my therapist's main mode of treating these behaviors was to throw me into the local mental hospital *after* I had cut myself—not before, mind you, because I was not allowed to call her—only afterward, when the deed was done. Never once, though, not once, in the three years that I saw this woman did she ever ask me what the cutting was about or ask why I did it.

"In fact, it was her rule that I not talk about what had happened to me—that I was to shrink it down, push it away, and not look at it. I was told not to speak of it because it was 'upsetting' to me. Also too 'upsetting' to me was to have contact with my family. She asked that I not speak to or be around my parents because they could get in the way of the healing. So this dynamic was set up in which I was not able to talk about what I needed to, I was not able to see or talk to my support system, not able to have real feelings or work through them, and if I refused to try to push it away or shrink it down, I was told to leave her office. The anger festered and grew in me like black mold."

Beth cringed as she told us about her frustration during this time. She was disconnected from her support system and found herself in another system that called cries for help "crazy." Beth found it an impossible position. This went on until she was sent to an inpatient unit and found someone who would truly listen to her: "For the first time in years, there was someone who was willing and wanting to listen to me and to my story. She was not afraid of the hard stuff, and she listened with her heart. I was able to talk to this woman about what I had been through as a child. The connection between Judy and me grew and flourished. I thrived."

Yet then, after Beth went home, Beth's therapist cut off Beth's connection with Judy. It was framed as "professional boundaries," but Beth experienced it as a profound betrayal. Part of Beth's reaction we have already talked about.

"And in that very moment," she said, "with those words, I felt myself falling down into a black chasm. A feeling of coldness washing over me—much as it felt every time a doctor administered anesthesia before surgery—a feeling that I had just died. I fell into a black void of nothingness.

"The guilt consumed me, night and day. I had dreams of my therapist raping me repeatedly. I stopped talking. I sat in our therapy sessions with a blanket over my head—not willing to let her see me ever again, not wanting to see her."

For several years, Beth was blind to her therapist's betrayal. Although she was angry with her therapist, she could not allow herself to call the actions wrong. There was always the nagging doubt that maybe she was crazy. But then came the day when Beth could really allow herself to feel the depths of betrayal and begin to change things. At this point, Beth had moved to a town thirty miles away and was commuting to see her therapist. She had also entered a sexual abuse survivor group: "And then one summer day, as I sat with the blanket over my head, I heard her tell me that I just needed to shrink it all down. I felt my body respond in a way I've never felt before. It started with a little spark in my belly that grew stronger as it traveled up through me and out my mouth. My voice was as strong as I have ever heard it before.

"'I can't do this anymore.' The blanket was shed, and I got up and walked out into the sunshine and never looked back."

We are motivated to be blind to betrayal to maintain important connections and relationships, but as we grow, we realize, as Beth did with her therapist, that those relationships are false and confining. If we can let ourselves, and we have support for falling into that disoriented place, we can begin to truly find ourselves. There can be no healing without talking about the betrayal, disclosing it to someone else, whether a close friend or even a support group.

Beth's story is about success in facing her betrayal, as we'll see in the next chapter, but it was risky. Beth *could* have found herself in worse circumstances after walking out of her therapist's office—she could have found herself being treated as more and more "crazy," as she attempted to make her inner experience of betrayal one that could be shared in words. Instead, she found a person who could listen to her beyond her words and stay with her while she figured it all out. That story we share in chapter 11.

Telling May Risk More Betrayal

Telling and knowing can be risky because a bad response from others can constitute a new and harmful betrayal. The rape survivor who is blamed for being raped, the child abuse victim who is not believed—these individuals are experiencing profound betrayal.

This betrayal can be deeply damaging. If getting a bad response to a disclosure can be a profound betrayal, it also means that there can be disclosure or nondisclosure of this experience as well, with all of the related complications and implications.

Bad responses to disclosure come in many varieties. One very bad kind of response is called DARVO.[3] This stands for: **D**eny the behavior, **A**ttack the individual doing the confronting, and **R**everse the roles of **V**ictim and **O**ffender, such that the perpetrator is assigned (or assumes) the victim role and turns the true victim into an alleged offender. That is a very negative response for the survivor. Not only does DARVO likely cause psychological harm, but we suspect it also often leads to retraction or silence.

A perfect example of this is when a guilty person is accused of rape. When confronted with this, the accused person denies that rape occurred, explaining it as consensual and acting in an outraged, affronted way, painting himself as a hapless victim. The perpetrator goes on to describe the actual victim as a vindictive person. The perpetrator therefore paints a picture of the victim as an aggressor, deserving of being spurned. The person disclosing the rape is thus raped again.

There are other risks as well—marriages fail, relationships fall apart, family members fight with one another. If workers talk about betrayal on the job and become whistleblowers, they are likely to lose their jobs. One example that demonstrated the risks of disclosing betrayal actually happened to us.

First, some background. In late 1990, Jennifer Freyd started to remember some childhood abuse by her father. She was discreet with the information but did share it privately with her therapist, her husband, her parents, and a few close friends. One of the results of her telling about the betrayal was the formation of the False Memory Syndrome Foundation, founded by her parents. There were other insidious outcomes as well, and here is the story of one of them, told in Jennifer's voice. She is referring to an article (the "Jane Doe article") written by her mother and widely disseminated in 1991 and 1992.[4]

"The existence of this Jane Doe article first came to my attention in a most disturbing fashion. I was sitting in the office of my colleague Dr. Pamela Birrell in the fall of 1991, when she passed me a copy of the journal *Issues in Child Abuse Accusation*. She said the journal issue had mysteriously appeared in her mailbox, and she wondered what I thought about it. I lazily flipped through the journal and skimmed a few words here and there. When I got to the article 'How Could This Happen?' authored by 'Jane Doe,' I read a paragraph or two and was astounded to discover personal details about someone named 'Susan' who sounded remarkably like myself. Suddenly, my attention was riveted on the article.

"The article 'How Could this Happen?' is subtitled 'Coping with a False Accusation of Incest and Rape.' It tells the first-person story of a family facing a 'false accusation of childhood sexual abuse and rape by a grown daughter against her father.' The article chronicles the story of middle-aged parents confronted with an allegation of incest by their thirty-three-year-old daughter. Jane Doe proclaims her husband entirely innocent of the accusations. In support of her claim that the accusations are false, Jane Doe presents numerous intimate details about the daughter's history that are meant to discredit her daughter. Jane Doe does not accept responsibility for herself or her husband. Rather, Jane Doe levels most of the blame against her daughter's therapist, one particular book, and the field of clinical psychology.

"As I continued to read the article in my colleague's office, a deafening noise filled my ears. 'Oh, my God,' I thought, 'this is about me!' It was about me and yet not, in that some crucial details had been changed—not only names but details that made me, or the person in the story—sound less credible. I must have looked up about then and murmured to Pam, 'This is about me! I mean, really about me—my life!' Pam looked utterly confused. She must have wondered about my sanity at that moment."

Pam Birrell remembered, "In 1991, I did not know Jennifer Freyd very well yet. We had met as colleagues in the Psychology Department and were in the beginning stages of what has turned out to be an enduring and enriching friendship. And I don't recall why she was sitting in my office that day in 1991.

"At the time, I was a practicing clinician, as well as director of the Psychology Clinic in the Psychology Department. I was slowly becoming aware of the debate over 'false memories' that was beginning to grow. I was seeing people in my practice with a history of sexual abuse, but none with what were later to be called 'repressed memories,' so I wondered one day when an unknown and unsolicited journal showed up in my mailbox in the Psychology Department, with no hint as to who had put it there or why. It puzzled me at the time, but all I did was to put it on my desk to read later. The title of the journal was *Issues in Child Abuse Accusations*, and it appeared to be about people who had made false claims of child abuse. It seemed to have little to do with my interests or work, so I just identified it as one of those mysteries of life.

"All the same, when I was talking to Jennifer, I decided to show it to her to see if she had any clue as to why it had arrived in my mailbox. I had no reason to think that she would, but it seemed an interesting phenomenon for acquaintances to discuss.

"I do remember vividly the expression that came across her face as she looked through the issue. It went from curiosity to bewilderment to incomprehension. She looked at me, stunned. 'This is about me,' she said. I was now as stunned as she was."

Jennifer went on with her remembering: "'About you? What do you mean?' Pam Birrell asked me. Shaken, I explained that the article by Jane Doe, written by a supposedly falsely accused mother, contained numerous details that made it clearly about me. Although my identity was thinly disguised and some details fabricated, the match was undeniable. Incomprehension turned to horror and mortification, as I imagined that others might somehow read this article and recognize me. It was like having one's most personal diary put on display—only worse, because in this case the diary contained both true and fabricated highly personal details.

"In the days, weeks, and months that followed this surreal experience, I became aware of the substantial amount of correspondence that had been occurring between my parents and some of my colleagues. I learned that during the late summer and early fall of 1991, my mother had sent that article to some of my colleagues, including senior professors in my own department, during the very year in which my promotion to full professorship was being considered. Although the article was technically anonymous, in each of these cases in which my very own colleagues received the article, my mother's and my identity were made absolutely explicit, usually by the addition of a letter signed by my mother. I later learned that even before sending the Jane Doe article, my mother had begun phoning some of my department colleagues.

"In the fall of 1991, during the weeks that followed my discovering the 'Jane Doe' article, I learned that my parents and their collaborators had already begun to form their professional advisory board for the False Memory Syndrome Foundation. In the spring of 1992, they even invited me to join the FMFS professional advisory board. When I did not accept the invitation, I received a second invitation from my mother in April 1992 that included the argument 'the Advisory Board is shaping up to be prestigious enough so that you won't feel ashamed to belong.' Betrayal added onto betrayal—being asked to join an organization founded and designed to attack people like me, who had begun to remember betrayal.

"This period of intrusion from my parents into my professional life culminated in having numerous colleagues actually join the FMSF board. I was horrified, particularly when a colleague in my own department joined the board, and even more so when my prior undergraduate mentor joined the advisory board. I could not fathom why my colleagues would do this. Was I not credible? If not, why not? I had no prior scandal attached to my name, no history of fraud or dishonesty.

"I realize now that none of this would have happened if *I* had not first become aware of the earlier betrayals in my life. The False Memory Syndrome Foundation would not have been founded, and the subsequent betrayals by my colleagues would not have happened. And yet, I don't regret the remembering, for it led to much growth and knowledge. But more about that in chapter 13."

It's Difficult to Know, and It's Difficult to Disclose

Yes, disclosure is risky, but it is necessary for healing to take place. We asked Rebecca Brewerman, "What finally helped?"

She had this to say: "Being able to tell my story and not having someone tell me what to do and how to do it, but just listening, just being there for me. And being believed, 'cause I felt like I haven't been believed most of my life. . . . That's the main thing. And I could take risks to make my life better."

Disclosure—that is, the telling of trauma—and the impact of trauma are deeply interwoven issues. It makes sense that this inevitable intermingling of trauma and disclosure is all the more so true for interpersonal traumas with high degrees of betrayal, stigma, and secrecy. Indeed, we refer to such traumas in terms of disclosure—we refer to them as "unspeakable."

Disclosure can help us get emotional, legal, or financial aid. Without disclosure, it is very hard to find resources, healing is difficult to promote, and future trauma is very difficult to prevent. We know that silence is part of the problem, at both the individual and the societal level, and that interpersonal violence breeds in secrecy. So it is really puzzling that nondisclosure of trauma is so common.

Although disclosure does facilitate the receipt of these good things, delayed disclosure or even nondisclosure is the norm.[5] In fact, trauma is not easily discussed. It can be forgotten, it is highly stigmatized, and it can be taboo to talk about. It can also be truly risky to discuss trauma, as we've seen.

Nondisclosure is particularly pronounced in the case of sexual trauma perpetrated by someone close to us, which has all of those elements of betrayal, stigma, and secrecy. Research suggests that fewer than one in four survivors disclose immediately following sexual abuse.[6] A typical time span of eight to fifteen years from abuse onset to disclosure has been found.[7] For survivors who participate in research on trauma, that research participation experience is often the very first time that they disclose to anyone.[8]

Furthermore, most people who experience childhood sexual abuse do not disclose it until adulthood, and many never tell at all.[9] In addition, some studies have revealed a pattern of disclosure followed by recanting and redisclosure.[10] So when people do disclose, some take it back, and then some go on to disclose again. Nondisclosure, delayed disclosure, and retraction are particularly likely in cases in which the perpetrator is close to the victim.[11] We will come back to the context of this implicit risk of disclosure to crucial relationships.

Why Don't We Disclose?

People are aware of some of the reasons they do not disclose—the explicit reasons—but they are not fully aware of the implicit reasons. Explicit reasons relate to an awareness of risk in disclosure. People contemplating disclosure may reasonably fear a negative reaction. They fear not being believed, fear blame or reprisal, fear stigma, and fear that it will harm their loved ones.

There are also reasons for nondisclosure that may elude conscious awareness. Although these are also based on real risk, people may not be aware of the risk or the fact that they are being influenced by it. These *implicit reasons* are that crucial relationships may be lost in the disclosure of trauma. This brings us back to the core idea of betrayal blindness—that we need to protect necessary relationships and social systems. Disclosure can risk those necessary relationships.

Remember our earlier discussion of betrayal trauma? We talked about the idea that betrayal blindness may be a survival mechanism. According to betrayal trauma theory, betrayal blindness occurs when awareness of mistreatment would threaten necessary or apparently necessary relationships. This is because, by being aware, one is at risk of chasing away or scaring away the very people one depends on or causing those people to respond negatively. In that case, unawareness, forgetting, and nondisclosure may be seen as adaptive responses to this sort of betrayal trauma. In other words, by keeping silent the victim protects a relationship that is perceived to be necessary. To the extent that this is true, it creates a huge impediment to disclosure because disclosure may risk the necessary relationship.

Telling Can Help or Hurt, Depending on the Response

Other people's response when we tell about betrayal is crucial. It is not surprising that when people respond positively to trauma survivors' disclosure of their abuse, it can be helpful and healing. A positive response can lead to the survivors' growth of inner resources and feelings of being validated and cared for. However, research has revealed that when people respond negatively to disclosure, it has substantial potential to do harm to the survivor.[12] Negative responses include blaming the survivor, expressing disbelief, and showing lack of concern. Sarah Ullman, a professor in the Department of Criminology, Law, and Justice at the University of Illinois at Chicago, reported research with adult rape survivors that demonstrated that a negative response to disclosure can be profoundly destructive to survivors, at times apparently more harmful than the rape itself.[13]

Brian Marx, a psychologist and researcher at the National Center for PTSD, VA Boston Healthcare System, captured some of this potential for harm: "In our society, the validity of reports of sexual violence is often questioned, and survivors are blamed for their sexual assaults. Furthermore, the consequences of these experiences are often trivialized or ignored by family, friends, police, legal officials, and sometimes even mental health professionals. Unfortunately, such social conditions further create stigma and shame for survivors, thereby compounding the destructiveness of their experiences."[14] In other words, a negative response to a disclosure does much harm to the person who has already been harmed.

It is clear that no disclosure keeps us stuck, but negative response to disclosure can be even worse. It is a risk.

What about disclosure that receives neither a very good nor a very bad response? Is that sort of disclosure better or worse than no disclosure at all? Interestingly, research indicates that when survivors disclose their trauma and don't receive a response, this can be beneficial if it is clear all along to the person disclosing that no response will be provided.[15]

What is an example of disclosure with no response? One example is writing to yourself in a journal that you do not show to anybody at all. Participating in research on trauma is another context in which disclosure without response can occur. In trauma research, we often ask people to disclose things, and we essentially give them no response to their particular disclosure. Crucially, we often set up the research procedure in such a way that there is no opportunity to give any response at all. The expectations here are critical. Giving somebody no response could actually be a negative response if the person disclosing expects a response of some sort. For instance, if somebody discloses a betrayal trauma and his or her disclosure is met with a stony face, that is a negative response. But if people disclose in a context where they do not expect a response, that can be very different. For instance, research participants might each write an essay about their trauma experience, put it in an envelope, and drop the envelope through a slot into a sealed box. If the participants in this situation have not put any identifying marks on their essays and if they are told that their responses are entirely anonymous, they have just disclosed in a way in which they could not get any response at all, and presumably they do not expect any response. The data indicate that this is generally a positive situation for people, relative to no disclosure at all. In fact, this essay-writing task has been extensively explored in recent years. Pioneered by Jamie Pennebaker of The University of Texas, the "writing task," or "expressive writing," has been shown in many studies to improve the physical and mental well-being of participants.[16] This is an interesting discovery for psychology and good news for trauma researchers.

In most of the expressive-writing studies, mental and physical health has been measured as an outcome to writing a series of three or four essays about an upsetting event versus writing about less emotional topics. Under most conditions, the participants randomly assigned to write about an upsetting event show improvement in both their physical and their mental well-being. In one of our favorite studies in this line of research, Pennebaker worked with a group of middle-aged engineers who had recently been laid off.[17] Half of the engineers were randomly assigned to write about their feelings about losing their jobs, and the other half wrote about their plans for finding new jobs. The outcome measure in this case was success at finding a new job. Those engineers who had written about being laid off and their feelings about it were more likely to have found new employment than were those who had written on the seemingly more practical topic. This stunning result offers clear evidence that disclosure itself can be a good thing for people. Note that the engineers received no specific feedback to their disclosures in the research study, so they had no damaging negative responses. Rather, the disclosure apparently allowed the engineers to process their negative experience in ways that ultimately left them more able to gain new jobs, perhaps because their psychological health made them more attractive to future employers. It appears there is something in disclosure itself that is valuable, as long as there is not a negative response.

All of this research implies that the social context in which people disclose affects the process itself. Related to this, disclosure is often not a single event, but rather a process that is highly dependent on the reactions of others. People disclose usually not in one moment, but over some period of time, and they gauge how much more they want to disclose depending on the responses they get.

Melissa Foynes and Jennifer Freyd looked at disclosures as they occur in real time.[18] Most research on disclosure has used a retrospective methodology, where people have been asked about their history of disclosure and other people's responses to it. In contrast, we brought people into the laboratory in pairs. We asked people to come in with a friend and to disclose an event that they have not told their friend that was very distressing to them. We videotaped this and then coded the videotapes to see what occurred in that context. We also asked participants to complete pre- and post-questionnaires, so that we could look at how the disclosure experience affected them. The individuals in each pair of friends were randomly assigned to be a "discloser" or a "listener."

In this study, we found that a history of high-betrayal trauma was associated with having received (in the past) more negative responses to disclosure. We also discovered that, not too surprisingly, posture on the listener's part predicted outcome; when listeners leaned backward, this was associated with more negative responses to disclosure. Most interestingly, we found that the number of interruptions was quite predictive of a positive experience, with a moderate level of interruptions being best.

From this research, we developed some materials to help people be better receivers when others disclose traumatic experiences to them.

First, it is important to use attentive body language.

1. *Do not* make inappropriate facial expressions (examples: smiling when someone is discussing a sad topic; rolling the eyes; raising the eyebrows when hearing how someone coped) and *do not* move your body too much (examples: excessive fidgeting; playing with a cell phone).

2. *Do* sit in an alert posture (leaning forward or upright) and use gestures (nodding) that convey engagement.

3. *Do* maintain consistent, not constant or darting, eye contact (that is, look directly at the person for brief periods of 3 to 6 seconds, then look away briefly before reconnecting).

Second, it is important to use verbal skills that encourage the speaker to continue.

1. *Do not* change the topic or ask questions that are off-topic. This may seem like a way to decrease your anxiety or make the other person more comfortable, but it often has the opposite effect.

2. *Do* allow silence and convey that you are listening by using encouraging words such as *hmmm* and *uh-huh* periodically.

3. *Do* state/name/reflect back the emotion being described. It might also help you to imagine yourself in the speaker's place and look at the situation from his or her perspective (examples: "Wow, sounds like it was scary for you." "It seems like you feel really sad about that." "I feel like that must've made you angry.").

4. *Do* ask questions if you are confused, and try to ask questions that require more than one word. (Instead of "Was that scary?" or "Do you mean it wasn't that bad?" ask questions like: "Could you tell me a little bit more about that?" or "What was that like for you?" or "What do you mean when you say _____?")

Third, it is important to use words in ways that convey support.

1. *Do not* reassure the person in a way that might minimize his or her experience. (Examples: "That happened so long ago, maybe it would help to try move on." "It's not worth the energy to keep thinking about it." "Don't be scared.")

2. *Do not* make judgments or evaluations about the person's responses or decisions. (Examples: "Couldn't you do/say _____ instead?" "I don't think you should worry about it anymore." "I think it'd be better for you to _____." "Why don't you _____?")

3. *Do* validate the person's emotions in a genuine tone. (Examples: "If that happened to me, I can imagine I'd feel really overwhelmed, too." "Given that experience, it makes sense you'd feel/say/do _____." "I think many people with that experience would have felt similarly.")

4. *Do* point out the person's strengths. (Examples: "I'm amazed at how much courage that took." "You've done a great job at keeping everything in perspective." "I really admire your strength." "I'm impressed with how you've dealt with this.")

5. *Do* focus on the person's experience, rather than on your own, and give advice only when it is asked for.

In a follow-up study (which was then published before the original study, as sometimes happens in academic publishing), Melissa Foynes and Jennifer Freyd used these listening tips to see if they could help people become better listeners.[19] Pairs of friends were once again recruited to the lab. They were randomly assigned the roles of discloser and listener. As with the first study, the disclosers were asked to tell their friend something upsetting that they had not shared before. After the initial disclosure, they were randomly assigned either the listening tips or a control condition that consisted of healthy living tips. They then made a second disclosure. The disclosers rated how well the disclosures went, from their perspective. In addition, research assistants, unaware of the experimental conditions, coded and rated videotapes of all of the disclosures. The researchers found that the listening tips did improve the listeners' behavior, compared to the control condition, and the disclosers felt that they were better heard. This preliminary study suggests that listening skills can be taught.

Author James Carse got it right when he said, "A creative listener is not someone who simply allows me to say what I already want to say, but someone whose listening actually makes it possible for me to say what I never could have said, and thus to be a new kind of person, one I have never been before and could not have been before this directed listening."[20]

In this chapter, we have seen that without disclosure of trauma, healing and prevention are hampered, and yet nondisclosure of trauma is common. The reasons for nondisclosure are both explicit (for instance, fear of being blamed) and implicit (particularly, an often unconscious need to protect a relationship with the perpetrator). We have also seen that disclosure can lead to positive or negative outcomes relative to nondisclosure, depending on social response. A negative response to disclosure is often itself a fundamental betrayal and can at times be so severely harmful as to constitute a betrayal trauma. The disclosure process is both internal and external. Finally, we have seen that people can learn to be better listeners, and this can lead to healing.

A lot of what we talk about in this chapter is based on empirical research, to the extent possible, but clearly much remains to investigate. Future research is needed to study the psychology of disclosure and response to disclosure, to identify best responses and to discover how best to teach these best responses. We must continue to find ways to make the unspeakable safely speakable and thus promote healing and prevention.

We've discussed the importance of disclosure and how it can be risky. Yet for true healing to happen, we not only need to know about our betrayals and to face the pain of them, we also need to tell the story. Despite the risks, all of this is ultimately healing. The next chapter examines why and how this is true.

11

The Healing Power of Knowing

B etrayal is part of the human condition. It is ubiquitous and unavoidable. We all encounter betrayal in our lives—we are betrayer and betrayed. As we've described throughout this book, there are all kinds of betrayal and many ways that we remain blind to it. We are most likely to be blind to betrayal if we are vulnerable and don't have the power to name our own experience, tell our own story, or claim our own identity. When we are blind to it, we know that something is wrong in our lives but are not able to name it. We lose our power and identity. We become less trusting overall or too likely to trust the wrong people.

We become more and more ashamed of ourselves, for betrayal is also a statement—we are not worth caring about—and we come to believe it ourselves. We retreat into silence and isolation. We may have social interactions but cannot risk intimacy. We must shield our shame.

Betrayal and our blindness to it have societal implications as well. A society where betrayal and betrayal blindness are rampant is a society that cannot trust. When we can't trust our institutions, we become insulated and paranoid interest groups. Something fundamental is missing—the web of relations that holds us together. When healthy, that web holds societies together, and it holds individuals together. When the web is torn, we retreat into isolation, not even trusting ourselves. We find ourselves increasingly unable to have intimate and loving relationships with one another. We come undone.

In chapter 10, we discussed the risks of knowing and telling about betrayal. In this chapter and the next, we examine why knowing and telling about betrayal are so important, not only for our own personal healing and empowerment, but also for the healing of our culture and our world.

Power, Trust, and Betrayal

You will recall Beth from a prior chapter. She was finally able to leave the therapist who would not or could not be with her as she struggled to find words for her betrayal.

Remember what she said: "And then one summer day, as I sat with the blanket over my head, I heard her tell me that I just needed to shrink it all down. I felt my body respond in a way I've never felt before. It started with a little spark in my belly that grew stronger as it traveled up through me and out my mouth. My voice was as strong as I have ever heard it before.

"'I can't do this anymore.' The blanket was shed, and I got up and walked out into the sunshine and never looked back."

Beth had invested a lot in her therapist and the mental health system. She trusted her therapist to help her and to have her best interests at heart. In doing so, she gave her therapist the power to help her and, unfortunately, also the power to harm her. In shedding the blanket that blinded her, however, Beth found a kind of personal power.

Many people do not have this kind of personal power—the power of identity and story and meaning. Abused children do not have this power. Many women who have suffered betrayal trauma do not have this power. This power develops from close and trusting relationships with parents and others. Those who have been betrayed have their power taken away. They cannot tell their own stories, are not solid in their identity, and are increasingly isolated as they move into shame.

Robert did not have the power to name his story when he was an only child in an extremely stressed family. His father was an alcoholic and his mother chronically depressed. When Robert was in grade school, he was called home one day because his mother had attempted suicide. His father left Robert with her, not wanting to embarrass the family by calling in a doctor. Robert sat for hours, not knowing whether she would live or die. She did survive that time but succeeded in taking her own life when Robert was in high school. Robert had nowhere to turn. His father blamed him for his mother's death, and Robert grew up believing he was worthless, stupid, and trouble for everyone around him. His parents, who were supposed to care for him and nurture him, had betrayed and abandoned him.

It was not until years later, when Robert had descended into drug abuse and made a serious suicide attempt himself, that he began to open up to his minister. He expected scorn and derision and further blaming, and if his disclosures of guilt and worthlessness had been met that way, it surely would have been his undoing. Shame would have piled on shame, perhaps silencing him forever. Fortunately for Robert, his minister was able to hear his story without judgment or scorn. In telling his story, Robert gradually was able to understand his life in a different way. He began to see himself not as a worthless child who had driven his mother to suicide and let his father down, but as a child who had never had parental support and had had to find his way in the world the best way he could.

He found that he could begin to trust not only his minister, but himself as well. He began to see that what had looked "crazy" in his life, including his suicide attempt and drug abuse, had been attempts to avoid the awareness and pain of the betrayals in his life. As he became more and more able to face them, with the support of, first, his minister and then a growing circle of friends, Robert's life changed dramatically. When he began to trust himself, he found he could also begin to trust others. Or was it the other way around? Perhaps trusting others helped Robert trust himself. He would never know. He only knew that telling his story gave him the power and trust to begin to live for the first time.

In this newfound trust of himself and others, Robert was able to claim his own power—to tell his story, to claim his own emotions and reactions to what had been done to him, and to free himself from the corrosive bonds of shame. He found this power only through the healing power of disclosure.

Disclosure Can Be Effective in Healing

Jacques Sandulescu, the Romanian survivor of Russian work camps discussed in chapter 3, longed to have his story told.[1] He wrote his compelling description of survival and hope as a means to help himself and the world. His wife recounted how their return to Donbas years later and meeting others who had survived helped heal his trauma. Yet the true miracle happened on their return from Donbas, when Jacques got an e-mail from a thirteen-year-old boy named Josh Overton in Springfield, Oregon—a town that had recently been traumatized by a school shooting. Josh was asking for a fresh copy of Jacques's book *Donbas* for his teacher, Steve Hess, who was about to retire. It turned out that Steve Hess had read *Donbas* to his classes for twenty-eight years, and his copy was falling apart. Josh had been so gripped by the story of survival that he had been transformed from a marginal student with failing grades into a student not only earning A's, but also caring about school.

Jacques's wife, Annie Gottlieb, reported that getting in touch with Josh and his teacher transformed Jacques's life as much as returning to Donbas had. In her interview in *Oprah Magazine*, Annie reported, "Finally he knew he had been heard. 'This is the most popular book I've ever read to kids,' Steve Hess told him. I realized something new about Jacques: His story, more than his genes, is who he is and what he needs to pass on. He'd longed for children, but not of his body—children of his story."[2] He had not only had his story heard, but also seen its ability to change the lives of others, a truly healing experience.

The power of telling the story as a healing experience can also be seen with Cathy, Beth, and Rebecca. They, too, describe telling their stories and having them received and, in doing so, explain how this disclosure and its respectful reception is so healing. For speaking truth to be healing, it must be heard. As James Carse said:

> Whatever else we may be saying each time we address another, we are beseeching them, 'Listen to me. Please, listen.' Our very lives depend on that listening. This plea is not merely one of the things we utter in our speech, it is what we utter with the whole of our speech. We never speak except to be heard. When we are not heard we have not truly spoken. And when we cannot speak we have increasingly less to say, therefore less to ask for, and the lights of our being steadily darken.[3]

Let's go back to Beth's story: "It took close to twelve years to undo all the damage that three years with my old therapist and the 'system' had done to me. Fortunately, for me, I had found a bit of an unconventional therapist who was not a fan of medication or dogma therapy. She did not react out of fear. In fact, quite the opposite. The one time I cut myself fairly early on in therapy with her, her sympathetic reaction when she saw the cut on my face was, 'Oww, that looks like it really hurt.' And as I looked into her eyes and touched my own face, I thought, 'Yeah, it really did.' I never cut again.

"She was my rock and my sounding board. She was outraged at some of the things that my previous therapist had done—and that was so very healing and validating for me. She created a safe space for me to explore, vent, and ultimately release. She was there for me in ways that only now I can fully appreciate. The first few years were hard. There was much to undo—and I wasn't trusting at all—but through her patience and rock-steady presence, I was able to fully trust that she was going to be there for me, no matter what. And she was. She did it through building a relationship with me—not by slapping labels on me, not by recommending medication or hospitalization—she did it through her very presence, her willingness to let me lead and to trust that I knew where I was going and, when I did veer off, to hold space for me to come back on my own accord.

"At the end of nearly twelve years with this woman, it hit me one day how very much I had taken her for granted in my life. She helped me grow up and was there with me every step of the way in her steadfast way. And even though I don't see her anymore, I feel her presence, patience, and quiet love rooted deep within me, giving me strength and courage as I continue on my journey with the knowledge that I am whole."

Beth's disclosure of her betrayals and learning to trust again has led to profound healing, and Beth is thriving in her knowledge of her wholeness. It took a relationship where she could begin to trust again and her courage to take the risk of knowing and telling her story. It took a place where she could "explore, vent, and ultimately release" the emotions and the betrayals. She was then able to claim her power back, to resent the way she had been treated: "It took years and years to heal from this whole experience. In all honesty, as I look back, I don't think I was as 'sick' or 'crazy' as my first therapist and the system made me out to be. . . . I think the cutting was a product of not being heard and not being able to speak about it. I had come to her to try to understand the flashbacks. I knew deep within myself that I needed to get it out and not keep it inside anymore. . . . When people are told over and over again how sick they are—how dangerous they are to themselves—and are medicated at high doses so that their brains can't function and then are also isolated from their support systems, they do start acting crazy. I did lose myself for a while."

Betrayal can cause us to lose ourselves in the maelstrom of the opinions and treatment of others. Like Beth, we can find our way back to trust ourselves and others. In previous chapters, we met Rebecca, who described her difficulty trusting others. You may remember her comments about how it used to be: "I try people out; I semitrust a couple of people. Actually, three, besides my most recent therapist, whom I do trust. But yeah, I've just been let down so deeply, from infancy, that it's really hard to trust myself. And now that I have a peaceful life where I have myself, for the first time in my life, I don't like people messing that up. I feel like I have to have some control because most of my life I really didn't have any control. Or I didn't feel like I had any control."

Here is the difference that disclosure made to Beth: "Being able to tell my story and not having someone tell me what to do and how to do it, but just listening, just being there for me. And being believed, 'cause I felt like I haven't been believed most of my life. . . . That's the main thing. At this point, having gotten my emotional wounds relatively healed, I now hope to regain as much use as possible of my body and have a life. I have made enormous strides in gaining a good life for myself. After more than sixty years of pain, I now look forward to thirty years or so of joy and peace and creativity."

Cathy's Story:
The Importance of Safety and Hope

Now in her forties, Cathy was finally able to speak her truth. Her story continues from chapter 9, where she spoke of the profound dissociation that she learned to use during her horrific childhood. She spoke now about safety, trust, and hope. For her, it was first necessary to establish a sense of safety, which she found in her therapist's office (whom we'll call Carol): "It was all just trying to find a

safe place. And I didn't find that safe place until after I had my second child, and after I came and met Carol. Her office was the first
safe place. She was my first safe experience."

We asked, "What made it safe?"

"What made it safe . . . She didn't sit there and tell me pretty
much anything. Like, I walked in, and she was honest, she didn't
judge me. And I remember, and I look back and feel so bad because
I was such a brat to her. I grilled her: 'How do you know you can
handle this? What makes you think you can deal with a client like
this?' And she just sat there and rolled with all this anger and hostil-
ity, this snotty little child, and she never—at least, it never showed
if she did—she never judged me. She gave me this container, you
know, it's like we joked about the shit I left on the floor, that I could
just dump it. And she gave me permission to leave it there. She
never said, 'Now clean up your mess and do it right, and do it this
way; and what are you talking about? You should be this, and you
should do that.' She just sat there and looked at me, and I could see
she had this empathetic expression, and she let me have a safe place
to figure it out."

Cathy got thoughtful here. There was a lengthy silence before
she finally said something very important: "Man, I spent years in
therapy. And, you know, there's this part like a kid coming home. I
could come back and be like 'Wait a minute, what about this? What
about that? Oh, my God!' That was huge. When you're betrayed as
a child, you have no idea what a safe place is, you don't know they
exist—you have no concept. None. And then you have a place, and
not only is it safe, but, like I told you, there's so much of this stuff
I forgot because I could process it, I could do work, I could leave it
there, and the gift was I could go out that door and I could just be
a twenty-two-year-old mom struggling through a divorce with two
babies. And that was plenty to deal with. That was a lot. And I could
struggle with the issues of my faith. And I could struggle with 'Who
the fuck do I want to be when I grow up?' because by then my kids
will be, too. That's the biggest gift. That's the beginning: safety. You
can deal with everything else when you have a safe place to process
it. That's it. It's that simple."

Cathy needed to be safe before she could face the abuse and betrayal of her past. She needed that "container" to help her through
the free fall and disorientation of her troubled past that she described

as a darkness, and a time when she could begin to trust her own re-actions and not rely on the adults around her.

"It was like living in darkness and, you know—you keep growing because you're supposed to, there's gotta be light somewhere, and you find light, and it creates a hunger because it validates finding trust and finding safety, finding one person, one safe place, and you go back to the very earliest time when you first felt that 'Ugh, this is wrong.' You go flying backward through time to that moment, and you're like, 'I was right. This is wrong. This is wrong—I was right, I'm okay.' And then it starts the process of being able to go, 'I was right about this, too; I was right about this, too; I was right about this, too.' And you begin to gain confidence, and then you gain hope."

Here, Cathy named the second necessary ingredient for heal-ing—hope. For Cathy, as with Rebecca and Beth and others, trust could help her begin to build new bonds with others and with herself.

We asked, "You began to trust yourself?"

"A little bit, a tiny bit," she said. "Because you still have all this head stuff going on from what you're taught, but there's that seed of hope. And that seed of hope grows. And you start looking for signs, and it's very uncomfortable, and it's very painful, and it's very, very scary because you have one candle in however many years of experience of darkness of safety and trust. So it's a lot easier to go back into the darkness, you know, 'cause, 'Oh, this is comfortable and familiar,' and all that crap that we do; we repeat our cycles. But it gives you hope and that validation that you, at two years old, knew this felt bad—that stays with you, even if you make the choices over and over and over again to go into the comfort of the darkness and hide from your pain and take it easy and to not do the work, there's always that light. Now, that gift, if somebody gives you that gift, which Carol gave me, was a huge gift, was the biggest and most important gift I've ever been given in my life—I can't betray that gift. And that way, I can't continue to betray myself. Because . . . what happens happens. And it stops; eventually, you get to walk away, eventually you get away. Whether it's the twenty-year mar-riage or the abusive father, whoever it is, you get to walk away, but the lesson is: Are you going to start listening to yourself? And are you gonna honor that light? Or are you going to keep betraying yourself? Because that's what we do when we repeat the process."

Cathy was truly searching for herself amid the voices of betrayal and society. "We're taught to betray ourselves. That's how they can mess you up. My mother died when I was eight, you know? I got away from her pretty much scot-free, pretty easy, but man, she taught me really well on how to keep betraying myself. So then you get this head and guts war of 'What am I going to listen to?' because it's so much easier to listen to your head and TV and everybody else in society, and your family or your church—even with good intentions—tell you because they want to believe these things are safe, and maybe for them they are. But when you've had that, you know, you can't blindly trust anything. And that's where the judgment and confusion come in. So you hold onto that light, that little bit, and you keep searching frantically for more."

And Cathy's hope could begin to grow: "Hope. It's hope: 'There might be some more of this; wow, if I found one person like this, maybe there's more.' You don't want to open it too much. . . . You don't look at it directly. But it nourishes that. And if you find someone else who gives you a little bit of that, then it feeds it. It's so frail—it's not frail, it's very fragile, because there are so many other factors that can mess it up, and you do get caught up in your head. But actually, because you bury it so deep, it's very strong."

Safety and hope are necessary ingredients for healing—a healing that can happen only when we are able finally to tell our own story, to claim our identity, to name our own feelings. There is power in this gift of self. As you can see, Beth, Rebecca, and Cathy found healing in the telling of their stories.

Awareness and Parenting

Disclosure and the healing that can follow it can create a space not only for oneself but for relationships with others. Cathy came to therapy after years of being betrayed as a child, and at the time she had two small children. We asked her how awareness of her abuse and betrayals had affected her parenting. Here is part of her answer: "That's a great question—and it's a really hard question. You know, I had my kids so young, and I always joked, because I was too young to know better, but I knew they were gifts, and I knew that this was my one shot at getting it right. And here was this big, huge, screaming chance to get it right because I was a hard-core addict and a prostitute when I met George's [her first son] dad and got pregnant . . . and I knew I had to figure out something different, and the only thing I could think of was, 'Okay, my parents are crazy, and they messed me up, and my siblings are all horrible parents; I'm going to do everything different. Whatever they did, I'm going to do the exact opposite.' Literally. I know that my parents, in their own bizarre way, thought they loved me, but that wasn't love, real love. But you have this perfect, pure, clean—pure clean—light. It's the most amazing, beautiful thing. And George is still the most amazing, beautiful thing in my life. And this is the challenge I have with people who abuse their kids; I understand frustration—God, I've had frustration with those two—and anger and lack of self, but you always try to do better. And I have the firm belief that no matter what I did, after acknowledging the abuse, I did better than my parents."

"After acknowledging the abuse, I did better than my parents." That statement made by Cathy has been backed up by empirical research. What researchers have discovered is that *how* a mother talks about her own childhood is strongly related to the security of her infant.[4] It is important to note here that the mother need not have had a happy childhood but needs to be able to talk about her childhood in an emotionally available way. People who have not faced the betrayals in their lives will often brush off the question about their childhood with a shallow statement that it was okay or even good, but their words do not match the absence of feeling in their reply. Alternatively, those who have suffered betrayals and not faced them may not be able to talk about their childhood at all, except with many contradictions and lack of coherence, or they may report not remembering. Conversely, those who have faced their betrayals can talk about their childhood with lucidity and emotion, and these mothers were likely to have secure infants.

When we asked her to elaborate on the importance of knowing and dealing with her own abuse, Cathy continued, "Yes. This was abuse, this was betrayal. I had to make sense of it. I had to find a way of organizing it to . . . contain it. To keep it away from George, you know, to protect this purity. It's the same way with the internal light of the knowing: You form a container and you build barriers of protection around it, and then you can identify it, you can figure it out, and then you can let it go. . . . There was that feeling that George came from that light inside of me, so I knew that I had to contain it, but I couldn't confine it. So it's keeping it all separate."

For Cathy, knowing about her own abuse was necessary. "I don't know any other way. I don't know any other way. It's the hard part, but God, it opens all the doors of possibilities. But if you're a parent, you have to. You've got to. Otherwise, you're just going to repeat it. And intentions don't mean shit; you can have the best of intentions—the best of intentions and the purest of heart—you know, but if your daddy is telling you that he loves you, and he's having sex with you at ten years old, and you think that's love, you're going to end up somehow messing up. One way or another. And maybe you're not going to repeat the exact cycle of abuse, but you're going to skewer something for your children."

By facing her own traumatic past and coming to terms with it, Cathy was able to raise two beautiful sons who are not ignorant of what their mother went through, but who respect her for the strength to face it.

12

The Healing Power of Telling

There is a healing power in the trust and the hope that come with awareness, as Cathy has told us. Cathy found her way to wholeness only by facing her betrayal and the lies. Disclosure and respectful reception of that disclosure are truly a healing experience.

Just as individuals may benefit from becoming aware of past betrayals, so, too, can larger groups. One context in which this can occur is the workplace. In prior chapters, we talk about institutional betrayal. When an individual dares to shine a light on such betrayal, it can create a terrible shock wave of retaliation, but it can also lead to a greatly improved environment. An entire organization can improve its functioning and well-being through an honest look at the injustices and the unearned entitlements that had been previously keeping the workers from realizing their full potential. Or an entire school district might become more welcoming to disabled students, if a teacher dares to blow the whistle.

In 1998, Dr. Pamella Settlegoode was hired by Portland Public Schools as a physical education teacher on a probationary basis. She was hired specifically to teach students with disabilities in various schools in the district. Not long into her employment, Dr. Settlegoode became concerned about the treatment of disabled students. She was frequently unable to find a place to teach, and she often lacked safe equipment and materials. Settlegoode brought these concerns to her immediate supervisor, but she was told that no one else had complained, and nothing was done about her concerns. At the end of her first year, Dr. Settlegoode wrote to her supervisor's supervisor.[1] She sent a long letter explaining her concerns about what she called "[s]ystematic discrimination, mal-administration, access, pedagogy, curriculum, equity and parity," and "greatly compromised" federal law. "In sum," she wrote, "these sketches offer a portraiture of a form of education that is . . . all too familiar in this country. It wasn't all that long ago when Black African Americans took a back seat on the American School bus (though in Portland, there's still lots of 'Separate, but equal' to go around)." Ultimately, Settlegoode was dismissed from her job for being "difficult." She sued the Portland Public Schools, invoking Oregon's Whistleblower Act. A jury found for her, and she was awarded a large sum. The case was appealed and made its way to the 9th Circuit. The decision was upheld.

One of the issues that the 9th Circuit considered was the impact of Settlegoode's actions on the school environment. As the court noted, Settlegoode's letter

> prompted the teachers to discuss how better to cooperate with each other and how to improve physical education for disabled students. She explained in great detail the meeting that was held in response to the letter: The meeting notes further demonstrate that Settlegoode's letter brought the teachers together to help make positive changes to their department and the physical education program, and that many of the teachers agreed with Settlegoode. The notes describe the "[m]any legitimate issues" mentioned in the letter, such as "[a]ccessibility" and "[e]quipment needs," and say that Settlegoode "has a lot of 'guts'" and that the letter "will help us pull together, now we are on 'the same page.'" A reasonable jury could have found that Settlegoode's letter was harmonizing, rather than disruptive.

Prior to Dr. Settlegoode's courageous acts, the school district had been betraying its disabled students. This was clearly both institutional betrayal to the students and blindness to that betrayal. Although disclosure was risky (Dr. Settlegoode was fired), it also ultimately led to a profoundly positive outcome.

Facing Betrayal on the Societal Level
Leads to Justice

Awareness of betrayal can happen at a societal level as well. Only when we become aware of betrayal can we be moved to action. The betrayal and the betrayal blindness that surrounded the Nazi Holocaust caused gaping wounds in German culture that are still healing today. The Holocaust Museum and other memorials stand as disclosure in a time when there are still cries by Holocaust deniers for people to turn away from awareness. Societies devastated by betrayal, whether it is genocide, child sexual abuse, or domestic violence, must create ways for victims to speak. And we must bear witness to them.

It is here that we all have much to learn from the Truth and Reconciliation Commission, established in 1995 in South Africa after the fall of apartheid. The commission's purpose was to bear witness to the atrocities that had occurred in that country during the last half century. Its work not only bore witness to the betrayals that had happened, the commission also investigated human rights abuses, worked to restore victims' dignity, and planned for their rehabilitation. It was a wrenching experience for all involved. During these hearings, many stories of abuse and betrayal came to light, with victims being given the chance to tell their stories in public and to their abusers. Retired Anglican bishop Desmond Tutu wrote the following about his experience:

> We have been shocked and filled with revulsion to hear of the depths to which we are able to sink in our inhumanity to one another. Our capacity for the sadistic enjoyment of the suffering we have inflicted on one another. The refinement of cruelty in keeping families guessing about the fate and whereabouts of their loved ones, sending them carelessly on a run-around from police station to police station, to hospital and mortuary in a horrendous wild goose chase.

He also reported that as wrenching as the process was, there were rewards:

> But there is another side, a more noble and inspiring one. We have been deeply touched and moved by the resilience of the human spirit. People who by rights should have had the

stuffing knocked out of them, refusing to buckle under intense suffering and brutality and intimidation. People refusing to give up on the hope of freedom. Knowing they were made for something better than the dehumanising awfulness of injustice, oppression. Refusing to be intimidated to lower their sights. It is quite incredible the capacity people have shown to be magnanimous, refusing to be consumed by bitterness and hatred. Willing to meet with those who have violated their persons and their rights. Willing to meet in a spirit of forgiveness and reconciliation. Eager only to know the truth, to know the perpetrator so that they could forgive them. We have been moved to tears. We have laughed. We have been silent and we have stared the beast of our dark past in the eye. And we have survived the ordeal. And we are realising that we can indeed transcend the conflicts of the past. We can hold hands as we realise our common humanity. The generosity of spirit will be full to overflowing when it meets a like generosity. Forgiveness will follow confession and healing will happen and so contribute to national unity and reconciliation.

At the end of the process, the final report pointed out the importance of full disclosure of trauma and betrayal trauma:[2]

Although we may currently be experiencing fatigue about the consequences of the past, it remains true that if we do not deal with the past it will haunt and may indeed jeopardise the future. We need to remember that the Truth and Reconciliation Commission (the Commission) was established in large part because of the dangers of inappropriate forgetting. We acknowledged then and must remember now that moving forward requires acknowledgement of the past, rather than denial. To ignore the suffering of those found by the Commission to be victims would be a particular kind of cruelty. After all, it was the testimony of these victims that gave us a window onto how others saw the past and allowed us to construct an image of the future.

In the process of the hearings, we heard the now familiar refrain that telling the story brings relief. Again, we saw the healing power of disclosure.

The experience itself helped to break an emotional silence, started the process of integrating experiences that had been repressed or shut out for years, alleviated feelings of shame, and, in an atmosphere of acceptance, began to restore dignity and self-respect. One victim reported that he had literally been healed by the process of storytelling: "I feel that what has been making me sick all the time is the fact that I couldn't tell my story. But now it feels like I got my sight back by coming here and telling you the story."

It is striking that this victim who was quoted in the commission report said that by telling, he got his "sight back." In other words, he is no longer blind to betrayal and feels whole.

The commission ends with this important statement:

The challenge to us all is to honour the process and to take responsibility for shaping our future. If we ignore the implications of the stories of many ordinary South Africans, we become complicit in contributing to an impoverished social fabric—to a society that may not be worth the pain the country has endured.

Perhaps you are objecting that your country didn't have apartheid or that the abuses were suffered in South Africa. It may be that the abuses and betrayals that occur in America, for instance, are primarily within the home, such as child abuse and marital infidelity, but they are traumas and betrayal traumas nonetheless. In not knowing and not telling about betrayals and traumas that have been perpetrated in the home and the workplace, we ignore the implications of the stories of many ordinary Americans, and we "become complicit in contributing to an impoverished social fabric."

This issue of awareness about societal betrayal is closely related to the idea of a free press. James D. Wolfensohn, the former president of the World Bank, in a speech to the World Press Freedom Committee about the necessity of a free press, pointed out that "if there is no searchlight on corruption and inequitable practices, you cannot build the public consensus needed to bring about change."[3] In other words, without seeing the betrayal and expressing it freely, we cannot stop injustice.

Sean Bruyea's Story: Speaking Truth to Power

Sean Bruyea, formerly of the Canadian air force, sent us his story of betrayal and awareness: "As with most military members, I joined right out of high school. I was only seventeen. Like West Point and Annapolis, Canada's version known as the Royal Military College began the intense process of indoctrination early: upon the first day of entering university. Resisting indoctrination is often futile. It appeals to and resonates with the deep subconscious; the military indoctrinates because indoctrination makes loyal and effective followers.

"Essential to military indoctrination is the unswerving and reflex willingness to sacrifice one's life. In order to be willing to sacrifice my life for Canada and Canadians, I firmly believed that the government institutions were worthy of my sacrifice by being nothing less than perfect, noble, and sacred.

"After becoming disabled in the military, I was summarily released without the slightest economic, medical, or social support assistance. This was a serious blow to my perception of a perfect nation and government. However, I had to desperately cling to the perception that my disabilities were gained protecting, maybe not a perfect but at least a noble and honoured government system."

Sean Bruyea served as an intelligence officer in the Canadian air force for fourteen years and was deployed to Qatar during the first Gulf War (1990–1991). The personal consequences of that war were devastating for him. He became depressed and suffered from post-traumatic stress disorder, leaving him totally and perhaps permanently disabled. At the time, Sean had an unswerving belief in the system in which he had served honorably and was convinced that "government institutions were worthy of my sacrifice by being nothing less than perfect, noble, and sacred." As a result, when he was summarily dismissed from the military without any benefits or assistance, he began to question the institution that he had so staunchly supported. Yet he still couldn't face the betrayal and still needed to believe in "a noble and honoured government system."

Sean now understands that this is betrayal blindness, but it was a difficult process for him to realize the full extent of the betrayal. "The system established to purportedly assist disabled veterans was daunting in complexity, bureaucracy, delays, and ambiguously obscure requirements. This system, I learned, was geared more toward perpetuating arcane and bizarre internal processes than responding to the limits and needs of disabled veterans and their families.

"I believed that being an honorable government system, it was likely unaware of its failings or else it would have addressed them. I also believed that all I needed to do was point out the flaws and recommend improvements. Surely, I thought, once government knew of its shortcomings, it would respond quickly to fix them.

"Why should I believe anything different about the government system for which I was willing to die? It freely, repeatedly, and vociferously espouses sacred principles and rights, such as freedom of speech, freedom from discrimination based upon disability, equality, justice, and ethical service to the public. I never imagined that this system would break not only these principles but Canadian privacy laws, while organizing widespread resources of the bureaucratic machine to stop my cry to help other veterans from being heard."

In 2005, Sean began to stand up in public to halt a program to replace lifelong pensions for disabled veterans with one-time lump sums. Even though he was never going to be affected by the program, he wanted to protect others who would be given an "inadequate lump sum." He testified to the Senate and then to the House of Commons, urging them to stop this replacement. The legislation passed over his objections, and anyone who opposed the plan was threatened with being called a "veteran hater." After this initial speaking out, Sean was effectively deserted by two colleagues who had helped him in his initial stand, when they were both placed in highly lucrative positions in the government. In order to accept these positions, they had to adhere to confidentiality agreements that severely limited their ability to speak publicly on veterans' issues, leaving Sean as the sole opposing voice.

It was shortly after this that the retaliation started. "Bureaucrats in the department began denying and questioning my treatment, which had never been questioned for more than five years prior. Secretive audits of every aspect of my benefits were initiated, and delays for reimbursement for medical care placed great financial strain upon my wife and me."

At this time, Sean's nongovernment medical team came to his aid. They warned the department that improperly scrutinizing and questioning what had never been questioned was causing him harm. They also underscored that any actions to remove his treatment would have grim and possibly fatal consequences.

Sean continued, "As a result, certain non–medically trained officials in government concocted an increasingly devious plan. They would invite me alone to a meeting, wherein I would be instructed to immediately submit to a week-long (or more) inpatient psychiatric assessment at a Veterans Affairs facility. Results of this assessment had been provided to the minister more than three weeks prior to the planned meeting.

"Essentially, the planned assessment would conclude that all my treatment would cease. If I refused the treatment, the minister was told and apparently agreed that all my treatment would cease. All I was told was that this would be a friendly meeting, with no agenda. There was an important stipulation: my medical practitioners would not be allowed to attend."

Ultimately, Sean declined to attend any meeting that did not include his health care practitioners, and a change of government in 2006 brought this plan to a halt, and he personally appealed to the new prime minister.

He renewed his struggle to stop the lump-sum payments for veterans. "I believed that surely the new government would stop the legislation to replace lifelong pensions with lump sums. I contacted the minister's staff in an attempt to brief him before bureaucrats could get to him. Instead, my personal cellular telephone number was leaked by political staff to bureaucrats who wrote the new law. They called me and brazenly reported back to their bosses that they tried to stop me from seeing the new minister. These bureaucrats unabashedly wrote to each other of the conversation wherein they told me I would never succeed in stopping the new program.

"The Prime Minister's Office was then to call me days later. Not once but twice, they asked me to not hold a press conference that I had planned. I held the press conference anyway. The next day, the most powerful offices of the country, the prime minister, the Privy Council, the minister, and the most senior bureaucracy in Veterans Affairs held a meeting to deal with me and my press conference. What plan they implemented is still shrouded from public view, but the effect was to isolate me from having any substantive influence upon or any input into government."

Sean was devastated and discouraged. He strongly believed in his stand in support of future veterans and reached out to a previous military commander for a reference: "He refused to be a reference. His reason: I had been 'talking with the Washington media.' He was referring to an article in the *Washington Post* in the spring of 2006 which quoted me regarding the policy of not lowering flags for deceased military personnel returning from Afghanistan."

It was only then that Sean could begin to question the immense betrayal by the organization that had promised to protect him. "Even with a once close comrade abandoning, in effect, betraying me, the military indoctrination held fast. Nonetheless, I began to question all that I had sacrificed in uniform. In typical black-and-white military thinking, either the government was undeserving of my sacrifice or the government was still sacred and noble and I was somehow deserving of the reprisals, the rescinded loyalty, the intimidation, the betrayal.

"I was in an existential dilemma," he said. "Suffering PTSD and major depression, along with my physical disabilities, dragged me into a swirling suicidal vortex of confusion, self-loathing, terror, and worthlessness. Either I would succumb to the easy comfort of death, or I could emerge from self-loathing into a world that by now was a one-dimensional terrifying monochrome shade of betrayal."

Sean credited two things for his continuing struggle—the love of his wife and the rebirth of compassion within himself for those who would be affected by what he considered an unjust system. "I came to understand that I could not just feel, but some portion of me could actually 'be' compassion. I will admit it was not a large part of me, with so much pain, terror, anger, and confusion. However, the unswerving connection of my wife with me showed me that love, kindness, patience, all that makes our world a better place, is not something we just act out for others. Part of us actually becomes kind and patient, while a definable measure in us becomes loving.

"Calling out to change the system to protect others became my new noble cause. Even while I struggled with a depression-tattered ego and negligent self-worth, as only PTSD can warp our own perception of our value to others, I inched forward toward meaning and away from fear.

"I made a personal commitment to myself: I would attempt to prevent what happened to me from ever happening to another soldier less resourceful or fortunate than me.

"To do this, my first step must be stand up to government. I knew that confidential information surrounding the disabilities and benefits of veterans was the most personal and intimate information one could have on a proud veteran and once proud soldier. If this private part of their lives was taken from them and distorted in malicious proportions, I knew that so many of these fragile veteran soldiers would succumb to the inevitable messages of self-destruction. The heart of these messages is inevitably poisonous helplessness and humiliation, resulting from having lost control of the most intimate part of themselves.

"In effect, having someone or something else take away what is most important to us is akin to suffering a spiritual incontinence over which we are powerless to prevent the spilling of our souls. Wounded soldiers are especially vulnerable to such a powerless spiritual disease."

So Sean began to write. First, he wrote to senior bureaucrats (who never responded) and then to the public to bring awareness of a system that betrayed its promises to the most vulnerable, the most silent: disabled veterans and their families. He also began to collect evidence about what that system had done to him. "Days became months. In our cold, damp, and increasingly crowded basement, I sorted, read, and cried profusely, fighting against the pull to believe what distortions of me they freely passed around like confetti at a wedding. I fought to make sense of what has now become more than 20,000 pages that bureaucrats proudly wrote, shared, briefed, and filed away in their own personal vaults . . . all about me.

"Multiple senior bureaucrats, including the highest ranking, the deputy minister, opened dedicated files on me. Briefing notes for ministers were circulated like supermarket tabloids to more than 75 executive bureaucrats (Canada's department of Veterans Affairs has only 1,400 employees in its Head Office and only 4,000 employees total). Two ministers, a Parliamentary secretary, and even my member of Parliament either saw the Briefing Notes or were briefed according to their contents. The Prime Minister's Office, the highest office of our land, was even given similar information.

"Ultimately, more than 857 individuals (those whom I know of) shared and accessed private information on me.

"This was all too overwhelming, all too helpless, all too humiliating. I had to grow in order to survive. I had to believe that life was more than distorted medical summaries written by non–medically trained bureaucrats. I had to believe that my right to say no was more powerful and more sacred than any trite and inaccurate summary of what others thought I was. I am . . . I had to be, more than that."

Sean had to grow in order to survive the betrayal—something that all of us have to do to cope with such enormous grief and anger. And Sean did grow. In the face of his betrayal, Sean continued to collect documents and to speak out. He began to write articles to show the government that it could not push disabled soldiers around. More than forty published (newspaper) articles later, he enrolled in a Masters of Ethics program in Ottawa. Then he was selected to present three papers at an academic forum on Military and Veterans Health.

And the government? "Since my revelations of what became known as the privacy scandal came to public light, four senior executives intimately connected to this privacy scandal have resigned with full pension and benefits. However, a number of key culprits remain. Being the first individual to publicly call for an Ombudsman in 2004, I was relieved to see such an office was created in 2007. It is still quite powerless, and the will of the senior officer is less than admirable, but at least the office exists.

"I have also received confirmation that the interim public service integrity commissioner has reopened my complaint and determined that indeed the previous officer should never have refused to investigate. The office has determined that on four important counts, Veterans Affairs committed substantial wrongdoing. Will this integrity officer do something to change the system? I doubt it, but I will try my best to make sure he does.

"Has anyone been punished? Will any bureaucrat be dissuaded from doing the same to another? Have injured soldiers and veterans been treated with greater dignity? Has the program I originally criticized been rescinded?

"Sadly, no to all of these."

Sean may never be able to come to terms with the betrayal of the military and his government, but in becoming aware of and standing up to that betrayal, Sean has discovered new life in himself and has discovered new allies: "The media became an ally. It even became a friend and a compassionate advocate for not just me but for the very individuals I was trying to help: injured soldiers and their families. This was an incredible shift for a country that does much to ignore its veterans except during Remembrance

Day. Almost every editorial board of every major daily newspaper in Canada condemned the privacy violations. Newspapers, radio, and TV carried the story over a six-week period.

"With this information, normally passive Canadians came alive. They wrote letters to members of Parliament, they wrote letters to newspapers, and they wrote to me, encouraging me to keep fighting, to continue helping others. The Canadian government may have abandoned me, but many Canadians did not. I felt a sense of growing pride and maybe peace that perhaps my military sacrifice and my sacrifice to help other veterans were not in vain. The betrayal of the system became less monolithic and more a manifestation of greedy, small people. In contrast, so many more good people helped me stand up to those who would otherwise take my dignity.

"Will public education eventually change this culture of immunity in government? Will Canada sacrifice for its soldiers the way its soldiers sacrificed for Canada?

"I can only answer that I hope so. This may not be a definitive answer. However, remember it was hope that kept me alive in the darkest days when bureaucrats tried to silence my voice. It was hope that kept my wife and me close when we felt our most alone, and it was hope that has given us a new life, in more ways than we could have ever hoped for."

Sean's story is one of courage and compassion in the face of betrayal and retaliation. His story has much to teach all of us about the struggles of becoming aware of betrayal and facing it squarely.

On the floor of the Canadian House of Commons, Veterans Affairs minister Jean-Pierre Blackburn issued the apology.[4] Blackburn said that he and the government are "truly sorry for the needless suffering and anxiety caused by the dissemination of the medical and financial files among hundreds of public servants." Bruyea accepted the apology, wisely observing, "That helps a lot. . . . It's not about money, it's about fixing the system."[5]

Speaking out about betrayals is risky, but this awareness and honesty have the potential to fix the system. Silence keeps the injustices intact. As a society, we pay enormous attention to some suffering and ignore equally horrific suffering. We ignore suffering when we respond with betrayal blindness. This is understandable, given what we know of human psychology, but we can do better in this world by purposely paying attention to betrayal and righting the wrong.

13

Speaking Our Truth

In chapter 10, we began the telling of our story together, as friends and colleagues, and about the betrayal that happened when we were just getting to know each other. It was a confusing and disorienting time for both of us, much as betrayal and knowing betrayal were upsetting for Rebecca, Beth, Cathy, and others whose stories we have told.

Here is the rest of our story, first as told by Jennifer Freyd: "The situation became more and more difficult until finally in August 1993, eight months pregnant with my third child and by then a tenured full professor, I gave the one and only speech I have ever delivered that discussed my personal situation related to delayed memories. The context was another professional conference (in Ann Arbor, Michigan), where I gave an invited presentation: 'Personal and Theoretical Perspectives on the Delayed Memory Debate.' After presenting betrayal trauma theory, I turned to a very different presentation. My personal speech began this way:

> I will now break with tradition—at least, my tradition until today—and speak about my personal experience with some of the issues that are the focus of discussion at this conference. As many of you know, the False Memory Syndrome Foundation (FMSF) was founded, and is now directed, by my mother, Pamela Freyd. It is widely known that my

parents claim to be "falsely accused" of sexual abuse by their daughter.

Numerous newspaper stories about the FMSF have presented my parents' status as falsely accused. Just last month, on the NPR evening radio news show *All Things Considered*, the reporter, Wendy Schmelzer, said, "For the last year, Dr. [Pamela] Freyd has criss-crossed the country attending similar meetings; each time with the same message for her audience—'You are not alone. My husband and I were also falsely accused.'"

Not only is it widely known that my parents were accused of sexual abuse, and not only is it widely assumed that the accusation was "false," but the details of their story are also—most strangely—widely known. My mother published her version of being falsely accused under the name "Jane Doe," and this published story has been circulated widely. Many people learn of the Jane Doe story in such a way that they know it is about the Freyd family; others learn the story without knowing the identity of the characters but believing the details to be accurate. I find the latter situation unnerving; I find the former situation—where people get exposed to Jane Doe, thinking it is about me—horribly invasive and violating. As one clinician said at a national meeting recently about the FMSF: "There is persuasive evidence that this organization grew out of one family's feud that's overgrown its boundaries and come into the popular culture."

In speaking about personal matters today, I would like to offer my truth in the hope that it will inform you of aspects of the context out of which FMSF grew. I would never have chosen to be here today speaking about my personal life, were circumstances not what they are. I make this decision partly because I have already lost so much of my privacy, and in such an unclear and distorted way, that I have come to desire clarity and public truth as the lesser of two undesirable situations. I also speak about these matters today because I hope what I have to share will help, directly or indirectly, other abused children and adult survivors of abuse. I hope that speaking my truth is, in the end, healing for myself and for others.

The truth I wish to speak about today pertains to *patterns* of behavior. I will speak about a pattern of behavior my parents have exhibited toward me in my childhood and are continuing into the present: a pattern of boundary violation, a pattern of invasion and control, a pattern of inappropriate and unwanted sexualization, a pattern of family and relationship dysfunction, and a pattern of intimidation and manipulation.

Despite these unfortunate things that I will be talking about today, I would also like you to know that I consider myself privileged in many ways. Most fundamentally, I am privileged to be a part of the family my partner and I have created—a family that happens to include particularly lovable children.

Later on in the speech, I went on to say:

My parents have severely violated my privacy. They use the foundation in a personal way. Earlier this year, for instance, my mother wrote a personal letter to my mother-in-law on FMSF letterhead, signing the letter with her title as executive director. The letter, which is dated February 17, 1993, was hostile to my husband and me, included the name of my therapist, and implied that my mother-in-law might be "cut off from the grandchildren." This entirely unsolicited letter was deeply upsetting to my mother-in-law, a woman in her late seventies, living alone and with no desire to have contact with my parents (she had experienced my father as verbally abusive and had avoided contact with him long before my husband raised the topic of my childhood sexual abuse with her). With her letter, my mother included the FMSF brochure. This is embarrassing and painful to me. It is as if the weight of a whole foundation stands behind my mother's frenzied denial of my reality [of childhood sexual abuse].

Until now, . . . only one side of our family story has been made public, and my silence has been taken as complicity. And the very nature of the publicity has been such that there is no accountability. Jane Doe wrote an anonymous article—it could be about anyone. And yet an enormous number of people received that article with a cover letter from Pamela Freyd. Indeed, I get calls from investigative journalists, and some of them contact me fully aware that

"Jane Doe" is my mother. As one reporter pointed out to me, the February 1992 FMSF newsletter in fact indicates that the executive director is "Jane Doe" and then in subsequent letters that the executive director is Pamela Freyd. Colleagues have told me that they have received the Jane Doe article from my mother herself, in which she makes clear her identity as author. In other cases, I have been given copies of letters from my mother, or letters in response to my mother, making reference to Pamela Freyd as Jane Doe. I find this invasion of my privacy horrifying.

It would be bad enough if the Jane Doe story were accurate. But not only is my privacy invaded in this way, the article is defaming. In a recent electronic message from my father, he finally makes explicit acknowledgment of the untruths in the Jane Doe article. My father explains that a reporter he knows thinks "he can put together stuff from the Jane Doe article and the Darryl Sifford columns, but in both cases fictional elements were deliberately inserted, and—unless we go on record—the reporter has no way of determining what those are."

"Fictional" is rather an astounding choice of words. The Jane Doe article incorrectly states, for instance, that I was denied tenure at a previous university due to lack of major publications, and that as of 1990–91 I was not sufficiently productive. In fact, I moved to the University of Oregon in 1987, just four years after receiving my PhD, to accept a tenured position as associate professor in the Psychology Department, one of the world's best psychology departments, especially in the area of cognitive psychology. My previous university, also a fine university, was unwilling to match a tenure offer that was two years early but otherwise made an attempt to keep me from leaving for Oregon. The article also includes extensive discussion of my supposed sex life—a largely inaccurate discussion. My mother sent the Jane Doe article to my colleagues during my promotion year—that is the year my case for promotion to full professor was being considered. I was absolutely mortified to learn of this violation of my privacy and this violation of the truth.[1]

As a child, I experienced significant betrayals in my family of origin. I remained blind to that betrayal until my early thirties. When I did remember the betrayal, the consequences were profound. Some of those consequences were difficult to manage, largely because of the social response to my story being told. Although I did disclose my memories to a few people close to me, my story was broadcast widely beyond my wishes or control. On the one hand, close friends and some family members provided great support and allowed me to heal in a way I never would have without awareness, disclosure, and social support. On the other hand, my parents, some colleagues, and ultimately a national organization caused me significant suffering by their reaction to my private history.

Betrayal of this magnitude demands response. We were lucky. It was a betrayal that we could not be blind to and one that we were motivated to confront. Both of us were faculty members in a psychology department and had the power to name the betrayal and claim our voices, much as Cathy, Rebecca, and Beth have done.

Pamela Birrell's response was in the form of an open letter dated September 1, 1993, to the advisory board members of the False Memory Syndrome Foundation:

As a close friend of Jennifer Freyd, I have watched the development of the False Memory Syndrome Foundation (FMSF) from the beginning. Recently, Dr. Freyd eloquently and effectively documented the unwelcome intrusion of this organization, founded by her parents, into her professional life. . . . In addition, as a clinical psychologist, I have seen the damage done by this organization to survivors of *documented* sexual abuse as they struggle to establish their own reality and to deal with the overwhelming pain of their trauma. I can remain silent no longer.

I am writing this letter to ask all of you to examine your motives and to look at the consequences of your membership on the advisory board of this particular foundation. There are several reasons for membership on this particular board and therefore association with an organization of this type. They are as follows:

1. Advisory Board membership as an enhancement of professional life and credentials.

   I have heard board member Dr. George Ganaway state on two occasions that his affiliation with this organization in no way communicates his agreement or disagreement with the official stance of the organization.[2] In other words, he sees his board membership as neutral and entirely advisory in nature. I would hope that Dr. Ganaway and others of you on the board for this reason could see that this is not a neutral stance. I am sure that he would not be on the advisory board of *Paidika* (a Danish journal for and about pedophilia), even to advise them in the "right" direction. Membership noted in their publications implies agreement [with] and support [of] and, furthermore, offers scientific credibility to the "false memory syndrome" where none exists. An example of this can be seen in the popular press: "In March, 1992, a group of distinguished psychologists . . . banded together to form the FMSF." The author goes on to state the FMSF position in a way that is truly damaging to incest survivors. For example, the author states that the "better-trained, older psychiatrists do not believe that childhood memories of trauma can be repressed for any length of time, except in rare cases of brain damage."[3] This statement is not only damaging but patently untrue, as anyone aware of the literature will agree.[4]

2. Anger against psychotherapists and the field of psychotherapy.

   The FMSF emphasizes the harm being done by bad therapy and megalomaniac therapists.[5] This is a legitimate stance (although somewhat overstated, as I note below). Any profession in this country can benefit from constructive criticism, both from within and from outside its ranks, and therapists need to continually monitor their activities. But for those of you who are on the board for this reason, wouldn't it be more intellectually honest to join or form a group that specifically targets therapists and not their clients? The name, False Memory Syndrome, clearly implies that the person with the memories is, at worst, a liar and, at best, a naive and unwilling pawn in the hands of the malignant therapist.

I would like to add a parenthetical note here. There is no question that bad therapists exist and bad therapy happens, but it is important to remember that many of the memories of incest reported are recovered under normal circumstances, in and out of therapy. Although there is power in the transference, and therapists need to be aware of this, we just do not have the kind of power attributed to us. I often sit in my office with a client who is in great pain while he or she recounts uninvited and overwhelming memories of abuse. If I had the kind of power attributed to me by the FMSF, I would stop the pain and stop the memories as soon as I could. Therapists are not out to "make monsters." Good therapy assists in creating conscious and whole human beings who are able to deal with pain in their lives in a constructive manner.

3. To promote the scientific study of memory.

There are those of you who may feel that this "foundation" offers the opportunity and platform for the scientific study of memory. Can the goals of objectivity in science be met by an organization that appears dedicated to proving that memories of abuse are false? How many of you give the same credence to research on the effects of smoking done by the American Tobacco Institute, compared to that same research done by researchers supported by neutral grants at universities? The scientific study of memory needs to stay at universities and other institutions of basic research that are uncontaminated by a self-serving bias.

4. To help reunite families torn apart by claims of incest.

The goal of reuniting families is most worthy. It is hard to see family members accusing one another, while simultaneously longing for reconciliation. However, a foundation named the False Memory Syndrome Foundation is hardly the vehicle for this reunification, given that its very name contains an accusation and also denies the reality of at least one family member. FMSF may argue that this reality is not a true one because it was "implanted" by therapists, but in healthy families, members do not attack one another's reality. I think that the true absurdity of this can be seen in the invitation to Jennifer Freyd by her parents to join the advisory board of this organization.

It is a common phenomenon for people to become angry with their parents during the course of psychotherapy. It is also a common phenomenon for these same people to enter into a mature and conscious relationship with their parents later in therapy—at least, when those parents do not continue to attack their children's vulnerability. I know of cases where incest has occurred and yet reunion has been possible because of the parents' willingness to confront their own behavior and to remain in relationships without intrusion. This would be even more likely to happen in families where "false memories" have been "implanted."

The problem of abuse in our society is a complex one. It involves power, control, victimization, denial, and, most of all, pain. Peter Vaill has movingly described the pain in our organizations and in our culture: "We can't just share our pain and confusion with each other. . . . There is massive suppression of anguish going on in the organizations and communities of the developed world—no one's fault in particular; just a fundamental part of our culture. I think there is a lot of collective, but unexpressed, anguish in our modern organizations."[6] We, as a society, must find ways to experience and share this pain. There are no simple solutions. Some therapists have attempted to foreclose on the pain by attaching it to discrete memories. The FMSF has attempted to cover the pain by attacking the messenger. We need to somehow be able to go through the pain to find the meaning it holds for each of us.

I would ask that each of you consider carefully your particular motives for being associated with this organization and to decide whether your objectives are being met. Jennifer Freyd has been deeply hurt by this organization, as have many other survivors. Those dealing with real memories of incest are in turmoil, in pain, and in constant doubt of their own reality. They feel shameful, anxious, and frightened. It is often easier for them to believe that they are crazy than to face the truth of their past. This organization has done them a great disservice. It is particularly tragic because the needs of a small number of those [who are] truly falsely accused could have been met without causing such damage.[7]

Only two members of the board ever responded to the letter, and their responses were terse and uncompromising, basically stating that they did not see this side of the controversy at all and were not willing to engage in dialogue.

This is how it all began. Perhaps the clarity of this betrayal was its saving grace for us. We could no longer be blind. Speaking out was wrenching for both of us. We spoke out at a time when the powers of society and our profession were clearly aligned on the side of blindness and oppression of survivors. We feared and received reprisal, which included being disinvited to speaking engagements and getting threatening letters. We were even picketed outside the psychology building. It was a harrowing time, and we were tempted to retreat into our academic havens. We are truly glad we didn't. Only when blindness is gone can healing truly begin.

Betrayal can separate us from others, but betrayals when confronted can bring us together. This is what happened to us. Twenty years after encountering and then confronting the Jane Doe article, we continue to learn and discover together.

14

Now I See:
Facing Betrayal Blindness

Throughout this book, we have laid out the many ways that betrayal and betrayal blindness can separate us from one another, can silence us, and can create an atmosphere of distrust and hopelessness. It is only in facing betrayal and the pain of it that we can grow into ourselves and claim our own truth. All of the people who were brave enough to tell us their stories have both demonstrated the toxicity of betrayal and its blindness and also planted seeds of hope. They all have gone from isolation and despair to hope and at least the promise of intimacy in their lives. They are more comfortable in their own skins, and they are able to love and trust themselves and others more wholeheartedly. They have demonstrated the healing power of loving relationships and the importance of showing that love to each other. There is no single way of accomplishing this healing. Their stories, however, as well as the research we have described, point to some general guidelines to prevent and recover from betrayal and its blindness.

You picked up this book for a reason. Perhaps you are reading this book simply because you find the topic fascinating. Perhaps you work for an institution that has the power to betray, and you would like to create an environment where betrayal is addressed and blindness is confronted. Perhaps you know someone struggling with betrayal and its devastating effects. Perhaps you are grappling with a dawning awareness of betrayal and betrayal blindness in your own life.

If you are touched by betrayal in any of these ways, you may be wondering what you can do to confront, heal from, and prevent betrayal and its blindness. As we conclude this book, we'd like to offer some suggestions for awareness and healing. These suggestions are for people who have been betrayed, their friends and supporters, as well as those institutions and individuals who hold the power either to betray or to create a safer world. This is by no means an exhaustive list, but rather a starting place.

For Those Who Suspect
They Have Been Betrayed

If you suspect or know that you have been betrayed, first of all take care of yourself. Betrayal is pernicious, especially if you have been blind to it. Although that blindness helped you survive by protecting important relationships, you have likely paid a high price in harm to your well-being. If you have been blind to betrayal, you have likely developed habits of perception, habits of thought, and patterns of behavior that are geared more to the maintenance of necessary relationships than to freedom, intimacy, and healing. As a consequence, you may have trouble believing in yourself or forming safe and loving relationships. In general, you may not have developed habits that show self-caring and self-nurturing. Change might even seem impossible to you. Yet change is possible. Here are some places to start. Some of these are obvious, but others are less so.

The Role of the Body

In chapter 9, we describe research showing that exposure to traumatic betrayal has many toxic effects. This includes basic physical health. People who have been extensively betrayed tend not to be as physically healthy as those who have not had such a history. It is difficult to do the relational and emotional work of healing without first addressing your basic physical health.

First, it is important to have adequate sleep hygiene. You need to get sufficiently restful and uninterrupted sleep in order to heal the mind. Try to go to bed only you are when sleepy and wake up around the same time every day. Adhere to bedtime routines that will give your body cues that it is time to slow down and sleep. For example, you might try listening to relaxing music, reading something soothing, having a cup of caffeine-free tea, or doing relaxation exercises.

Second, you need to get sufficient exercise. Do what you like to do, as long as you are moving your body. Ride your bike, swim, dance, walk, do yoga, or do whatever physical activity brings you pleasure. It is hard to overestimate the benefits of exercise on your sense of well-being.

Third, make an effort to eat well and to eat foods that make your body thrive. This means eating a variety of whole foods. Most people find that they feel more energetic and healthy if they avoid excessive amounts of foods that are high in salt, saturated and trans fats, cholesterol, and added sugar. You may discover that eating a sufficient amount of protein (such as fish, beans, raw nuts, and seeds) and a large variety of fruits, vegetables, and whole grains gives your body a feeling of fullness and health.

If these measures—sleeping well, exercising, and adhering to a healthy diet—fail to bring a sense of good health, it is essential that you see a doctor to assess whether there are underlying conditions.

If you do attend to basic physical self-care, your body can be a powerful ally. Although we rarely think of our bodies as important in dealing with a psychological problem such as betrayal, in fact the body can be crucial in promoting our awareness and healing. A friend and colleague put it this way: "My biggest protection now against betrayal blindness is being more fully in my body and paying careful attention to what it is telling me. When I had my worst experiences of betrayal, I was numb and dissociated from my body. I've taken up a martial art, which has fast-tracked my awareness of what danger and threat feel like, because I need to notice them in training in order to be able to respond and not be blind to the realities of attack (even though it's a training attack, it's still a place in which I can get physically hurt!). I now know what I feel when my body's cheater detectors come online, and I've learned to stop and pay careful and close attention to those physical sensations."

Being in touch with our bodies is indispensable for overall health, overall healing, and becoming aware of betrayals.

The Role of Relationships

As important as a healthy body is for healing, equally important are healthy relationships. In simple terms, it is a good idea to stay away from people who feel toxic to you, spend time with people who feel safe to you, and seek out relationships in which you feel good about yourself.

Psychologist Belle Liang and her colleagues developed the "Relational Health Indices Scale."[1] We have found that the items from this scale provide useful information to assess the health of current relationships. Ask yourself some of the following questions (based on the Relational Health Index) about a friend:

1. Even when I have difficult things to share, I can be honest and real with my friend.
2. After a conversation with my friend, I feel uplifted.
3. The more time I spend with my friend, the closer I feel to him/her.
4. I feel understood by my friend.
5. It is important to us to make our friendship grow.
6. I can talk to my friend about our disagreements without feeling judged.
7. My friendship inspires me to seek other friendships like this one.
8. I am comfortable sharing my deepest feelings and thoughts with my friend.
9. I have a greater sense of self-worth through my relationship with my friend.
10. I feel positively changed by my friend.
11. I can tell my friend when he/she has hurt my feelings.
12. My friendship causes me to grow in important ways.

If you answered yes to all or most of these questions, then you are likely in a healthy relationship with your friend. However, if you answered no to many of them, the relationship may not be one in which you can grow and heal. Perhaps you can change this relationship. You might find that if you model the behaviors you want from your friend, some positive changes will naturally occur. If you cannot repair your current friendships, find friends or perhaps a therapist to create a relationship in which you can answer these questions affirmatively.

Another way of thinking about this was suggested to us by our friend and colleague. Here is what she said: "I've also learned to notice when I'm having a long argument with someone else in my head. That's a data point that I am being unseen and unheard and could be at risk of being betrayed. If I'm in those conversations with someone, I know that I need to pay attention to how I'm silencing myself in the relationship and move toward unsilencing."

Do you ever feel silenced in this way in your current relationships? Perhaps it is time to either speak up or seek a relationship in which you don't feel silenced.

Yet another way of thinking about this is in terms of the dependence you may have in certain relationships. Relationships that you feel you "cannot live without" and those in which you feel psychologically, financially, or physically dependent on someone else are potentially relationships in which blindness develops. Dependency in relationships is not necessarily a bad thing. In fact, we are all dependent on others. Interdependence is healthy. However, sometimes extreme dependency can be toxic, increasing the probability of betrayal and betrayal blindness. You might ask yourself if you are comfortable with your level of dependency on a particular relationship. If not, is it possible for you to become less dependent? Either way, it is wise to be aware that dependency can potentially make you prone to betrayal blindness.

The Role of Disclosure

In chapter 11, we discuss the healing that comes from knowing and telling about betrayal. We also discuss the importance of disclosing only when it is safe. Ideally, you can find someone who will listen to you nonjudgmentally and will support you as tell your story. Research we discuss in chapter 10 also suggests that you might get benefits from telling your story in a private way, perhaps by writing in a journal. Words, whether spoken or written, can be a powerful way to communicate a betrayal story, but they are not the only way. Music, art, and dance can be used to express a betrayal experience.

Some people have been particularly creative in figuring out ways to disclose and tell their stories. Lana R. Lawrence, an accomplished photographer, found it helpful to work through her history of betrayal using flow charts. Flow charts are both visual and well-suited for recording facts. Lana experienced a number of severe childhood betrayals at the hands of caregivers, as well as subsequent and intersecting betrayals when she tried to get help for the initial injuries. She was able to capture the sequence of events, their complex interactions, and the scope of the betrayals by creating flow charts. "I think that flow charts are a really good way of visualizing the

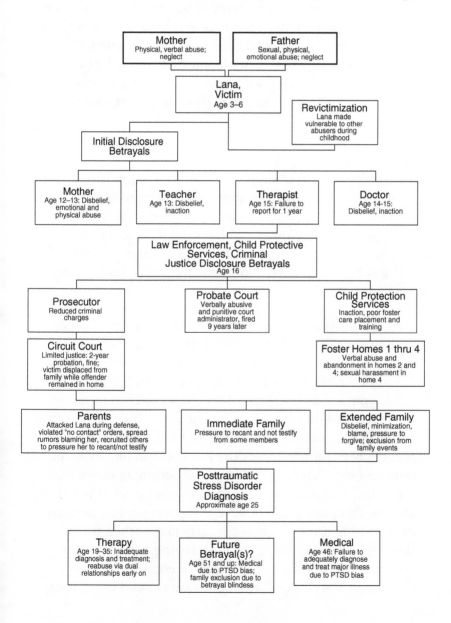

initial trauma and then the subsequent traumas that might follow. I've done it for each parent and began with each disclosure in my teens and then through the court system, the family losses/betrayals, religion, the educational system, mental health system and medical system betrayals, and so on. I am sure there will be categories in the future, as I wonder if betrayals related to the initial trauma can span a lifetime."

In disclosing your story to another person, the way that he or she listens is crucial. Later in this chapter, we discuss ways that friends and other supportive people can be good listeners. Knowing what good listening consists of should help you select others to whom you can safely tell your story. Remember that you can be harmed by someone who does not listen to you respectfully and nonjudgmentally.

Understanding the Process

Even with all of this in place—a healthy body, supportive relationships, and safe disclosure—healing from betrayal and its blindness is challenging. It is not a simple process of telling and then knowing. Jennifer M. Gómez and Laura Noll, doctoral students in clinical psychology, recently captured some of this complexity and offered the following advice for someone newly confronting betrayal blindness.

> First, understand that betrayal blindness has served a purpose in your life. Particularly with family members or others you must coexist with, you may have been experiencing what we call "rotating betrayal blindness." This occurs when you are aware of the betrayal at one moment but then later find that you speak, act, or feel as if you were not aware that there has been betrayal in the relationship. Removing betrayal blindness does not occur in one moment, once and for all. It is more likely that becoming fully aware takes time and that you will rotate in and out of blindness. During this time, you will need a support system, perhaps even outside professional help, particularly when the relationship has been lifelong or long-lasting, in order to help you endure the pain of fully acknowledging the relationship for what it is (laced with betrayal and good times, too),

as opposed to what your betrayal blindness allowed you to believe.

Betrayal blindness has indeed served a purpose in your life. It has kept you safe at times when there was no safety. Although overcoming blindness is ultimately one of the most healing things you can do, it does have its costs. You may find yourself falling into that free fall we described earlier, not knowing what or whom to trust. Only you will know if this is the time to take on this challenge. Trust yourself, find others you can trust, and understand that you might not be ready yet.

If you do decide that the time is right to confront betrayal and betrayal blindness in your own life, and you are confident you are addressing your need for a healthy body, supportive relationships, and safe disclosure, be gentle with yourself. This will be hard work and will take time. Take as long as you need. During this period, do things that bring beauty and joy to you. Each person has his or her own delights. We find spending time in nature, playing or listening to music, and reading a good book to be among the ways we can find that rejuvenating beauty and joy.

For Friends and Supporters

William Schumacher, a beginning therapist, told us the following: "As I've seen clients in the clinic, I've been struck by how powerful disclosing trauma can be. Being an active and supportive listener goes a long way in helping trauma survivors heal."

What does active and supportive listening look like? In chapter 10, we review research by Melissa Foynes and Jennifer Freyd on effective listening. That research included teaching people some basic listening skills. Here are some suggestions, based on the educational materials the researchers developed.

First, it is important to use attentive body language. This means demonstrating that you are interested through your facial expressions, posture, and eye contact. Second, use words that encourage the speaker to continue. For example, do not change the subject or ask questions that are off topic. This may seem like a way to decrease your anxiety or make the other person more comfortable, but it often has the opposite effect. It is okay to allow silence and to convey that you are listening by using encouraging sounds such as "hmmm" and "uh-huh" periodically. Try to reflect back the emotion being described. For instance, you might let your face convey the sadness you are feeling and express it by saying, "Wow, that is very tragic." It might also help to imagine yourself in the speaker's place and to look at the situation from his or her perspective. It is okay to ask questions if you are confused. Finally, remember to focus on the experience of the person disclosing, rather than on your own. Give advice only when it is requested.

One important goal is for you, the listener, to comprehend the speaker's story and communicate your attention and understanding.

Third, remember to use words in a way that conveys support. At the same time, try to avoid reassuring the person in a manner that might minimize his or her experience. For example, it is not helpful to say, "That happened so long ago, maybe it would help to try move on," or "It's not worth the energy to keep thinking about it," or even, "Don't be scared." Similarly, avoid expressing judgments or evaluations about the story you are hearing. What does help is validating the person's emotions in a genuine tone. For example, you might say, "If that happened to me, I can imagine I'd feel really overwhelmed, too." It is also beneficial to point out the person's strengths. Comments such as "I'm amazed at how much courage that took" and "I really admire your strength" can be healing. Just as a good listener conveys attention and understanding, it is also essential to show caring and support.

True listening goes beyond such concrete suggestions. As we described earlier, stories of betrayal so often begin in fragmented and sometimes implausible ways.[2] They evoke strong reactions in us, from compassion to outright rejection. They scare us, they anger us, and they never leave us untouched. It is easy to distance ourselves or become vicariously traumatized by these stories. Therefore, it is tempting to settle for a technique of listening that helps the teller of the narrative create a clearer and more factual narrative. Yet true listeners must be willing to go further, seeking emotional depth and truth, rather than merely focusing on surface particulars and facts. It is hard for listeners to reserve judgment and remain emotionally present as an individual struggles to express the emotional truth embedded in experiences of betrayal. However, you will find that doing so creates a true healing environment.

An effective listener must care enough to be involved and be affected by what is heard. It is often painful for the listener, as well as for the speaker. Douglas Steere gives us this warning: "For the listener who knows what he or she is about, there is a realization that there is no withdrawal halfway. There is every prospect that he or she will not return unscathed. . . . A friend of mine who has spent many years in listening admits that in the course of it, he has learned something of the 'descent into Hell' and is quite frank in confessing that for him each act of listening that is not purely mechanical is a personal ordeal. Listening is never cheap."[3]

True listening is never cheap, but it is powerful. It will help those who have been betrayed reconnect with themselves and with others so that they can form deep relationships.

Deep relationships offer the greatest potential for growth and healing, as well as for harm. Therapist Laure Kahn has identified the emotion of "love" as central to these most powerful relationships, whether they are the ones in which harm occurs or the ones in which healing occurs.[4]

The traumatizing of love occurs when a child's experience of love, caring, and affection collides with his or her experiences of abuse and betrayal. The union of love, trust, and safety becomes fractured, while notions of love and betrayal become linked in tragic partnership.

Kahn goes on to observe that healing relationships manifest the best qualities of love, such as care, commitment, trust, knowledge, responsibility, and respect. Love, commitment, respect, and support are important in our personal relationships. Conveying these qualities through good listening and active support can make all the difference. Good relationships are the matrix in which healing occurs.

For Institutions and Powerful Others

We have addressed what victims of betrayal and their supports can do. It is equally important for those in authority, institutions and individuals alike, to face their power to betray and its devastating consequences. Healthy individuals and healthy institutions create communities in which all members can thrive and grow. It is up to the institutions to assess their strengths and shortcomings in preventing betrayal and in facing the consequences when those betrayals do occur.

In chapter 4, we describe research by Carly Smith and Jennifer Freyd that looks at one particular kind of institutional betrayal: that of failing to prevent or responding poorly to reports of sexual assaults within the institutional environment. This is an issue that has profoundly troubled institutions ranging from churches to universities to the military. Smith and Freyd developed the Institutional Betrayal Questionnaire to measure the types of policies and behaviors that fail to prevent assaults or that support those who report being assaulted. As we explain in chapter 4, the researchers found that these institutional failures related to worse psychological distress for victims of sexual assault. Fortunately, these flaws are easily remedied. If you are a decision maker in an institution, you might ask yourself how well your institution is doing on the matter of sexual assault.[5]

> Are you taking proactive steps to prevent this type of experience?
>
> Are you creating an environment in which this type of experience seems like no big deal?
>
> Are you creating an environment in which this experience seems likely to occur?
>
> Are you making it difficult for people to report the experience?
>
> Are you responding adequately to the experience, if reported?
>
> Are you covering up the experience?
>
> Are you punishing victims for reporting this experience (e.g., with loss of privileges or status)?

If all institutions engaged in self-study using questions like these, a particularly harmful type of institutional betrayal could be prevented. With safeguards in place, victims would feel secure reporting their complaints. Both actual acts of betrayal and blindness toward those acts would be much less frequent.

Sexual harassment and violence are one kind of betrayal that institutions must face. Governments, communities, and institutions have the power to betray in many ways, from exploiting employees and denying basic civil rights to failing to protect whistleblowers. The institutions may have policies that directly betray individuals, or they may turn a blind eye when wrongdoings are reported. These failures harm individuals, while also eating away at the fabric of communities.

Institutions can take steps to prevent and respond to betrayal. First, institutions can establish explicit policies and procedures. This might include creating a specific position or committee that is responsible for assessing the potential for betrayal and taking appropriate steps to reduce the prevalence of betrayals and to respond to victims. Second, institutions can educate individuals about the effects of betrayal and betrayal blindness and what to do to prevent them. (Imagine a world in which this education was part of the standard curriculum.) Third, institutions can respond supportively to individuals who report being the victims of betrayal. This might begin by acknowledging that a betrayal has occurred. Individuals need this acknowledgment, because they are often unprepared for their psychological reactions to betrayal.

Fourth, and most crucially, institutions must protect the whistleblower. They must support and even cherish those who challenge authority by raising difficult truths. Beware an institution that labels these people "insubordinate"! The duty of an institution is much like that of a good friend or another supportive person: listen well. Listening well means being attentive, respectful, and supportive to both victims and whistleblowers. In this way, institutions can provide a safe environment for accounts of betrayal to be told and thus create the context for victims to heal and institutions to thrive.

Final Words

We began this book by asking you, the reader, about your experiences with betrayal. We hope that our examples and our research evidence have helped you understand those experiences of betrayal and your responses to them. We can heal from betrayal, as individuals and as a society, but we must first recognize the power of betrayal and how easy it is to be blind to it. We can move from relationships based on power and control to mutual relationships of trust and safety, if we are willing to be vulnerable, take risks, and listen to one another as we all tell our stories. We can all begin to be new people, creating a new society together.

Recommended Reading

Angelou, M. *I Know Why the Caged Bird Sings*. New York: Random House, 1969.

Belford, B., L. A. Kaehler, and P. Birrell. "Relational Health as a Mediator between Betrayal Trauma and Borderline Personality Disorder." *Journal of Trauma and Dissociation* 13 (2012): 244–257.

Birrell, P. J., and J. J. Freyd. "Betrayal Trauma: Relational Models of Harm and Healing." *Journal of Trauma Practice* 5(1) (2006): 49–63.

Bowlby, J. *A Secure Base: Parent-Child Attachment and Healthy Human Development*. New York: Basic Books, 1988.

Briere, J. N. *Therapy for Adults Molested as Children: Beyond Survival*, rev. 2nd ed. New York: Springer, 1996.

Brown, L. S. *Subversive Dialogues: Theory in Feminist Therapy*. New York: Basic Books, 1994.

Brown, L. S., and J. J. Freyd. "PTSD Criterion A and Betrayal Trauma: A Modest Proposal for a New Look at What Constitutes Danger to Self." *Trauma Psychology, Division 56, American Psychological Association, Newsletter* 3(1) (2008): 11–15.

Courtois, C. A. *Healing the Incest Wound: Adult Survivors in Therapy*, 2nd ed. New York: W. W. Norton and Company, 2010.

DePrince, A. "Social Cognition and Revictimization Risk." *Journal of Trauma & Dissociation* 6(1) (2005): 125–141.

DePrince, A. P., L. S. Brown, R. E. Cheit, J. J. Freyd, S. N. Gold, K. Pezdek, and K. Quina, "Motivated Forgetting and Misremembering: Perspectives from Betrayal Trauma Theory." In R. F. Belli, ed., *True and False Recovered Memories: Toward a Reconciliation of the Debate (Nebraska Symposium on Motivation 58)*. New York: Springer, 2012, 193–243.

Foynes, M. M., and J. J. Freyd. "The Impact of Skills Training on Responses to the Disclosure of Mistreatment." *Psychology of Violence* 1 (2011): 66–77.

Freyd, J. J. *Betrayal Trauma: The Logic of Forgetting Childhood Abuse.* Cambridge, MA: Harvard University Press, 1996.

Gobin, R. L., and J. J. Freyd. "Betrayal and Revictimization: Preliminary Findings." *Psychological Trauma: Theory, Research, Practice, and Policy* 1 (2009): 242–257.

Goldsmith, R. E., M. R. Barlow, and J. J. Freyd. "Knowing and Not Knowing about Trauma: Implications for Therapy." *Psychotherapy: Theory, Research, Practice, Training* 41 (2004): 448–463.

Herman, J. L. *Trauma and Recovery.* New York: BasicBooks, 1992.

Kauffman, J., ed. *Loss of the Assumptive World.* New York: Taylor and Francis, 2002.

Koss, M. "Rape: Scope, Impact, Interventions, and Public Policy Responses." *American Psychologist* 48 (1993): 1062–1069.

Pennebaker, J. W. *Opening Up: The Healing Power of Expressing Emotions.* New York: Guilford Press, 1997.

Sandulescu, J. *Donbas: A True Story of an Escape across Russia.* Lincoln, NE: Iuniverse.com, 2000.

Schulhofer, S. J. *Unwanted Sex: The Culture of Intimidation and the Failure of Law.* Cambridge, MA: Harvard University Press, 1998.

Stewart, J. B. *Blind Eye: How the Medical Establishment Let a Doctor Get Away with Murder.* New York: Simon & Schuster, 1999.

Tutu, D. *No Future without Forgiveness.* New York: Doubleday, 1999.

Notes

Preface

1. K. Kendall-Tackett, "The Health Effects of Childhood Abuse: Four Pathways by Which Abuse Can Influence Health," *Child Abuse & Neglect, 26* (2002): 715–729; J. Read, J. van Os, A. P. Morrison, and C. A. Ross, "Childhood Trauma, Psychosis and Schizophrenia: A Literature Review with Theoretical and Clinical Implications," *Acta Psychiatrica Scandinavica 112* (2005): 330–350.
2. J. J. Freyd, B. Klest, and A. P. DePrince, "Avoiding Awareness of Betrayal: Comment on Lindblom and Gray (2009)," *Applied Cognitive Psychology 24* (2010): 20–26.

Chapter 1: Blind to Betrayal

1. J. J. Freyd, "Blind to Betrayal: New Perspectives on Memory for Trauma," *Harvard Mental Health Letter, 15*(12) (1999): 4–6.
2. R. E. Goldsmith, M. R. Barlow, and J. J. Freyd, "Knowing and Not Knowing about Trauma: Implications for Therapy," *Psychotherapy: Theory, Research, Practice, Training, 41* (2004): 448–463.

Chapter 2: Children Betrayed

1. This description of Judy, like that of Kayla below, is based on our experience with psychotherapy clients; it does not represent any one person. Many descriptions in this book, particularly where a client's own words are used, are based on actual people. We will indicate in each case whether the description is based on a single person or is a composite.
2. J. W. Tebbel, *From Rags to Riches: Horatio Alger Jr. and the American Dream* (New York: Macmillan, 1963).

3. B. Lamb (interviewer) and F. Wu (interviewee), *Yellow: Race in America beyond Black and White* (interview transcript, 2002), http://booknotes .org/Watch/168640-1/Frank+Wu.aspx.

Chapter 3: The Wide Reach of Betrayal Blindness

1. G. Sheehy, *Hillary's Choice* (New York: Random House, 1999).
2. A. Jarecki et al., *Capturing the Friedmans* (United States: HBO Video, 2003).
3. S. Pinker, *The Stuff of Thought: Language as a Window into Human Nature* (New York: Viking, 2007).
4. S. O'Rinn, V. Lishak, R. T. Muller, and C. C. Classen, "Betrayal and Its Associations with Memory Disturbances among Survivors of Childhood Sexual Abuse" (under review).
5. A. Jarecki et al., *Capturing the Friedmans* (United States: HBO Video, 2003).
6. S. J. Schulhofer, *Unwanted Sex: The Culture of Intimidation and the Failure of Law* (Cambridge, MA: Harvard University Press, 1998).
7. H. Jung, "Eugene Probation Officer Pleads Guilty to Sex Assault of Woman He Supervised," *Oregonian*, April 28, 2011, http://www .oregonlive.com.
8. United States Attorney's Office, District of Oregon, "Former United States Probation Officer Sentenced to 10 Years," press release, 2011, http://www.justice.gov/usao/or/PressReleases/2011/20110718_ Walker.html.
9. N. de Fabrique, S. J. Romano, G. M. Vecchi, and V. B. Van Hasselt, "Understanding Stockholm Syndrome," *FBI Law Enforcement Bulletin* 76(7) (2007): 10–16.
10. N. de Fabrique, V. Van Hasselt, G. Vecchi, and S. Romano, "Common Variables Associated with the Development of Stockholm Syndrome: Some Case Examples," *Victims & Offenders* 2 (2007): 91–98.
11. J. Sandulescu, *Donbas: A True Story of an Escape across Russia* (Lincoln, NE: Iuniverse.com, 2000).
12. Office of the Inspector General, "The California Department of Corrections and Rehabilitation's Supervision of Parolee Philip Garrido," 2009, retrieved July 13, 2011, http://www.oig.ca.gov/ media/reports/BOI/Special%20Report%20on%20CDCRs%20 Supervision%20of%20Parolee%20Phillip%20Garrido.pdf.
13. C. Moskowitz, "Bonding with a Captor: Why Jaycee Dugard Didn't Flee," August 31, 2009, http://www.livescience.com/7862-bonding-captor-jaycee-dugard-flee.html.

14. Office of the Inspector General, "The California Department of Corrections and Rehabilitation's Supervision of Parolee Philip Garrido," 2009, retrieved July 13, 2011, http://www.oig.ca.gov/media/press_releases/2009/Corrections%20Failed%20to%20 Properly%20Supervise%20Parolee%20Phillip%20Garrido.pdf.

Chapter 4: Blind Adherence
1. A. Hill, *Speaking Truth to Power* (New York: Doubleday, 1997).
2. C. L. Powell, "Remarks to the United Nations Security Council," February 5, 2003, New York City, U.S. Department of State, http://web.archive.org/web/20070109235502/http://www.state.gov/secretary/former/powell/remarks/2003/17300.htm.
3. Zurbriggen, E. L. (2005). Lies in a Time of Threat: Betrayal Blindness and the 2004 U.S. Presidential Election. *Analyses of Social Issues and Public Policy, 5*, 189–196.
4. United States Department of Labor, "Family and Medical Leave Act" (n.d.), http://www.dol.gov/whd/fmla/index.htm.
5. D. Dalby and R. Donadio, "Irish Report Finds Abuse Persisting in Catholic Church," *New York Times*, July 13, 2011, http://nytimes.com.
6. R. Riegel, "Lives Were Ruined by What They Did," *Independent*, July 14, 2011, http://www.independent.ie/.
7. C. P. Smith and J. J. Freyd, "Nowhere to Turn: Institutional Betrayal Exacerbates Traumatic Aftermath of Sexual Assault," poster presented at the 27th Annual Meeting of the International Society for Traumatic Stress Studies (ISTSS), Baltimore, Maryland, November 3–5, 2011.
8. See http://your4state.com/fulltext?nxd_id=262542. The full Freeh report can be found at: http://pahomepage.com/images/Multi_Media/pahomepage/nxd_media/dox/pdf/2012_07/REPORT_FINAL_071212.pdf.
9. D. Jamail, "Rape Rampant in U.S. Military," *Al-Jeezera English*, December 24, 2010, http://english.aljazeera.net.
10. ACLU, "SWAN and ACLU File Lawsuit Seeking Military Sexual Trauma Records Withheld by Federal Government," press release, 2010, http://www.aclu.org/womens-rights/swan-and-aclu-file-lawsuit-seeking-military-sexual-trauma-records-withheld-federal-gov.
11. A. W. Burgess and L. L. Holmstrom, "Coping Behavior of the Rape Victim," *American Journal of Psychiatry 133* (1976): 413–418; J. M. Heidt, B. P. Marx, and J. P. Forsyth, "Tonic Immobility and Childhood Sexual Abuse: A Preliminary Report Evaluating the Sequelae of Rape-Induced Paralysis," *Behaviour Research and Therapy 43* (2005): 1157–1171.

12. A. P. DePrince, L. S. Brown, R. E. Cheit, J. J. Freyd, S. N. Gold, K. Pezdek, and K. Quina, "Motivated Forgetting and Misremembering: Perspectives from Betrayal Trauma Theory," in R. F. Belli, ed., *True and False Recovered Memories: Toward a Reconciliation of the Debate* (Nebraska Symposium on Motivation 58) (New York: Springer, 2012), 193–243.

13. J. W. Schooler, "Discovering Memories of Abuse in the Light of Meta-Awareness," *Journal of Aggression, Maltreatment, & Trauma 4* (2001): 105–136.

14. D. M. Elliott, "Traumatic Events: Prevalence and Delayed Recall in the General Population," *Journal of Consulting and Clinical Psychology 65* (1997): 811–820.

15. R. M. Bolen and M. Scannapieco, "Prevalence of Child Sexual Abuse: A Corrective Meta Analysis," *Social Service Review 73* (1999): 281–313; D. M. Fergusson, L. J. Horwood, and L. J. Woodward, "The Stability of Child Abuse Reports: A Longitudinal Study of the Reporting Behavior of Young Adults," *Psychological Medicine 30* (2000): 529–544.

16. E. Jonzon and A. Lindblad, "Disclosure, Reactions, and Social Support: Findings from a Sample of Adult Victims of Child Sexual Abuse," *Child Maltreatment 9* (2004): 190–200; D. Smith, E. J. Letourneau, B. E. Saunders, D. G. Kilpatrick, H. S. Resnick, and C. L. Best, "Delay in Disclosure of Childhood Rape: Results from a National Survey," *Child Abuse & Neglect 24* (2000): 273–287.

17. S. J. Ceci, S. Kulkofsky, J. Z. Klemfuss, C. D. Sweeney, and M. Bruck, "Unwarranted Assumptions about Children's Testimonial Accuracy," *Annual Review of Clinical Psychology 3* (2007): 311–328; D. M. Elliott, and J. Briere, "Forensic Sexual Abuse Evaluations in Older Children: Disclosures and Symptomatology," *Behavioural Sciences and the Law 12* (1994): 261–277.

18. M. M. Foynes, J. J. Freyd, and A. P. DePrince, "Child Abuse: Betrayal and Disclosure," *Child Abuse & Neglect: The International Journal 33* (2009): 209–217; T. D. Lyon, "False Denials: Overcoming Methodological Biases in Abuse Disclosure Research," in M. E. Pipe, M. E. Lamb, Y. Orbach, and A. C. Cederborg, eds., *Disclosing Abuse: Delays, Denials, Retractions and Incomplete Accounts* (Mahwah, NJ: Erlbaum, 2007), 41–62.

19. J. J. Freyd, F. W. Putnam, T. D. Lyon, K. A. Becker-Blease, R. E. Cheit, N. B. Siegel, and K. Pezdek, "The Science of Child Sexual Abuse," *Science 308* (2005): 501.

20. J. L. Herman, *Trauma and Recovery* (New York: Basic Books, 1992).

21. I. H. Frieze S. Hymer, and M. S. Greenberg, "Describing the Crime Victim: Psychological Reactions to Victimization," *Professional Psychology: Research and Practice 18* (1987): 299–315; M. Koss, "Rape: Scope, Impact, Interventions, and Public Policy Responses," *American Psychologist 48* (1993), 1062–1069.

22. N. P. Yuan, M. P. Koss, and M. Stone, *The Psychological Consequences of Sexual Trauma*, Harrisburg, PA: VAWnet, a project of the National Resource Center on Domestic Violence/Pennsylvania Coalition against Domestic Violence, March 2006, retrieved May 15, 2008, from http://www.vawnet.org.

23. S. Ullman and H. Filipas, "Ethnicity and Child Sexual Abuse Experiences of Female College Students," *Journal of Child Sexual Abuse 14* (2005): 67–89.

24. B. P. Marx, "Lessons Learned from the Last Twenty Years of Sexual Violence Research," *Journal of Interpersonal Violence 20* (2005): 225–230.

25. J. L. Herman, *Trauma and Recovery* (New York: BasicBooks, 1992).

26. Carrier, P. *Holocaust Monuments and National Memory Cultures in France and Germany since 1989: The Origins and Political Function of the Vél' d'Hiv' in Paris and the Holocaust Monument in Berlin* (New York: Berghahn Books, 2005).

27. J. Chirac, 1995, http://www.sncfhighspeedrail.com/wpcontent/uploads/2010/10/Chirac1995.pdf.

Chapter 5: Why Blindness?

1. J. Tooby and L. Cosmides, "The Psychological Foundations of Culture," in J. Barkow, L. Cosmides, and J. Tooby, eds., *The Adapted Mind: Evolutionary Psychology and the Generation of Culture* (New York: Oxford University Press, 1992), 19–136.

2. Definition from *Encyclopedia Britannica*: Fight-or-flight response: response to an acute threat to survival that is marked by physical changes, including nervous and endocrine changes that prepare a human or an animal to react or to retreat. The functions of this response were first described in the early 1900s by American neurologist and physiologist Walter Bradford Cannon.

3. L. S. Brown and J. J. Freyd, "PTSD Criterion A and Betrayal Trauma: A Modest Proposal for a New Look at What Constitutes Danger to Self," *Trauma Psychology, Division 56, American Psychological Association, Newsletter 3*(1) (2008): 11–15.

4. J. J. Freyd, B. Klest, and C. B. Allard, "Betrayal Trauma: Relationship to Physical Health, Psychological Distress, and a Written Disclosure Intervention," *Journal of Trauma & Dissociation 6*(3) (2005): 83–104.

5. R. Goldsmith, J. J. Freyd, and A. P. DePrince, "Betrayal Trauma: Associations with Psychological and Physical Symptoms in Young Adults," *Journal of Interpersonal Violence* 27 (2012): 547–567.

6. A. P. DePrince, L. S. Brown, R. E. Cheit, J. J. Freyd, S. N. Gold, K. Pezdek, and K. Quina, "Motivated Forgetting and Misremembering: Perspectives from Betrayal Trauma Theory," in R. F. Belli, ed., *True and False Recovered Memories: Toward a Reconciliation of the Debate* (*Nebraska Symposium on Motivation 58*) (New York: Springer, 2012), 193–243.

7. R. Goldsmith, J. J. Freyd, and A. P. DePrince, "Betrayal Trauma: Associations with Psychological and Physical Symptoms in Young Adults," *Journal of Interpersonal Violence* 27 (2012): 547–567; F. W. Putnam, "Ten-Year Research Update Review: Child Sexual Abuse," *Journal-American Academy of Child and Adolescent Psychiatry* 42 (January 1, 2003): 269–278.

8. J. J. Freyd, B. Klest, and C. B. Allard, "Betrayal Trauma: Relationship to Physical Health, Psychological Distress, and a Written Disclosure Intervention," *Journal of Trauma & Dissociation*, 6(3) (2005): 83–104; L. A. Kaehler and J. J. Freyd, "Borderline Personality Characteristics: A Betrayal Trauma Approach," *Psychological Trauma: Theory, Research, Practice, and Policy 1* (2009): 261–268; S. S. Tang and J. J. Freyd, "Betrayal trauma and gender differences in posttraumatic stress," *Psychological Trauma: Theory, Research, Practice, and Policy* (in press).

9. A. P. DePrince and J. J. Freyd, "The Intersection of Gender and Betrayal in Trauma," in R. Kimerling, P. C. Ouimette, and J. Wolfe, eds., *Gender and PTSD* (New York: Guilford Press, 2002), 98–113.

10. L. R. Goldberg and J. J. Freyd, "Self-Reports of Potentially Traumatic Experiences in an Adult Community Sample: Gender Differences and Test-Retest Stabilities of the Items in a Brief Betrayal-Trauma Survey," *Journal of Trauma & Dissociation* 7(3) (2006): 39–63.

11. J. Briere and D. M. Elliott, "Prevalence and Psychological Sequelae of Self-Reported Childhood Physical and Sexual Abuse in a General Population Sample of Men and Women," *Child Abuse and Neglect* 27 (2003): 1205–1222.

12. L. R. Goldberg and J. J. Freyd, "Self-Reports of Potentially Traumatic Experiences in an Adult Community Sample: Gender Differences and Test-Retest Stabilities of the Items in a Brief Betrayal-Trauma Survey," *Journal of Trauma & Dissociation* 7(3) (2006): 39–63.

13. B. K. Klest, *Trauma, Posttraumatic Symptoms, and Health in Hawaii: Gender, Ethnicity, and Social Context*, doctoral dissertation, University of Oregon, 2010.

Chapter 7: Mental Gymnastics

1. K. Rausch and J. F. Knutson, "The Self-Report of Personal Punitive Childhood Experiences and Those of Siblings," *Child Abuse & Neglect* 15(1–2) (1991): 29–36.
2. C. Boyd, "The Implications and Effects of Theories of Intergenerational Transmission of Violence for Boys Who Live with Domestic Violence," *Australian Domestic & Family Violence Clearinghouse Newsletter 6* (2001a): 6–8.
3. M. Platt, J. Barton, and J. J. Freyd, "A Betrayal Trauma Perspective on Domestic Violence," in E. Stark and E. S. Buzawa, eds., *Violence against Women in Families and Relationships*, vol. 1 (Westport, CT: Greenwood Press, 2009), 185–207.
4. A. P. DePrince, "Social Cognition and Revictimization Risk," *Journal of Trauma and Dissociation 6* (2005): 125–141.
5. T. L. Messman-More and P. J. Long, "Child Sexual Abuse and Revictimization in the Form of Adult Sexual Abuse, Adult Physical Abuse, and Adult Psychological Maltreatment," *Journal of Interpersonal Violence 15*(5) (2000): 489–502.
6. K. A. Becker-Blease, K. Deater-Deckard, T. Eley, et al., "A Genetic Analysis of Individual Difference in Dissociative Behaviors in Childhood and Adolescence," *Journal of Child Psychology and Psychiatry 45* (2004): 522–532; K. A. Becker-Blease, J. J. Freyd, and K. C. Pears, "Preschoolers' Memory for Threatening Information Depends on Trauma History and Attentional Context: Implications for the Development of Dissociation," *Journal of Trauma & Dissociation 5*(1) (2004): 113–131; A. P. DePrince and J. J. Freyd, "The Intersection of Gender and Betrayal in Trauma," in R. Kimerling, P. C. Ouimette, and J. Wolfe, eds., *Gender and PTSD* (New York: Guilford Press, 2002), 98–113.

Chapter 8: Insights from Research

1. J. J. Freyd, A. P. DePrince, and D. Gleaves, "The State of Betrayal Trauma Theory: Reply to McNally (2007)—Conceptual Issues and Future Directions," *Memory 15* (2007): 295–311.
2. E. Bernstein and T. Putnam, "Development, Reliability, and Validity of a Dissociation Scale," *Journal of Nervous and Mental Disease 174* (1986): 727–735.
3. J. J. Freyd, B. Klest, and C. B. Allard, "Betrayal Trauma: Relationship to Physical Health, Psychological Distress, and a Written Disclosure Intervention," *Journal of Trauma & Dissociation 6*(3) (2005): 83–104.
4. J. R. Stroop, "Studies of Interference in Serial Verbal Reactions," *Journal of Experimental Psychology 18*(6) (1935): 643–662.

5. J. J. Freyd, S. R. Martorello, J. S. Alvarado, A. E. Hayes, and J. C. Christman, "Cognitive Environments and Dissociative Tendencies: Performance on the Standard Stroop Task for High versus Low Dissociators," *Applied Cognitive Psychology* 12 (1998): S91–S103.

6. A. P. DePrince and J. J. Freyd, "Dissociative Tendencies, Attention, and Memory," *Psychological Science* 10 (1999): 449–452.

7. A. P. DePrince and J. J. Freyd, "Dissociative Tendencies, Attention, and Memory," *Psychological Science* 10 (1999): 449–452.

8. A. P. DePrince and J. J. Freyd, "Forgetting Trauma Stimuli," *Psychological Science* 15 (2004): 488–492; A. P. DePrince and J. J. Freyd, "Memory and Dissociative Tendencies: The Roles of Attentional Context and Word Meaning in a Directed Forgetting Task," *Journal of Trauma & Dissociation* 2(2) (2001): 67–82.

9. K. A. Becker-Blease, J. J. Freyd, and K. C. Pears, "Preschoolers' Memory for Threatening Information Depends on Trauma History and Attentional Context: Implications for the Development of Dissociation," *Journal of Trauma & Dissociation* 5(1) (2004): 113–131.

10. G. E. Tsai, D. Condie, M. T. Wu, and I. W. Chang, "Functional Magnetic Resonance Imaging of Personality Switches in a Woman with Dissociative Identity Disorder," *Harvard Review of Psychiatry* 7 (1999): 119–122.

11. A. DePrince, "Social Cognition and Revictimization Risk," *Journal of Trauma & Dissociation* 6(1) (2005): 125–141; J. J. Freyd, B. Klest, and C. B. Allard, "Betrayal Trauma: Relationship to Physical Health, Psychological Distress, and a Written Disclosure Intervention," *Journal of Trauma & Dissociation* 6(3) (2005): 83–104.

12. R. Goldsmith and J. J. Freyd, "Awareness for Emotional Abuse," *Journal of Emotional Abuse* 5(1) (2005): 95–123.

13. Brian Murphy, "Molester Built Trust Slowly," *Detroit Free Press*, September 3, 1998.

14. I. L. Janis, *Victims of Groupthink: A Psychological Study of Foreign-Policy Decisions and Fiascoes* (Boston: Houghton Mifflin, 1972).

15. "China: Tiananmen's Unhealed Wounds," 2009, Human Rights Watch, http://www.hrw.org.

16. B. Glauber, "Trusted Doctor Found to Be a Killer," *Register-Guard*, February 9, 2000, 7A.

17. J. B. Stewart, *Blind Eye: How the Medical Establishment Let a Doctor Get Away with Murder* (New York: Simon & Schuster, 1999).

Chapter 9: Betrayal Blindness Is Toxic

1. L. A. Kaehler and J. J. Freyd, "Borderline Personality Characteristics: A Betrayal Trauma Approach," *Psychological Trauma: Theory, Research, Practice, and Policy 1* (2009): 261–268; J. J. Freyd, B. Klest, and C. B. Allard, "Betrayal Trauma: Relationship to Physical Health, Psychological Distress, and a Written Disclosure Intervention," *Journal of Trauma & Dissociation 6*(3) (2005): 83–104.

2. P. J. Birrell and J. J. Freyd, "Betrayal Trauma: Relational Models of Harm and Healing," *Journal of Trauma Practice 5*(1) (2006): 49–63; B. Belford, L. A. Kaehler, and P. J. Birrell, "Relational Health as a Mediator between Betrayal Trauma and Borderline Personality Disorder," *Journal of Trauma & Dissociation 13*(2) (2012): 244–257.

3. J. J. Freyd, A. P. DePrince, and E. L. Zurbriggen, "Self-Reported Memory for Abuse Depends upon Victim-Perpetrator Relationship," *Journal of Trauma & Dissociation 2*(3) (2001): 5–16; J. J. Freyd, B. Klest, and C. B. Allard, "Betrayal Trauma: Relationship to Physical Health, Psychological Distress, and a Written Disclosure Intervention," *Journal of Trauma & Dissociation 6*(3) (2005): 83–104.

4. J. A. Chu and D. L. Dill, "Dissociative Symptoms in Relation to Childhood Physical and Sexual Abuse," *American Journal of Psychiatry 147*(7) (1990): 887–892.

5. B. Plattner, M. A. Silvermann, A. D. Redlich, V. G. Carrion, M. Feucht, M. H. Friedrich, and H. Steiner, "Pathways to Dissociation: Intrafamilial versus Extrafamilial Trauma in Juvenile Delinquents," *Journal of Nervous and Mental Disease 191*(12) (2003): 781–788.

6. J. Lavino, "Guest Commentary: Forgiveness—The Ultimate Revenge," *Camera*, August 2, 2011, http://www.dailycamera.com.

7. J. J. Freyd, *Betrayal Trauma: The Logic of Forgetting Childhood Abuse* (Cambridge, MA: Harvard University Press, 1996).

8. J. J. Freyd, A. P. DePrince, and E. L. Zurbriggen, "Self-Reported Memory for Abuse Depends upon Victim-Perpetrator Relationship," *Journal of Trauma & Dissociation 2*(3) (2001): 5–17.

9. T. Schultz, J. L. Passmore, and C. Y. Yoder, "Emotional Closeness with Perpetrators and Amnesia for Child Sexual Abuse," *Journal of Child Sexual Abuse 12*(1) (2003): 67–88.

10. J. A. Sheiman, "Sexual Abuse History with and without Self-Report of Memory Loss: Differences in Psychopathology, Personality, and Dissociation," in L. M. Williams and V. L. Banyard, eds., *Trauma & Memory* (Thousand Oaks, CA: Sage, 1999), 139–148.

11. V. J. Edwards, R. Fivush, et al., "Autobiographical Memory Disturbances in Childhood Abuse Survivors," *Journal of Aggression, Maltreatment, & Trauma 4* (2001): 247–264.

12. J. J. Freyd, B. Klest, and C. B. Allard, "Betrayal Trauma: Relationship to Physical Health, Psychological Distress, and a Written Disclosure Intervention," *Journal of Trauma & Dissociation 6*(3) (2005): 83–104.

13. R. Goldsmith, J. J. Freyd, and A. P. DePrince, "Betrayal Trauma: Associations with Psychological and Physical Symptoms in Young Adults," *Journal of Interpersonal Violence 27*(3) (in press): 524–544.

14. V. J. Edwards, J. J. Freyd, S. R. Dube, R. F. Anda, and V. J. Felitti, "Health Outcomes by Closeness of Sexual Abuse Perpetrator: A Test of Betrayal Trauma Theory," *Journal of Aggression, Maltreatment & Trauma 21* (2012): 133–148.

15. A. P. DePrince, *Trauma and Posttraumatic Responses: An Examination of Fear and Betrayal*, doctoral dissertation, University of Oregon, 2001.

16. J. A. Atlas and D. M. Ingram, "Betrayal Trauma in Adolescent Inpatients," *Psychological Reports 83* (1998): 914.

17. S. C. Turell and M. W. Armsworth, "A Log-Linear Analysis of Variables Associated with Self-Mutilation Behaviors of Women with Histories of Child Sexual Abuse," *Violence against Women 9* (2003): 487–512.

18. M. Okuda, M. Olfson, D. Hasin, B. F. Grant, K.-H. Lin, and C. Blanco, "Mental Health of Victims of Intimate Partner Violence: Results from a National Epidemiologic Survey," *Psychiatric Services 62*(8) (2011): 959–962.

19. A. P. DePrince and J. J. Freyd, "The Intersection of Gender and Betrayal in Trauma," in R. Kimerling, P. C. Ouimette, and J. Wolfe, eds., *Gender and PTSD* (New York: Guilford Press, 2002), 98–113.

20. S. S. Tang and J. J. Freyd, "Betrayal Trauma and Gender Differences in Posttraumatic Stress," *Psychological Trauma: Theory, Research, Practice, and Policy* (in press).

21. J. J. Freyd, B. Klest, and C. B. Allard, "Betrayal Trauma: Relationship to Physical Health, Psychological Distress, and a Written Disclosure Intervention," *Journal of Trauma & Dissociation 6*(3) (2005): 83–104; R. L. Gobin and J. J. Freyd, "Betrayal and Revictimization: Preliminary Findings," *Psychological Trauma: Theory, Research, Practice, and Policy 1* (2009): 242–257.

22. A. Campbell, "Oxytocin and Human Social Behavior," *Personality and Social Psychology Review 14*(3) (2010): 281–295; A. Charuvastra and M. Cloitre, "Social Bonds and Posttraumatic Stress Disorder," *Annual Review of Psychology 59* (2008): 301–328.

23. J. S. Seng, "Posttraumatic Oxytocin Dysregulation: Is It a Link among Posttraumatic Self Disorders, Posttraumatic Stress Disorder, and Pelvic Visceral Dysregulation Conditions in Women?" *Journal of Trauma & Dissociation 11*(4) (2010): 387–406.

24. American Psychiatric Association, *Diagnostic and Statistical Manual of Mental Disorders* (4th ed., text rev.) (Washington, DC: American Psychiatric Association, 2000).

25. L. A. Kaehler and J. J. Freyd, "Borderline Personality Characteristics: A Betrayal Trauma Approach," *Psychological Trauma: Theory, Research, Practice, and Policy 1* (2009): 261–268; L. A. Kaehler and J. J. Freyd, "Betrayal Trauma and Borderline Personality Characteristics: Gender Differences," *Psychological Trauma: Theory, Research, Practice, and Policy* (in press).

26. B. Belford, L. A. Kaehler, and P. Birrell, "Relational Health as a Mediator between Betrayal Trauma and Borderline Personality Disorder," *Journal of Trauma & Dissociation* (submitted).

27. R. L. Gobin and J. J. Freyd, "Betrayal and Revictimization: Preliminary Findings," *Psychological Trauma: Theory, Research, Practice, and Policy 1* (2009): 242–257.

28. A. DePrince, "Social Cognition and Revictimization Risk," *Journal of Trauma & Dissociation 6*(1) (2005): 125–141.

29. R. L. Gobin and J. J. Freyd, "Betrayal and Revictimization: Preliminary Findings," *Psychological Trauma: Theory, Research, Practice, and Policy 1* (2009): 242–257.

30. R. L. Gobin and J. J. Freyd, "Betrayal and Revictimization: Preliminary Findings," *Psychological Trauma: Theory, Research, Practice, and Policy 1* (2009): 242–257.

31. J. J. Freyd, *Betrayal Trauma: The Logic of Forgetting Childhood Abuse* (Cambridge, MA: Harvard University Press, 1996).

32. R. Gobin, "Partner Preferences among Survivors of Betrayal Trauma," in *Trauma, Attachment, and Intimate Relationships*, guest editors Eileen Zurbriggen, Robin Gobin, and Laura Kaehler, a Special Issue of the *Journal of Trauma & Dissociation 13*(2) (2012, in press).

33. K. C. Pears, J. Bruce, P. A. Fisher, and K. K. Hyoun, "Indiscriminate Friendliness in Maltreated Foster Children," *Child Maltreatment 15*(1) (2010): 64–75.

34. R. Yehuda, S. L. Halligan, and R. T. Grossman, "Childhood Trauma and Risk for PTSD: Relationship to Intergenerational Effects of Trauma, Parental PTSD, and Cortisol Excretion," *Development and Psychopathology 13*(3) (2001): 733–753.

35. R. E. Heyman and A. M. S. Slep, "Do Child Abuse and Interparental Violence Lead to Adulthood Family Violence?" *Journal of Marriage and Family 64*(4) (2002): 864–870.

36. J. Goodwin, T. McCarthy, and P. DiVasto, "Prior Incest in Mothers of Abused Children," *Child Abuse and Neglect 5*(2) (1981): 87–95.

37. N. A. Cort, C. Cerulli, S. L. Toth, and F. Rogosch, "Maternal Intergenerational Transmission of Childhood Multitype Maltreatment," *Journal of Aggression, Maltreatment and Trauma 20*(1) (2011): 19–38.

38. A. C. Hulette, L. A. Kaehler, and J. J. Freyd, "Intergenerational Associations between Trauma and Dissociation," *Journal of Family Violence 26* (2011): 217–225.

39. M. L. King, *Beyond Vietnam: A Time to Break Silence*, speech presented at Riverside Church in New York City, 1967.

Chapter 10: The Risks of Knowing

1. J. J. Freyd, "Shareability: The Social Psychology of Epistemology," *Cognitive Science 7* (1983): 191–210.

2. J. J. Freyd, "Betrayal-Trauma: Traumatic Amnesia as an Adaptive Response to Childhood Abuse," *Ethics & Behavior 4* (1994): 307–329.

3. J. J. Freyd, "Violations of Power, Adaptive Blindness, and Betrayal Trauma Theory," *Feminism & Psychology 7* (1997): 22–32.

4. Jane Doe, "How Could This Happen?: Coping with a False Accusation of Incest and Rape," *Issues in Child Abuse Accusations 3* (1991): 154–165. (*Issues in Child Abuse Accusations* was self-published by Ralph Underwager, a prominent defense witness who became a founding member of the FMSF advisory board, and his wife, Hollida Wakefield. Underwager later resigned from the FMSF board after publicity was drawn to his quote in an interview published in *Paidika: The Journal of Paedophilia* that included: "Paedophiles can boldly and courageously affirm what they choose. They can say that what they want is to find the best way to love.")

5. E. Jonzon and A. Lindblad, "Disclosure, Reactions, and Social Support: Findings from a Sample of Adult Victims of Child Sexual Abuse," *Child Maltreatment 9* (2004): 190–200; D. Smith, E. J. Letourneau, B. E. Saunders, D. G. Kilpatrick, H. S. Resnick, and C. L. Best, "Delay in Disclosure of Childhood Rape: Results from a National Survey," *Child Abuse & Neglect 24* (2000): 273–287.

6. M. Hébert, M. Tourigny, M. Cyr, P. McDuff, and J. Joly, "Prevalence of Childhood Sexual Abuse and Timing of Disclosure in a

Representative Sample of Adults from Quebec," *Canadian Journal of Psychiatry* 54(9) (2009): 631–636.

7. E. Somer and S. Szwarcberg, "Variables in Delayed Disclosure of Childhood Sexual Abuse," *American Journal of Orthopsychiatry* 71 (2001): 332–341.

8. D. W. Smith, E. J. Letourneau, B. E. Saunders, D. G. Kilpatrick, H. S. Resnick, and C. L. Best, "Delay in Disclosure of Childhood Rape: Results from a National Survey," *Child Abuse & Neglect* 24(2) (2000): 273–287.

9. D. W. Smith, E. J. Letourneau, B. E. Saunders, D. G. Kilpatrick, H. S. Resnick, and C. L. Best, "Delay in Disclosure of Childhood Rape: Results from a National Survey," *Child Abuse & Neglect* 24(2) (2000): 273–287.

10. T. Sorenson and B. Snow, "How Children Tell: The Process of Disclosure in Child Sexual Abuse," *Child Welfare* 70(1) (1991): 3–15.

11. M. M. Foynes, J. J. Freyd, and A. P. DePrince, "Child Abuse: Betrayal and Disclosure," *Child Abuse and Neglect* 33 (2009): 209–217; L. C. Malloy, T. D. Lyon, and J. A. Quas, "Filial Dependency and Recantation of Child Sexual Abuse Allegations," *Journal of the American Academy of Child & Adolescent Psychiatry* 46(2) (2007): 162–170; T. D. Lyon, "Child Sexual Abuse: Disclosure, Delay, and Denial," in Margaret-Ellen Pipe, Michael E. Lamb, Yael Orbach, and Ann-Christin Cederborg, eds., *Child Sexual Abuse: Disclosure, Delay, and Denial* (Mahwah, NJ: Lawrence Erlbaum Associates, 2007), 41–62.

12. A. J. Jacques-Tiura, R. Tkatch, A. Abbey, and R. Wegner, "Disclosure of Sexual Assault: Characteristics and Implications for Posttraumatic Stress Symptoms among African American and Caucasian Survivors," *Journal of Trauma & Dissociation* 11(2) (2010): 174–192.

13. S. Ullman and C. Najdowski, "Prospective Changes in Attributions of Self-Blame and Social Reactions to Women's Disclosures of Adult Sexual Assault," *Journal of Interpersonal Violence* 26(10) (2011): 1934–1962; C. E. Aherns, "Being Silenced: The Impact of Negative Social Reactions on the Disclosure of Rape," *American Journal of Community Psychology* 38 (2006): 263–274; S. Ullman, "Is Disclosure of Sexual Traumas Helpful?: Comparing Experimental Laboratory versus Field Study Results," *Journal of Aggression, Maltreatment, and Trauma* 20(2) (2011).

14. B. P. Marx, "Lessons Learned from the Last Twenty Years of Sexual Violence Research," *Journal of Interpersonal Violence* 20(2) (2005): 225–230.

15. S. J. Lepore, J. D. Ragan, and S. Jones, "Talking Facilitates Cognitive-Emotional Processes of Adaptation to an Acute Stressor," *Journal of*

Personality & Social Psychology 78(3) (2000): 499–508; S. E. Ullman, "Correlates and Consequences of Adult Sexual Assault Disclosure," *Journal of Interpersonal Violence* 11(4) (1996): 554–571.

16.　E. M. Gortner, S. S. Rude, and J. W. Pennebaker, "Benefits of Expressive Writing in Lowering Rumination and Depressive Symptoms," *Behavior Therapy* 37(3) (2006): 292–303; B. K. Klest and J. J. Freyd, "Global Ratings of Essays about Trauma: Development of the GREAT Code, and Correlations with Physical and Mental Health Outcomes," *Journal of Psychological Trauma* 6(1) (2007): 1–20.

17.　S. P. Spera, E. D. Buhrfeind, and J. W. Pennebaker, "Expressive Writing and Coping with Job Loss," *Academy of Management Journal* 37(3) (1994): 722–733.

18.　M. M. Foynes and J. J. Freyd, "An Exploratory Study Evaluating Responses to the Disclosure of Stressful Life Experiences as They Occurred in Real Time," *Psychological Trauma: Theory, Research, Practice, and Policy* (in press).

19.　M. M. Foynes and J. J. Freyd, "The Impact of Skills Training on Responses to the Disclosure of Mistreatment," *Psychology of Violence 1* (2011): 66–77.

20.　J. P. Carse, *The Silence of God: Meditations on Prayer* (San Francisco: HarperSanFrancisco, 1995).

Chapter 11: The Healing Power of Knowing

1.　J. Sandulescu, *Donbas: A True Story of an Escape across Russia* (Lincoln, NE: Iuniverse.com, 2000).

2.　A. Gottleib, "Journey to Healing," *O, The Oprah Magazine*, October 2001, http://www.oprah.com.

3.　J. P. Carse, *The Silence of God: Meditations on Prayer* (San Francisco: HarperSanFrancisco, 1995).

4.　There are several studies, which are reported by John Bowlby. J. Bowlby, *A Secure Base: Parent-Child Attachment and Healthy Human Development* (New York: Basic Books, 1988).

Chapter 12: The Healing Power of Telling

1.　*Settlegoode v. Portland Public Schools*, 362 F. 3d 1118 (9th Cir. 2004).

2.　Truth and Reconciliation Commission Final Report, 2003, www.info.gov.za/otherdocs/2003/trc/2_7.pdf.

3.　J. D. Wolfensohn, "Voices for the Poor," speech given at the World Press Freedom Committee in Washington, 1999.

4.　S. Munroe, "Government Apologizes to Veteran Sean Bruyea," *Canada Online*, October 26, 2010, http://canadaonline.about.com.

5.　J. O'Neill, "Betrayed Veteran Receives Gov't Apology," *Edmonton Journal*, October 26, 2010, http://www2.canada.com.

Chapter 13: Speaking Our Truth

1. J. J. Freyd, "Theoretical and Personal Perspectives on the Delayed Memory Debate," in *Proceedings of the Center for Mental Health at Foote Hospital's Continuing Education Conference, Controversies around Recovered Memories of Incest and Ritualistic Abuse* (Ann Arbor, MI: Foote Hospital, 1993), 69–108.

2. G. Ganaway, "Town Meeting: Delayed Memory Controversy in Abuse Recovery," Panel presented at the Fifth Anniversary Eastern Regional Conference on Abuse and Multiple Personality, June 1993, Alexandria, VA (1993a); G. Ganaway, Panel presented at The Center for Mental Health at Foote Hospital's Continuing Education Conference: "Controversies around Recovered Memories of Incest and Ritualistic Abuse," August 1993, Ann Arbor, MI (1993b).

3. M. Gardner, "Notes of a Fringe Watcher: The False Memory Syndrome," *Skeptical Inquirer 17*(3) (1993): 370–375.

4. J. Herman, *Trauma and Recovery* (New York: Basic Books, 1992); J. Herman and E. Schatzow, "Recovery and Verification of Memories of Childhood Trauma." *Psychoanalytic Psychology 4* (1987): 1–16.

5. R. Ofshe and E. Watters, "Making Monsters," *Society* (1993): 4–16.

6. P. B. Vaill, "The Rediscovery of Anguish," *Creative Change 10*(3) (1990): 18–24.

7. P. Birrell, "An Open Letter to the Advisory Board Members of the False Memory Syndrome Foundation," *Moving Forward Newsjournal 2*(5) (1993): 4–5.

Chapter 14: Now I See

1. B. Liang, A. Tracy, C. A. Taylor, L. M. Williams, J. V. Jordan, and J. B. Miller, "The Relational Health Indices: A Study of Women's Relationships," *Psychology of Women Quarterly 26* (2002): 25–35.

2. P. J. Birrell and J. J. Freyd, "Betrayal Trauma: Relational Models of Harm and Healing," *Journal of Trauma Practice 5*(1) (2006): 49–63.

3. D. Steere, *On Listening to Another* (New York: Harper & Row, 1964).

4. L. Kahn, "The Understanding and Treatment of Betrayal Trauma as a Traumatic Experience of Love," *Journal of Trauma Practice 5*(3) (2006): 57–72.

5. The questions are based on the IBQ developed by Smith and Freyd. C. P. Smith and J. J. Freyd, "Nowhere to Turn: Institutional Betrayal Exacerbates Traumatic Aftermath of Sexual Assault," poster presented at the 27th Annual Meeting of the International Society for Traumatic Stress Studies (ISTSS), Baltimore, Maryland, November 3–5, 2011.

Index

A

abandonment, 10–15
"ableism," 21
alexithymia, 92
Allard, Carolyn, 102
All Things Considered (NPR), 154
anxiety
    betrayal trauma theory
        and, 58
    childhood betrayal and, 12
    sexual trauma and, 39
    See also mental health
apartheid, 143–145
Armsworth, M. W., 103
Atlas, J. A., 103
attachment
    caregiver dependence and,
        53–54
    Stockholm syndrome and,
        28–34
attention, dissociation and, 86–92
Avila-Smith, Susan, 41–42
avoidance, 20–24
awareness
    consciousness of betrayal,
        84–85

disclosure about betrayal,
    114–118
healing and, 138–140
See also consciousness of
    betrayal

B

Bay of Pigs, groupthink and, 93
Becker-Blease, Kathy, 90
Belford, Brent, 107–108
betrayal, preventing, 171–173.
    See also healing
betrayal blindness
    avoidance and, 20–24
    "blindness," context, 21–22
    consent and, 24–28
    defined, 4, 21–22
    "rotating," 167
    Stockholm syndrome and,
        28–34
    See also betrayal trauma
        theory
Betrayal Detection Measure, 109
*Betrayal Trauma: The Logic of
    Forgetting Child Abuse*
    (Freyd), 101

betrayal trauma theory
  attachment system and, 53–54
  cheater detectors, 54–55
  consciousness of betrayal,
    67–70
  example, 49–53
  fight, flight, freeze response,
    55–61
  institutional betrayal and,
    35–36, 43–46
  social contracts, 53, 54–55
  theory development, 49
  two-dimensional model for
    traumatic events, 57
Bhagwati, Anuradha, 41–42
Birrell, Pamela
  Betrayal Detection Measure,
    109
  on BPD, 106–108
  on disclosure risk, 119–122
  on False Memory Syndrome
    Foundation (FMSF),
    157–161
Blackburn, Jean-Pierre, 152
blame
  institutional betrayal in court,
    25, 42–46
  self-blame, 10–15
borderline personality disorder
  (BPD)
  betrayal trauma theory
    and, 58
  relationships affected by
    betrayal and, 106–108
brain, dissociation and, 91–92.
    See also memory; mental
    health
Brief Betrayal Trauma Survey
  (BBTS), 58–61, 109

Bruyea, Sean, 146–152
bystanders, institutional betrayal
  and, 46–48

C

Capturing the Friedmans (docu-
    mentary), 20–21, 23–24
caregiver dependence, attach-
    ment and, 53–54
Carse, James, 129, 133
Catholic Church, sexual abuse
    and, 37–38
Centers for Disease Control
    (CDC), 102
cheater detectors, 54–55
children
  betrayal of, generally, 10–19
  child pornography, 20–21
  cycle of violence, 81–83, 111
  dissociation and childhood
    abuse, 101
  Trauma Symptom Checklist
    for Children, 103
Chirac, Jacques, 47–48
Chu, James, 101
Clinton, Bill, 20
Clinton, Hillary, 20
Communist Party of China
    (CPC), 94
Condie, Don, 91
consciousness of betrayal, 62–70,
    71–83, 84–95
  alexithymia, 92
  awareness, 84–85
  dissociation, 86–92
  domestic violence and, 71–83
  groupthink, 93–94
  meta-cognition, 85

perpetrator grooming and, 92–93

trust and, 94–95

consent, 24–28

"Corrections Failed to Properly Supervise Parolee Philip Garrido" (Shaw), 34

Cosmides, Leda, 55

court cases, institutional betrayal and, 25, 42–46

cycle of violence, 79, 81–83, 111

D

Dahmer, Jeffrey, 40

DARVO (Deny, Attack, Reverse, Victim, Offender), 119

delayed disclosure, 44–46

dependence, on abuser, 81–83

depression
  betrayal trauma theory and, 58
  childhood betrayal and, 12
  See also mental health

DePrince, Anne
  dissociation, 88–90
  memory impairment and perpetrator-victim relationship, 101–102
  mental health effects of betrayal, 102, 103
  revictimization, 108

diet, healthy, 164

Dill, Diana, 101

Diocese of Cloyne (Ireland), 37–38

directed forgetting paradigm, 89

disclosure, 114–129
  awareness and, 114–118

constructive response to, 124–129

for healing, 132–135, 141–142, 143–145, 146–152, 166–167

listening skills for, 126–129, 169–171

negative response to, 118–124

victim reaction to assault and, 44–46, 76–83

dissociation
  betrayal trauma theory and, 58
  defined, 86–92
  Dissociative Experiences Scale (DES), 86–88, 101
  dissociative identity disorder, 86, 91, 99–101
  divided attention, 89–91

"Doe, Jane" (Pamela Freyd), 119–122, 153–161

domestic violence
  consciousness of betrayal and, 71–83
  cycle of violence and, 79, 111
  mental health effects of betrayal, 103

Donbas: A True Story of an Escape across Russia (Sandulescu), 29–32, 132–133

Dugard, Jaycee Lee, 32–34

E

Edwards, Valerie, 102

Elliott, Diana, 43–44

employers, betrayal by, 36–37, 141–142, 146–152

exercise, as beneficial, 164
expressive writing, 125–126

F

False Memory Syndrome
  Foundation (FMSF),
  119–122, 153–161
Family Medical Leave Act
  (FMLA), 36
FBI, 25, 27, 29
females. *See* gender (of victims)
fight, flight, freeze response, 55–61
financial issues
  domestic violence and, 81
  infidelity and, 5
flow charts, 166–167
Foynes, Melissa, 126–129,
  169–171
French Roundup, 47–48
Freyd, Jennifer
  *Betrayal Trauma: The Logic of
    Forgetting Child Abuse*, 101
  betrayal trauma theory devel-
    oped by, 49 (*See also*
    betrayal trauma theory)
  on BPD, 106–108
  Brief Betrayal Trauma Survey
    (BBTS), 58–61
  consulting by, 24, 25, 26, 27
  directed forgetting paradigm,
    89–90
  Dissociative Experiences
    Scale (DES), 86–88
  on effect of betrayal on
    society, 111
  on False Memory Syndrome
    Foundation (FMSF),
    153–157

Institutional Betrayal
  Questionnaire (IBQ), 172
on listening skills, 126–129,
  169–171
on memory impairment and
  perpetrator-victim relationship, 101–102
on mental health effects of
  betrayal, 102
personal experience of,
  119–122, 153–161
on PTSD, 104
on revictimization, 108–110
Sandulescu interview by,
  30–32
on selective attention and
  divided attention, 88–91
shareability theory, 115–116
Freyd, Pamela ("Jane Doe"),
  119–122, 153–161
Friedman, Arnold, 20–21, 23–24
Friedman, Elaine, 21, 23–24
Friedman, Howard, 23–24

G

Ganaway, George, 158
Garrido, Phillip Craig, 32–34
gender (of victims)
  betrayal trauma theory and,
    58–61
  gender socialization, 81–83
  infidelity and, 8
  mental health effects of
    betrayal and, 103–104
genocide, bystanders to, 47–48
girls. *See* gender (of victims)
Gobin, Robyn, 108–110
Goldberg, Lewis, 58–61

Goldsmith, Rachel, 102
Gómez, Jennifer M., 167
Gottlieb, Annie, 30–32, 133
government, cover-up by, 93–94
groupthink, 93–94

H

healing, 130–140, 162–173
   awareness, parenting, and, 138–140
   disclosure for, 132–135, 141–142, 143–145, 146–152, 166–167
   institutional betrayal and, 171–173
   physical health for, 163–164
   power and trust for, 131–132
   process of, 167–169
   role of relationships in, 165–166
   safety and hope for, 135–138
   shame and, 130–131
   support system for, 169–171
Herman, Judy, 46
Hess, Steve, 133
Hill, Anita, 35
hippocampus, 91–92
Holocaust
   effects of betrayal on society and, 110–111, 112, 143
   Vel' d'Hiv Roundup (French Roundup), 47–48
Holton, Dwight C., 28
hope, healing and, 135–138
"How Could This Happen?" ("Doe"), 119–122, 153–161
Hulette, Annmarie, 111

I

Independent (Ireland), 37–38
indiscriminate friendliness, 110
individuals, toxic effects of betrayal on, 96, 97–105. *See also* mental health
infidelity, 1–9, 64–70
Ingram, D. M., 103
institutional betrayal, 35–48
   betrayal trauma theory and, 35–36, 43–46
   bystanders and, 46–48
   by Catholic Church, 37–38
   in court, 25, 42–46
   disclosure for healing, 141–142, 143–145, 146–152
   effect on society, 111
   by employers, 36–37
   groupthink and government cover-up, 93–94
   military sexual trauma (MST), 40–42
   research on, 38–40
   sexual harassment, 27–28
Institutional Betrayal Questionnaire (IBQ), 38, 172
intimate partner violence. *See* domestic violence
Iraq War, 35
Issues in Child Abuse Accusation, 119–122

J

Jamail, Dahr, 40–42
Janis, Irving, 93
Jeezera English, Al-, 40–42

justice system, institutional
    betrayal in court, 25, 42–46

K

Kaehler, Laura, 106–107, 111
Kahn, Laure, 171
kidnapping, Stockholm syn-
    drome and, 28–32
King, Martin Luther, Jr., 112
Klest, Bridget, 61, 102
"knowing." *See* consciousness of
    betrayal
knowledge isolation, 86. *See also*
    dissociation

L

Lawrence, Lana R., 166–167
levels of betrayal effects, 96–113
    individual, 96, 97–105
    relationship, 96, 105–110
    society, 96–97, 110–113
Lewinsky, Monica, 20
Liang, Belle, 165
listening skills, for disclosure,
    126–129, 169–171

M

Marx, Brian, 45, 124–125
maternal revictimization, 111
Mattingly, Michael, 93
memory
    avoidance and, 24
    betrayal trauma theory
        and, 58
    dissociation and, 86–92
    effects of betrayal on, 101–102

meta-memory, 80
    suspicion and, 8
    victims' reaction to assault,
        43–46
mental health
    anxiety, 12, 39, 58
    betrayal trauma theory and,
        58
    borderline personality disor-
        der (BPD), 58, 106–108
    depression, 12, 58
    dissociative identity disorder,
        86, 91, 99–101
    as effect of betrayal on indi-
        viduals, 102–103
    gender and post-traumatic
        stress disorder (PTSD),
        103–104
    post-traumatic stress disor-
        der, 110–111, 124–125, 146
meta-cognition, 85
military sexual trauma (MST),
    40–42
Moskowitz, Clara, 33

N

National Center for PTSD, VA
    Boston Healthcare System,
    124–125
National Epidemiologic Survey
    on Alcohol and Related
    Conditions, 103
National Family Violence Survey,
    111
Nazis. *See* Holocaust
neutral condition, 87
New York Times, 37
Noll, Laura, 167

nondisclosure, 44–46
NPR, 154
nutrition, 164

O

Okuda, Mayumi, 103
Oregon Research Institute, 61
Overton, Josh, 133
oxytocin dysregulation, 104–105

P

parents
    as betraying, to children,
        10–15 (*See also* children;
        perpetrators)
    parenting and healing,
        138–140
Park, Sandra, 42
passivity, during sexual assault,
    43–46
Paterno, Joe, 39–40
Pennebaker, Jamie, 125–126
Pennsylvania State University
    (Penn State), 39–40
perpetrators
    cycle of violence and, 79,
        81–83, 111
    grooming of victim by,
        92–93
    known to victim, 44–45,
        101–102
physical health
    betrayal trauma theory and
        illness, 58, 104–105
    healing and, 163–164
Pinker, Steven, 22
Platt, Melissa, 11

Portland (Oregon) Public
    Schools, 141–142
post-traumatic stress disorder
    (PTSD)
    betrayal trauma theory and, 58
    gender and, 103–104
    military and betrayal
        blindness, 146
    National Center for PTSD,
        VA Boston Healthcare
        System, 124–125
    societal effects of betrayal,
        110–111
Powell, Colin, 35
power
    disclosure and, 146–152
    healing and, 131–132
"psychic numbing," 47

R

racial discrimination
    example, 15–18
    Truth and Reconciliation
        Commission (South
        Africa), 112–113, 143–145
    See also Holocaust
"rape myths," 25
Relational Health Indices
    Scale, 165
relationships
    healthy, 165–166
    toxic effects of betrayal on,
        96, 105–110
retraction, 44–46
revictimization, 27–28, 108–110,
    111
romantic partners, choice of, 109
"rotating" betrayal blindness, 167

S

safety, healing and, 135–138
Sandulescu, Jacques, 29–32, 132–133
Sandusky, Jerry, 39–40
Schmelzer, Wendy, 154
Schneider, Andrew, 42
Schulhofer, Stephen, 26
Schumacher, William, 169
selective attention, 88–91
self-mutilation, 103, 116–118, 133–135
Service Women's Action Network (SWAN), 41–42
Settlegoode, Pamela, 141–142
sexual abuse
    Catholic Church and, 37–38
    childhood betrayal and, 12–15
    criminal cases, 24–27
    nondisclosure and, 123
    victims' reaction to, 43–46
    See also institutional betrayal
shame, felt by victim, 10–15, 130–131
shareability theory, 115–116
Shaw, David R., 34
Sheehy, Gail, 20
Shipman, Harold, 94–95
sleep hygiene, 163–164
Smith, Carly, 38, 111, 172
social contracts, 53, 54–55
society
    justice for betrayal and, 143–145
    oppression in (See institutional betrayal)
    social betrayal, 57
    toxic effects of betrayal on, 96–97, 110–113
spousal betrayal
    domestic violence, 71–83, 103, 111
    infidelity, 1–9, 64–70
Steere, Douglas, 171
Stockholm syndrome, 28–34
Stroop tasks, 86–88
structural equation modeling, 104
support system, importance of, 5–6, 169–171
Swango, Michael ("Doctor Death"), 94–95

T

Tang, Shin Shin, 104
Thomas, Clarence, 35
Tiananmen Square protests (China), government cover-up and, 93–94
tonic immobility, 56
Tooby, John, 55
trauma, defined, 49. See also betrayal trauma theory
Trauma Symptom Checklist for Children, 103
trust
    as "blinding," 8
    consent and, 26
    healing and, 131–132
    institutional betrayal and, 38–40
    need for, 94–95
    perpetrator grooming and, 92–93
    social contracts and, 53, 54–55

violation of, 18–19
Truth and Reconciliation
  Commission (South Africa),
  112–113, 143–145
Tsai, Gouchual, 91
Turell, S. C., 103
Tutu, Bishop Desmond, 143–144

U

Ullman, Sarah, 124
University of California, Santa
  Cruz, 35–36
University of Illinois at Chicago,
  124
University of Oregon, 156
University of Texas, 125–126
*Unwanted Sex: The Culture of
  Intimidation* (Schulhofer), 26
U.S. Department of Defense,
  41–42
U.S. Department of Veterans
  Affairs, 41–42

V

VA Boston Healthcare System,
  124–125

Vel' d'Hiv Roundup (French
  Roundup), 47–48
Veterans Administration
  (Canada), 146–152
victim psychology
  consciousness of betrayal and,
  77–83
  institutional betrayal in court,
  25, 42–46
  revictimization, 108–110

W

Walker, Mark, 27–28
Washington Post, 149
Wolfensohn, James D., 145
women. *See* gender (of victims)
Women Organizing Women,
  41–42
World War II. *See* Holocaust
writing task, 125–126
Wu, Frank, 17–18, 24

Z

Zurbriggen, Eileen, 35–36,
  101–102

CPSIA information can be obtained
at www.ICGtesting.com
Printed in the USA
LVHW040827040323
740927LV00005B/477